SUPPORTING HIGHER EDUCATION 4.0 WITH BLOCKCHAIN

T0384802

This book explores the current and future impacts of blockchain technologies, such as cryptocurrency, on the education system. Blockchain is a disruptive technology based on a shared, distributed ledger, where transactions are registered by consensus in a network of peers, using cryptographic mechanisms that render the records virtually immutable and, ideally, enable transparency, auditability, and resilience. What role, then, could it play in fostering transformative approaches such as student-centred teaching and learning, distributed learning environments, and lifelong learning? This book provides essential perspectives into blockchain applications and challenges within education and offers a broader view of blockchain technology against existing information and communication technologies used in education. Spanning the effects on institutions, students, and the labour market, these chapters offer critical reviews and analyses of current research, practical first-hand applications of blockchain in education, and original conceptual models.

Grażyna Paliwoda-Pękosz is Associate Professor in the Department of Informatics at Krakow University of Economics, Poland.

Piotr Soja is Associate Professor in the Department of Informatics at Krakow University of Economics, Poland.

SUPPORTING HIGHER EDUCATION 4.0 WITH BLOCKCHAIN

Critical Analyses of Automation, Data, Digital Currency, and Other Disruptive Applications

Edited by Grażyna Paliwoda-Pękosz and Piotr Soja

NEW YORK AND LONDON

Designed cover image: © Getty Images

First published 2024
by Routledge
605 Third Avenue, New York, NY 10158

and by Routledge
4 Park Square, Milton Park, Abingdon, Oxon, OX14 4RN

Routledge is an imprint of the Taylor & Francis Group, an informa business

© 2024 selection and editorial matter, Grażyna Paliwoda-Pękosz, Piotr Soja; individual chapters, the contributors

ISBN: 978-1-032-32897-3 (hbk)
ISBN: 978-1-032-33212-3 (pbk)
ISBN: 978-1-003-31873-6 (ebk)

DOI: 10.4324/9781003318736

Typeset in Times New Roman
by SPi Technologies India Pvt Ltd (Straive)

CONTENTS

Editors and Contributors   *vii*
Acknowledgements   *xi*

Blockchain technology in Education 4.0: An introduction   1
Grażyna Paliwoda-Pękosz and Piotr Soja

1 Towards Education 4.0: Challenges and opportunities   7
   Paweł Konkol and Dariusz Dymek

2 Blockchain as a disruptive technology in Education 4.0   37
   Janusz Stal and Dariusz Put

3 Supporting the management of educational
   institutions using blockchain   62
   Jan Trąbka and Mariusz Grabowski

4 Management of student-centred learning with blockchain   94
   Mariusz Grabowski and Paweł Konkol

5 Addressing labour market challenges with blockchain   119
   Dariusz Put and Jan Trąbka

6 Teaching blockchain: The case of the MSc in
   Blockchain and Digital Currency of the University
   of Nicosia   150
   Marinos Themistocleous

7 Academic certificates issued on blockchain: The case
   of the University of Nicosia and Block.co   166
   Marinos Themistocleous, Klitos Christodoulou and Elias Iosif

8 Blockchain's impact on education: Current landscape
   and prospects for the future   179
   Dariusz Dymek and Janusz Stal

Index   *200*

EDITORS AND CONTRIBUTORS

Grażyna Paliwoda-Pękosz is Associate Professor at the Department of Informatics, Krakow University of Economics (KUE), Poland. She holds a postdoctoral degree (habilitation) and Ph.D. in economics from KUE, and MSc in computer science and mathematics from the Jagiellonian University of Krakow, Poland. Her main research interests include applications of ICT in education and ICT for development. Grażyna has published in *Information Systems Management, Industrial Management & Data Systems, Information Technology for Development, Technological and Economic Development of Economy*, and in conference proceedings such as AMCIS, ICEE, ISD, and ICCE. She has served as a reviewer for a number of journals including *Journal of Supercomputing, Information Systems Management, Information Technology for Development, Journal of Enterprise Information Management*, and *Technology in Society*. Grażyna has acted as Programme/Organisational Committee member in numerous international conferences, including AMCIS, EMCIS, and ICTM.

Piotr Soja is Associate Professor at the Department of Informatics, Krakow University of Economics (KUE), Poland. He holds a postdoctoral degree (habilitation) and Ph.D. in economics from KUE. His research interests include enterprise systems, ICT for development, and ICT for active and healthy ageing. Piotr has published in *Enterprise Information Systems, Industrial Management & Data Systems, Information Systems Management*, and *Information Technology for Development*, among many other journals, as well as in numerous conference proceedings such as AMCIS, HICSS, and ISD. He is member of the Editorial Board of several journals, including *Frontiers in Blockchain, Information Technology for Development*, and *Journal of Enterprise Information Management*. He has acted as Programme/ Organisational Committee member in numerous international conferences, including AMCIS, EMCIS, EuroSymposium, and ICTM. Currently, Piotr serves as president of the Polish Chapter of AIS.

Dr. Klitos Christodoulou is Assistant Professor at the Department of Digital Innovation, University of Nicosia, Cyprus (UNIC). Klitos obtained his Ph.D. in computer science from the School of Computer Science at the University of Manchester, UK. He is also the research manager at the Institute For the Future (IFF) and the scientific lab leader of the Distributed Ledgers Research Centre (DLRC) at IFF; a centre that aims towards fostering academic research on blockchain. His research interests span both data management challenges, with a focus on machine learning techniques, and distributed ledger technologies, with an emphasis on blockchain ledgers. His current research activities focus on distributed ledger technologies and blockchain ledgers. He has published more than 30 scientific papers in the area of data integration, machine learning, and distributed ledgers. He is also an Associate Editor at the *Frontiers in Blockchain* journal and acts as the Principal Investigator for several EU research grants.

Dr. Dariusz Dymek is Associate Professor at the Department of Computational Systems, Krakow University of Economics (KUE), Poland. He received his Ph.D. degree and a postdoctoral degree (habilitation) from the Faculty of Management of KUE. He has a strong business experience. For several years he was vice president of an IT company which was a leader on the Polish market in the Data Warehouse and Business Intelligence areas. Dariusz is an author of several dozen publications in the field of IT systems architecture, IT project management, software quality, blockchain, and theoretical aspects of software engineering. The papers have been published in Polish and English-language conferences, journals, and monographs. Dariusz Dymek currently gives lectures on data modelling, Data Warehouse, software quality, and IT project management at undergraduate and postgraduate level in Polish and English.

Dr. Mariusz Grabowski is Associate Professor at the Department of Computational Systems, Krakow University of Economics (KUE), Poland. He received his Ph.D. degree and a postdoctoral degree (habilitation) from the Faculty of Management of KUE. Mariusz is an author of numerous publications in the field of information systems. The papers have been published in Polish and English-language conferences, journals and monographs including the Americas Conference on Information Systems, European Mediterranean & Middle Eastern Conference on Information Systems, and Springer. Mariusz currently gives lectures on introduction to information systems, information systems security, e-business and e-commerce at undergraduate level, and IT governance at postgraduate level.

Dr. Elias Iosif is Assistant Professor at the Department of Digital Innovation, University of Nicosia, Cyprus (UNIC). Dr. Iosif also serves as Associate Head at the same department, as well as scientific lab co-leader at the Distributed Ledgers Research Centre, Institute For the Future, UNIC. He is teaching at the MSc in Blockchain and Digital Currency offered by UNIC, which is the first degree programme globally on blockchain. Also, he is participating in several European Commission funded projects focused on blockchain technologies. Dr. Iosif has a Ph.D. degree in Electronic and Computer Engineering. His areas of expertise include blockchain and metaverse, machine learning, and human language technologies (natural language processing, spoken dialogue systems). He has experience in the respective startup ecosystem. He has authored/co-authored over 70 peer-reviewed scientific publications. Dr. Iosif is the co-author of two award-winning research works focusing on text sentiment analysis and consensus algorithms.

Dr. Paweł Konkol is Assistant Professor at the Department of Computational Systems, Krakow University of Economics, Poland. He holds a Ph.D. in management and his teaching and research interest is focused on integrated management information systems, e-commerce, blockchain, and IT systems in education. Dr. Paweł Konkol is the author/co-author of articles in the field of the implementation of IT systems at higher education institutions, blockchain, agile methodologies in IT project management, and criteria of the selection of methods of IT project implementation. His papers were published in Polish and international conference proceedings and monographs.

Dr. Dariusz Put is Associate Professor at the Department of Computational Systems, Krakow University of Economics, Poland. He holds a Ph.D. in economics and a postdoctoral degree (habilitation) in management. His areas of research include databases, information integration, organisation processes improvement and integration, blockchain, data science, and machine learning. Dariusz Put has published several dozen academic papers and coursebooks and has taken part in over 30 scientific conferences concerning the above-mentioned research areas.

Dr. Janusz Stal is Associate Professor at the Department of Informatics, Krakow University of Economics, Poland. He holds a Ph.D. in economics and habilitation degree in management and quality studies from the Krakow University of Economics. His research areas include mobile technology, mobile knowledge management, applications of ICT in education, and cloud computing. Janusz Stal has published articles in *Information Technology for Development*, *Journal of Enterprise Information Management*, and numerous conference proceedings of AMCIS, EMCIS, ECIME, SIGCSE/SIGCUE, IIS, ICEEE, and ICEL.

Prof. Marinos Themistocleous is Associate Dean of the School of Business, Director at the Institute For Future (IFF), and the scientific coordinator of the world's leading Blockchain and Digital Currency MSc programme at the University of Nicosia, Cyprus. Before joining the University of Nicosia, he worked for Brunel University, London and the University of Piraeus, Greece. He has held visiting positions at Bocconi University, Milan, and IE University, Madrid. He served as a member of the Parallel Parliament of Cyprus and president of the Digital Economy and Digital Governance Committee. Marinos serves as advisor and consultant and has collaborated with many organisations in the USA, UK, EU, and UAE in areas like blockchain, metaverse, digital transformation, information systems integration, eHealth, e-business, e-government, and smart cities. He has authored more than 175 refereed journal and conference articles, 9 books and has received citations and awards of excellence. His research has attracted funding from various organisations. Marinos is on the editorial board of academic journals and conferences, and in the past, he served as managing editor of the *European Journal of Information Systems* (EJIS).

Dr. Jan Trąbka is Assistant Professor at the Krakow University of Economics, Poland, and he holds a Ph.D. in economics from the same university. He works at the Department of Informatics. His research interests include analysis and design of information systems (especially in content management and business process management areas), business process modelling, accounting systems, and ERP systems. Jan is the author of several articles and conference papers (presented at AMICIS, PoEM, SIGSAND/PLAIS EuroSymposium). In his business life he has been involved in business analysis and pre-implementation requirement analysis projects (ERP, Workflow, BPMS, ECM). In the past, he worked as a project manager for Asseco Group and for several years he managed projects in logistics, medicine, and IT sectors.

ACKNOWLEDGEMENTS

The Project has been financed by the Ministry of Science and Higher Education within the "Regional Initiative of Excellence" Programme for 2019–2022. Project no.: 021/RID/2018/19. Total financing: 11 897 131.40 PLN. The book editors would like to thank all authors for their valuable contributions and the interviewees from the University of Nicosia, Cyprus, for sharing their first-hand experience with teaching and implementing blockchain technology at their university. Special thanks are also addressed to Artur Pękosz and Monika Pękosz for their help during proofreading. Last but not least, the editors would like to thank Daniel Schwartz, editor at Taylor & Francis, for his guidance throughout the publication process.

BLOCKCHAIN TECHNOLOGY IN EDUCATION 4.0

An introduction

Grażyna Paliwoda-Pękosz and Piotr Soja

This book explores how blockchain technology can reshape education. In so doing, it aims to recognise the state-of-the-art in the area of blockchain applications in education, investigate the possibilities of future use, evaluate the impact of blockchain on the educational ecosystem, and give a broader view of blockchain technology in comparison with existing Information and Communication Technologies (ICT) used in education. In particular, it investigates the potential of blockchain technology to support the idea of Education 4.0.

Blockchain is a disruptive technology based on a shared, distributed ledger, where transactions are registered by consensus in a network of peers, using cryptographic mechanisms that render the records virtually immutable. Such a solution enables transparency, auditability, and resilience. The most prominent and well-known application of this technology is in cryptocurrencies, with Bitcoin being the most famous example. However, there are other blockchain-based innovative experiments in high-profile areas such as healthcare, financial services, transport, and management (Cunha et al., 2021; Frizzo-Barker et al., 2020).

Blockchain also has the potential to transform the educational domain, supporting the implementation of Education 4.0, the concept that emerged in recent years as a response to the changes in society and economy related to globalisation and the constant development of ICT. Education 4.0 is an approach to learning related to the fourth industrial revolution and involves the transformation of education through advanced digital technology and automation (Joshi, 2022). The Forth Industrial Revolution, or in other words Industry 4.0, describes a new industrial revolution centred around cyber-physical

DOI: 10.4324/9781003318736-1

systems and the trend towards digitisation, automation, and the increasing use of ICT in the manufacturing environment (Oesterreich & Teuteberg, 2016; Olsen & Tomlin, 2020). In essence, Education 4.0 is a new education shift aimed at the values represented by Industry 4.0 and focuses on adaptive learning to enable students to develop the skills needed on the present labour market (Stroe, 2022).

Although blockchain has been explored in numerous fields, the research works that investigate blockchain applications in education are still scarce. This also refers to the book publications concerning blockchain in education. On top of that, already published books tend to focus on individual aspects of blockchain applications (e.g., distance learning, certificate issuance) and do not approach the topic in a comprehensive way that would provide a bigger picture of the existing environment, targeting Education 4.0 challenges. These include, among other things, student-centred teaching and learning, distributed learning, lifelong learning, and the role of disruptive ICT.

The main topics of investigation in the field of blockchain for education are in line with the Gartner report "4 Ways Blockchain Will Transform Higher Education" published on 16 October 2019, which identified four main paths of blockchain applications in education, i.e. record keeping, business processes, digital assets, and a new business model (Gartner, 2019). However, those are very general and call for further development and examination. Indeed, blockchain, as an emerging and disruptive technology, requires investigation into the new possibilities of its applications. Future will show which of them are worth implementing, but at the current stage of technology development the overview of blockchain technology in education in a broader context is valuable and desirable.

Therefore, the current book strives to deal with the topic in a multi-faceted way, considering the standpoints of the three main education stakeholders: educational institutions, students, and the labour market. To this end, it investigates the potential role of blockchain in the existing educational ecosystem and evaluates the possibilities of transforming this environment. Not only the bright sides of blockchain but also the threats that might be involved with this technology adoption are discussed. In the critical evaluation of the role of blockchain in education, the book also draws from practice by presenting a number of first-hand insights from the University of Nicosia, Cyprus, the world's leading university in blockchain teaching and educational applications (Bitcoin.com, 2016; Buntinx, 2017; NOWPayments, 2020). Overall, the book consists of eight chapters, of which six chapters critically evaluate the role of blockchain in education, and two chapters describe real-life applications of blockchain technology in a university.

Chapter 1 provides a broad overview of the contemporary educational environment. In so doing, Paweł Konkol and Dariusz Dymek discuss the challenges related to Education 4.0 from the viewpoints of its main stake-holders, i.e. the labour market, higher educational institutions, and students. They put special attention to the need of competence-based learning that requires an introduction of new learning methods and forms, supported by disruptive technologies, e.g., augmented reality, artificial intelligence, cloud computing, big data, and blockchain.

Next, in Chapter 2, Janusz Stal and Dariusz Put outline the fundamentals of blockchain technology. This chapter provides a reference point for other chapters that discuss various aspects of blockchain technology applications which need to refer to some technology-related underpinnings of block-chain. More specifically, in the chapter, the concept of Distributed Ledger Technology, on which the idea of blockchain is based, is presented. Further-more, the consensus algorithms and the concept of smart contracts are out-lined. Finally, a critical evaluation of blockchain's potential for reshaping education is delivered.

The focus of Chapter 3 is educational institutions, which are one of the three main stakeholders of education. The educational institutions' percep-tion of blockchain-based applications is evaluated. Starting with the outlin-ing of the concept of business process management, Jan Trąbka and Mariusz Grabowski discuss the prospects of supporting this idea by blockchain. They summarise the current state of blockchain endeavours in this area and discuss the future possibilities. One of the most valuable contributions of this chapter is setting a big picture by mapping blockchain applications onto a two-dimensional plot, with the first dimension considering the time-span of benefits (short-term versus long-term), and the second related to the pro-cess orientation of an organisation (internal versus external).

The student's standpoint has been given the main attention in Chapter 4. To this end, Mariusz Grabowski and Paweł Konkol outline one of the main principles of Education 4.0, i.e. student-centred learning. They present the most important concepts related to this idea, such as distributed learning and lifelong learning, and discuss how these can be supported by blockchain technology. Special attention is paid to accessing educational content, which is strongly related to the protection of intellectual property rights. It appears that blockchain technology can be especially useful in enforcing these rights.

In Chapter 5, Dariusz Put and Jan Trąbka discuss the expectations, chal-lenges, and needs of the contemporary labour market in the light of Industry 4.0. In this way, the authors examine the perspective of the third main stake-holder of Education 4.0. Special attention is paid to the changes in industry that result in the appearance of new jobs, the decline in some traditional occupations, and the need of lifelong and competency-based learning. These require competency-based management and validation of different kinds of certificates, as expected by employers. This area also appears promising for blockchain applications, and the authors present the architecture of a block-chain-based system for competence management.

Following the discussion of the main blockchain concepts and education stakeholders' perspectives elaborated in the previous chapters, Chapter 6 by Marinos Themistocleous presents hands-on experience with the development of the world's first course related to blockchain at the University of Nicosia, Cyprus. It should be noted that this course was supported from the very beginning by some blockchain-based solutions; e.g. graduates received blockchain-based certificates and were allowed to pay tuition fees in crypto-currencies. The motto of the University of Nicosia: "Think big", cited in the lessons learnt section, can be a great and encouraging takeaway from this chapter.

Continuing the reflections on the lessons learnt from a real-world use of blockchain, Chapter 7 focuses on the issuance of blockchain-based certificates at the University of Nicosia. Marinos Themistocleous, Klitos Christodoulou, and Elias Iosif present Block.co – a platform developed at the University for this purpose. The platform's main goal is not to use blockchain just for the sake of using it but to show that blockchain can meet the requirements of a decentralised system for the issuance of certificates. This approach is in line with the needs of graduates, the labour market, and educational institutions, as discussed in the previous chapters.

Chapter 8 is the concluding chapter, in which Dariusz Dymek and Janusz Stal deliver a critical evaluation of the existing and potential areas of block-chain applications in education. To this end, the chapter provides an overview of the factors that need to be taken into account when the use of blockchain is considered. The authors' opinion which deserves the readers' special attention is as follows:

> *Blockchain technology has a potential to support higher education institutions in their shift towards Education 4.0. However, it might be a time-consuming process. Ongoing projects that use blockchain play a significant role in this transformation. Their failure can slow down the process of blockchain technology adoption, but their success will most likely attract more institutions and make the whole community more open to blockchain applications.*

In our opinion, this can be a concluding remark of the book as a whole.

We believe that the book makes an important contribution to the popularisation of blockchain technology in the educational context, which is especially important in the light of this generally underdeveloped subject and restricted scope of existing books. The book's comprehensive character would be valuable for readers with various backgrounds, including researchers and practitioners. Researchers will gain a broad outline of the considerations associated with education transformation with the use of blockchain that can guide their research. Practitioners will obtain a comprehensive overview of the possibilities and ideas for applications, including insights into first-hand experience with blockchain applications at a university. In particular, the book will be interesting for policy makers at the university and governmental level (e.g. the Ministry of Education), university IT departments, companies that develop software for universities, and software suppliers. Furthermore, since blockchain technology is still in the process of entering university curricula, the book may also be useful for postgraduate students. By the same token, selected chapters (e.g., Chapters 1, 2, 8) can also be used as supplementary reading for undergraduate students within courses such as Computer Science, Information Systems, Management, and Pedagogy.

In short, the current book critically evaluates blockchain's potential for reshaping education. To this end, on the one hand, the most promising areas are delineated, and on the other hand, the most challenging issues are outlined. As a result, the book would be helpful in raising awareness about the role of blockchain in education and in gaining a broader insight into the future role of blockchain in educational institutions.

References

Bitcoin.com. (2016). *Students Graduate from First Ever Blockchain Master's Program.* Retrieved Feb. 8, 2023, from: https://news.bitcoin.com/students-graduate-block chain-masters/

Buntinx, J. P. (2017). *Top 5 University Bitcoin Courses.* Retrieved Feb. 8, 2023, from: https://themerkle.com/top-5-university-Bitcoin-courses/

Cunha, P. R., Soja, P., & Themistocleous, M. (2021). Blockchain for development: a guiding framework. *Information Technology for Development, 27*(3), 417–438.

Frizzo-Barker, J., Chow-White, P. A., Adams, P. R., Mentanko, J., Ha, D., & Green, S. (2020). Blockchain as a disruptive technology for business: A systematic review. *International Journal of Information Management, 51*, 102029.

Gartner. (2019, October, 16). *4 Ways Blockchain Will Transform Higher Education.* Gartner Report. Retrieved Feb. 8, 2023, from: https://www.gartner.com/smarter withgartner/4-ways-blockchain-will-transform-higher-education

Joshi, N. (2022, March, 31). *Understanding Education 4.0: The Machine Learning-Driven Future of Learning.* Forbes. Retrieved Feb. 4, 2023, from: https://www. forbes.com/sites/naveenjoshi/2022/03/31/understanding-education-40-the-machine-learning-driven-future-of-learning/

NOWPayments. (2020). *Top 5 Universities Offering Courses in Blockchain in 2020.* Retrieved Feb. 8, 2023, from: https://www.unic.ac.cy/top-5-universities-offering-courses-in-blockchain-in-2020-4/

Oesterreich, T. D., & Teuteberg, F. (2016). Understanding the implications of digitisation and automation in the context of Industry 4.0: A triangulation approach and elements of a research agenda for the construction industry. *Computers in Industry*, *83*, 121–139.

Olsen, T. L., & Tomlin, B. (2020). Industry 4.0: Opportunities and challenges for operations management. *Manufacturing & Service Operations Management*, *22*(1), 113–122.

Stroe, A. C. (2022). Digitalization of Romanian education system: Is Romania ready to embrace Education 4.0? *Informatica Economica*, *26*(3), 16–25.

1

TOWARDS EDUCATION 4.0

Challenges and opportunities

Paweł Konkol and Dariusz Dymek

1.1 Introduction

Nowadays, the higher education sector faces various challenges related to the social and economic transformation linked with Industry 4.0 and widespread digitalisation of almost every professional activity and occupation. Social aspects of the labour market evolution over the recent years have been associated with new generations entering the workforce (Millennials, Generation Z, Generation Alpha) combined with rapid development of new Information and Communications Technologies (ICT) and their impact on the economy (Bielińska-Dusza & Gierałt, 2021). These factors influence the higher education sector which must transform in order to adapt to new conditions. This adaptation should meet the expectations coming from different stakeholders, including students (as future employees) and employers. These expectations refer more to specific, sometimes narrow, practical competences and skills, rather than general, theoretical knowledge.

Technology and innovation can be perceived as an important driver for transformation in the higher education area whose aim is to ensure high responsiveness to labour market demands by educating goal-oriented graduates able to adapt to the rapidly changing requirements and ready to continuously acquire new knowledge and skills within the lifelong learning framework (Hong & Ma, 2020). Since digitalisation is accelerating, the problem of insufficient supply of graduates with relevant digital skills and competences is observed in different countries. A good illustration of this problem is data from the European Digital Economy and Society Index (DESI) which show that only 54% of Europeans aged between 16 and 74

DOI: 10.4324/9781003318736-2

have at least basic digital skills (European Commission, 2022). This is one example of indicators which characterises external environment in which higher education operates and shifts towards Education 4.0. This is an approach to learning that is related to the fourth industrial revolution and considers transforming education through advanced digital technology and automation (Joshi, 2022). Education 4.0 includes a new education shift aimed at values represented by Industry 4.0 and focuses on adaptive learning to enable students develop skills needed in the present labour market (Stroe, 2022). This shift is based on the conviction that present employers concentrate less on conceptual and theoretical knowledge, but rather on how future employees can adapt and integrate this general knowledge with new technologies, having capabilities to up-skill, re-skill, and pursue lifelong learning (Hong & Ma, 2020). Continuous education helps to remain professionally agile. Looking from the perspective of Industry 4.0 transformation, one of the challenges to the current workforce and new generations of employees is the process automation and predictions of its influence on the labour market. Education offering short and long learning paths helps to limit and avoid potential risks linked with automation.

The importance of Education 4.0 transformation has also been recognised by the World Economic Forum which estimates that a global enhancement in students' collaborative problem-solving capacity to the average level of today's top 10 scoring countries should yield an additional $2.54 trillion in increased productivity to the global economy (World Economic Forum, 2022).

This chapter presents the concept of Education 4.0 in the context of the changes taking place in society and economy and shows how these changes affect higher education. Section 1.2 describes the current social and economy phenomena and the challenges created by the ongoing changes to education. In response to these challenges, new concepts of functioning in the area of higher education were developed (described in Section 1.3), supported by new forms and methods of teaching (Section 1.4). As discussed in Section 1.5, such an answer would not be possible without new technologies that increase the scope of activities of educational organisations, thus allowing them to adapt to changing conditions.

1.2 Education 4.0 ecosystem

1.2.1 Fourth Industrial Revolution and its influence on education

The Fourth Industrial Revolution (4IR), often referred to as the Industry 4.0, is a common name for economic and social changes resulting from the widespread digitisation of production processes and services, the beginning of which dates back to the end of the 20th century (Davis, 2016). But despite its name, its effects extend far beyond the industry. The following quotation is a good illustration of that phenomenon (Schwab, 2016, p. 109):

> *In the fourth industrial revolution, digital connectivity enabled by software technologies is fundamentally changing society. The scale of the impact and the speed of the changes taking place have made the transformation that is playing out so different from any other industrial revolution in human history.*

The important aspect of 4IR transformation is the combination of technologies which results in blurring the boundaries between physical, digital, and biological spheres (Xu, David, & Kim, 2018). The results of 4IR are deep changes in the labour market. The high dynamics of transformation associated with the adaptations of new technologies makes employers alter their expectations towards current and future employees, which in turn translates into a change in expectations towards educational institutions.

The challenges faced by education are well described by the famous quote of Richard Riley, the former American Secretary of Education (Ton-Quinlivan & Hackwood, 2017, p. 3):

> *We are currently preparing students for jobs that don't yet exist ... using technologies that haven't been invented ... in order to solve problems we don't even know are problems yet.*

The key aspect here is the dynamic change of professions with new types of jobs arising in different domains and specialisations. According to the World Economic Forum 65% of children who begin their school education nowadays will work in professions that yet do not exist at present (World Economic Forum, 2016).

This is not the first time that education has faced challenges, although it might be the first time when changes have been so quick. Throughout recent history, educational institutions went through various periods of transformation. Looking at past evolution of education and dividing it into stages, four main periods can be distinguished. The first one, referred to as Education 1.0, was focused mainly on the needs of agricultural society; the second, Education 2.0, on the needs of industrial society; and the third one, referred to as Education 3.0, on transformation oriented on how to take advantage of technology. The aim of the next stage, Education 4.0, is to meet the needs of an era of innovations (Himmetoğlu, Ayduğ, & Bayrak, 2020). These innovations not only represent a fundamental change for the industrial sector but also evoke various changes in the way people live and work.

Taking into account the dynamic character of the labour market, the challenges that contemporary education is facing can be summarised as follows (Dimitrova, Madzhurova, Raychev, & Stoyanova, 2022):

- increased demand for advanced-level cognitive skills (e.g., problem-solving, critical thinking, and advanced communication);
- increased demand for lifelong learning as employees often must change career paths throughout their professional lives;
- expecting higher educational institutions to act as the platform for the development of innovation.

Summing up, the transformation towards Education 4.0, forced largely by 4IR processes, is associated with significant changes in the labour market. These changes have a great impact on higher educational institutions and demand to rethink the way and methods of providing education for students.

1.2.2 New generations on the labour market

Transformation of the labour market refers to changes in expectations of new generations who enter workforce. Generation Y or Generation Z may serve as good examples of the challenge posed by young employees to employers. Generation Y refers to the group of people born between 1981 and 1994/96. An important feature related to representatives of Generation Y, often referred to as Millennials, is the growing impact of Internet on their everyday life. They are team-oriented, have high hopes for themselves and others, and are sociable and ready for changes (Pysarevskyi et al., 2022). Generation Z represents the latest wave of young employees starting their professional career and includes the people born between 1995 and 2012. One of the most important characteristics of this cohort is digitalisation. Generation Z is the first global generation whose life began in the world determined and dominated by digital technologies, making Generation Z representative digital experts since their childhood. Constant access to the Internet when reaching and consuming information is one of the typical features of this generation (Machov et al., 2021). Generation Z (also called post-millennials and centennials) may be also described by a higher level of individualism, multitasking and entrepreneurial skills (Pysarevskyi et al., 2022).

These new generations entering the labour market also bring new expectations, demands, and attitudes towards building their professional career and shaping their work–life balance. Taking representatives of Generation Y into consideration and comparing this cohort with the previous ones, including their parents, it is important to mention different approaches referring to job perception and the role of the employer. This includes, for instance, willingness to spend less time on professional activity and perceiving free time as more important than additional working hours (Robak, 2017). These kinds of changes raise the challenge to employers who have to meet different expectations of young professionals; for example, developing an organisational culture supporting work–life balance.

Considering present changes in individual preferences, flexibility of work schemes needs to be broadened (OECD, 2017). In these new circumstances, the old question of how many hours we spend at work turns into whether the required task is finished. Focus on result, not on workload, makes jobs easier and customised and creates more flexible conditions regarding the place and pace of work. However, a side effect of this might be blurring the boundary between personal and professional life, which creates the significant challenge both for employees and employers: how to develop working conditions allowing work–life integration (e.g., combining family and working responsibilities). Similar expectations can also be observed in higher education institutions (HEIs), where students want to link the education with gaining a professional experience, often starting their first job during their studies. Furthermore, many countries are facing problems with a persistent gap between the skills and knowledge needed on the market and those possessed by graduates entering workforce (Malik & Venkatraman, 2017). This poses a challenge to both labour market institutions and HEIs regarding the anticipation of future demands in order to prepare and transform existing educational programmes and teaching methods. It is expected that HEIs will put more stress on very specific, limited set of skills and competences, rather than concentrate on some general knowledge from a given discipline. In particular, this is true for studies in the area of IT, where HEIs compete on the educational market with training institutions providing very narrow and specific trainings (recognisable by employers) which fit directly into the current demands of the labour market.

1.2.3 Possibilities of educational processes automation

An important element of IR4 is automation, which can lead to the redefinition of some professions or even causing them to disappear from the labour market. Hawksworth, Berriman and Goel (2018) point out three basic waves of how automation processes may look like over the next few decades:

1. Algorithm wave – related to automation of basic, simple computational tasks and analysis of structured data in fields concerning finance, communication, and information. This first wave is already underway.

2. Augmentation wave – concerning communicating and exchanging information based on dynamic technological support, automation of repeatable tasks like filling in forms, and analysis of unstructured data in semi-controlled environments. These processes are already going on but will intensify in the coming years.
3. Autonomy wave – related to automation of physical labour and manual dexterity, working out problems in dynamic real conditions, like manufacturing and transport (e.g., autonomous cars). This wave is already in the development stage, but its full maturity is expected in 2030s.

Automation exerts strong pressure on the entire economy and the shape of the labour market. In this context, the question about the impact of automation on education can appear. Can automation support education in facing the challenges posed by the changing labour market? To answer this question, a closer look at activities linked with educational processes and their characteristic in the context of automation is necessary. Figure 1.1 presents such a characteristic in comparison to other sectors.

Compared to other sectors, the characteristic of tasks and skills in the education sector shows that they have rather low automatability potential since, compared to average, they are more focused on social skills or management, the areas which are difficult to be replaced by technology and machines. Obviously, automation will have an impact on educational processes, but this impact will not affect education as strongly as many other sectors (Hawksworth, Berriman, & Goel, 2018).

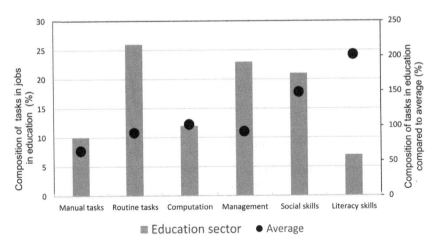

FIGURE 1.1 Composition of tasks involved in jobs in education.

Source: Based on (Hawksworth, Berriman, & Goel, 2018).

It should be underlined that the automation of processes through digitalisation, combined with globalisation, beside positive impact, also creates various problems. The one related to education and training is the disappearance of some professions with another new ones being created at the same time. This means that there is the necessity for continuous transformation of study programmes, both in terms of content and methods used, with the increasing use of ICT tools facilitating flexibility in many aspects (e.g., distance learning, individual study paths). Hence, looking at these changes from the perspective of HEIs, one of the main challenges for the future is how to equip graduates with such skills and knowledge that will ease the navigation in this technology-driven environment. Considering dynamic character of changes, the emphasis has to be put on the development of the lifelong learning opportunities offering ways to acquire skills needed at various stages of an individual's professional career.

1.2.4 Higher education institutions in the changing environment

Looking generally at the education market, an increasing number of students reflects the growing importance of HEIs in society. Taking into account past two decades, global participation in higher education by the year 2020 reached 228 million students, as compared to 82 million in 1995 (Higher education in a changing and challenging world, 2022). Transformation of higher education based on advanced digital technologies facilitates provision of educational resources and knowledge for such a wide population of students at different levels. The move towards distance learning has taken place in the worldwide tertiary education, with some important limitations and obstacles encountered. One of them refers to the fact that low-income countries are the place of living for 96% of the 2.9 billion people who have never used the Internet (Higher education in a changing and challenging world, 2022). Increasing popularity of distance learning also moves the attention to the general growing importance of remote work in the labour market. In the era of globalisation and common access to the Internet, it is easy to search for manpower worldwide. Splitting jobs into lower-level tasks, allows the possibility to hire employees to perform individual tasks, without the necessity to create more formal relationships. It results in enlarging the sector of freelancers or the platform economy (e.g., Upwork, Freelancer, Guru) (Pongratz, 2018).

The pace of transformation towards Education 4.0 has been accelerated by the COVID-19 pandemic. In addition, preferences of Generation Z students, discussed in Section 1.2.2, also contributed to changes in expectations towards an educational system that can be summarised as follows (Fisk, 2017):

- diverse time and place (more opportunities to learn at different places and times, e-learning tools and methods),
- personalised learning (adaptation of the study programme and methods to the capabilities of a student, increasing importance of mentoring),
- project-based learning and assessing of students' progress (learning based on project and teamwork approach),
- field experience (more opportunities oriented on practical skills),
- data interpretation (increasing importance of competencies in data analysis).

It should be noted that HEIs operate in the growing competitive environment, which raises challenges especially to the public higher education sector. HEIs compete for new students, budget, and subsidies, as well as for the academic staff. What is more important, competition in the higher education sector evolves in such a way that it refers not only to individuals or countries but also to institutional level, turning universities into real competitors (Musselin, 2018). From this perspective of the growing competitiveness, the term marketisation of higher education is used to describe trends of providing higher education based on a pure market basis. This generally may be perceived as a method of ensuring balance between the demand and supply of student education, scientific research, and other activities of higher education institutions based on price mechanism (Brown, 2015). In this context, it is worth mentioning that the emerging competition from organisations is not directly included in the education sector (in particular, public education). They offer their own programmes and courses whose scope and form are driven by market needs or are aimed at promoting their own methods and tools. For instance, Oracle Academy (academy.oracle.com) or Microsoft Imagine Academy (microsoft.com/en-gb/education/imagine-academy) offers many complete programmes or individual courses based on their own software.

Competitiveness refers also to distance learning educational market where HEIs have to compete with various institutions offering non-degree training programmes which are nowadays growing in popularity (Morris, Ivancheva, Coop, Mogliacci, & Swinnerton, 2020). For instance, in some areas like IT, the market of training courses is very extensive, and some training programmes are regarded by employers as comparable to formal HEIs' degree courses.

Considering generation-related changes, today's students often start their studies with detailed expectations for their future professional career path.

This causes a change in the role of students in the educational process, from passive listeners to active participants who have their own requirements and expectations that the HEIs should meet. The answer of HEIs to this challenge is the idea of student-centred learning, which is included in the Education 4.0 concept. Student-centred learning underlines the need to provide students with higher level of autonomy, independence, and control over their learning experiences (Lathika, 2016). In the student-centred learning approach, students are perceived as the owners of their learning processes. They build learning opportunities and have the possibility to reconstruct knowledge in a dynamic way based on an open-ended learning environment (Lee & Hannafin, 2016). Compared to the past decades, when traditional, externally directed learning in which students' engagement and participation were more passive, in student-centred learning student's role is more active. This approach provides more opportunities to develop soft skills and competences necessary for the project team collaboration. These types of skills are prerequisite for the effective team collaboration and are essential to succeed in project realisation in different business sectors and to facilitate the spread of necessary knowledge across organisations.

HEIs that change their teaching methods towards student-centred approach concentrate on skills and practices that facilitate lifelong learning and an independent problem-solving approach. More emphasis is put on students' interests, enabling them to decide what and how will they learn. This method of education provision transforms a teacher into a facilitator of the educational process for an individual student during their study track, rather than for a class or group perceived as a whole.

Student-centred learning needs efficient methods and tools facilitating adjustment of teaching programmes to present and future needs of the labour market. The higher education system should be more responsive to labour market needs providing graduates with relevant competencies and employability perspectives (OECD, 2019). Apart from the labour market or employers' needs, this adjustment may also be seen from the perspective of students' expectations for education. Education more tailored for individual requirements should provide counselling and recommendation for students based on their prior educational achievements. Introduction of student-centred learning approach may be enhanced by the usage of different teaching methods, and at the same time, implementing various new ICT tools and technologies in the teaching processes. These methods include computer-supported collaborative learning, problem-based learning, active learning, and cooperative learning (Judi & Sahari, 2013).

One of the important challenges to stakeholders of the labour market, mainly employers and educational institutions, considers verifications of educational achievements and diploma. This challenge is enforced by globalisation and the mobility of workers. Looking from the point of view of HEIs, it is necessary to provide fast and reliable methods for employers to verify documents that job candidates present as the proof of their academic achievements. HEIs issue various documents like transcripts, diploma supplements, and other documents that provide potential employers and other institutions with deeper understanding of student achievements. However, employers encounter difficulties on how to guarantee that these documents are real and not fraudulent, taking into account that the level of fraud in this area is high. According to the statistics from the United Kingdom (HEDD, 2021), about 30% of students and graduates cheated by fabricating or exaggerating their academic achievements. Another data for the United Kingdom shows that half of large businesses and small- and medium-sized enterprises have encountered an employment candidate who cheated about degree qualifications, presenting a false degree or by inflating their grade (Half of UK employers have been victims of degree fraud, 2019).

Furthermore, an important problem is an educational black market offering fake degrees and diplomas. This can lead to serious consequences like in the case of police in Brazil, where new police staff joined the forces presenting fake diplomas (Lepiane et al., 2019). In the United States, problem of fake diplomas has existed for a long time. According to an estimation from 2011 by Attewell and Domina (2011), 6% of bachelor's degrees and 35% of associate degrees in the United States were fake. Frauds referring to educational documents relate to other aspects like misrepresenting achievements, changing grades, and inflating work experience. These kinds of problems with frauds are deepened by the fact that some institutions issuing documents disappear from the market or have problems with their archives storing documents. This also affects students who are not able to validate their achievements.

All these challenges create additional, unnecessary costs for companies with regard to verification procedures. According to estimations for the United Kingdom, on average, companies' spendings to address these issues account for £ 40 000 (Henle, Dineen, & Duffy, 2019; Awaji & Solaiman, 2022). Therefore, various stakeholders in the labour market (educational institutions, companies, human resources, and recruitment agencies) should be interested in implementing new digital solutions improving practices in this field. When considering verification of educational achievements by the labour market, digital technologies such as blockchain may be used to provide learners with better access and ownership of their qualifications with accompanying documents and certificates.

Education 4.0 transformation takes place in the environment which is characterised by the mobility of students and staff. This raises another challenge considering verification of students' achievements related to mobility.

Mobility-related processes are not only managed at intra-organisational level but also refer to many interactions and recognition procedures between HEIs from different countries. In order to provide more transparency and accountability in this area, HEIs need efficient tools to control access to students' data, maintaining the appropriate level of privacy and security. This is the domain in which new digital technologies such as blockchain may produce positive effects. The recent example can be the Erasmus Without Paper, the digital solution for higher education institutions whose aim is to provide methods to connect and exchange data between institutional Erasmus+ mobility management systems for the better management of international students' mobility. In case of students' mobility experience blockchain may be used for the management of certificates attesting courses completed at host institutions.

1.3 Competency-based learning

1.3.1 Impact of the labour market on learning approaches

Common requirements for present employees include the ability to acquire new skills, solve problems, effectively work in team and quickly embrace new technologies and methods of operations. This increases the responsibility of higher education institutions which have to concentrate more on the development of practical skills rather than the transfer of general theoretical knowledge. This more holistic approach to the learning process better prepares graduates to apply knowledge to real-life problems. An emphasis on more competency-based education is linked with the requirements towards higher education institutions to offer more practice-oriented approach (Bauer, 2021). This orientation on practice does not refer only to hard skills but also to soft ones which are perceived as the very important asset of employees, and higher educational institutions have to put emphasis on their development among students. As stated in the famous adage, "You get hired for hard skills, but get fired for soft skills", they form the important part of an employee's professional portfolio. Helping students to develop soft skills is probably the greatest challenge faced by higher education today (Pérez et al., 2020). The competency-based learning concept has been developed to respond to these challenges. This transformation of educational entities is enhanced at regional and international level. Various regulations at European level which underline the need for more competency-based education may serve as examples (European Union, 2018). Looking at competences from different standpoints, some level of ambiguity can be observed. The general concept of competences refers to knowledge, skills, and experience (Serafin, 2016), whereas more detailed distinctions indicate competences as the category embracing not only skills but also knowledge, abilities, and broader predispositions (OECD, 2005). The distinction between behavioural and technical competencies has also been underlined, where the former may be associated with soft skills, like teamwork or leadership (Armstrong & Taylor, 2014). The topic related to competencies and skills in the light of the labour market transformation is discussed in Chapter 5.

One of the challenges to the labour market is how to effectively manage competencies and provide convenient methods of their verification. Various new ICT solutions and technologies may be used to improve these processes, with blockchain being one of the most promising examples (Dymek, Konkol, Stal, Put, & Trąbka, 2020). Competence-oriented teaching relates with the shift to more practice-oriented study programmes or teaching methods and closer links with external stakeholders from the labour market. It is also associated with an enhancement of work–life relevance of higher education as the way to meet the demands of the labour market (Bauer, 2021). The emphasis on competences leads to the growing importance of student-centred approach, in which the learning scope and the speed of the learning paths are adjusted to various students in a more individual way (see Section 1.2.4). Combining this with an increasing number of students, it becomes clear that without the support of ICT technologies these goals will not be achievable. Competency-based teaching should be based on data analyses to build individual learning paths or monitor progress and achievements of an individual student. These analyses may be supported by advanced business intelligence functionalities offering various tools like student's progress dashboard presenting data from different perspectives.

1.3.2 Industry 4.0 and the focus on skills in education

A paradigm shift towards competency-based curriculum is accelerated by various demands addressed at HEIs. Many of them belong to the consequences of the Industry 4.0 transformation. Hence, the Education 4.0 should be analysed from the perspective of methods and ways used by HEIs trying to align educational processes with the needs raised by Industry 4.0 processes (Bonfield, Salter, Longmuir, Benson, & Adachi, 2020). Present-day students do not necessarily look for vast and complete encyclopaedic knowledge and broad multi-angle analyses but rather concentrate on specific skills and methods to complete particular tasks. The European Union funded project called "The University for the Future", launched by HEIs, companies and public bodies, aims to bridge the actual gap in the present higher education offer from the perspective of digitalisation processes. The emphasis is put on a better cooperation between HEIs, business sector, and public authorities as the response to Industry 4.0 transformation. Table 1.1 presents the skills

TABLE 1.1 Competencies in Industry 4.0.

Engineering	Management	Design and innovation
Data science and advanced (big data) analytics	Technology awareness	Understanding the impact of technology
Novel human–machine interfaces	Change management and strategy	Human–robot interaction and user interfaces
Digital-to-physical transfer technologies, such as 3-D printing	Novel talent management strategies	Tech-enabled product and service design
Advanced simulation and virtual plant modelling	Organisational structures and knowledge	Tech-enabled ergonomic solutions and user experience
Closed-loop integrated product and process quality, control and management systems	The role of managers – more as teamwork facilitators than task assigners	
Data communication and networks and system automation	Tech-enabled processes: Forecasting and planning metrics, scheduling	
Real-time inventory and logistics optimisation systems	Business analysis	
Artificial Intelligence, robotics, automation, programming	Digital skills	
Information Technologies Mechatronics, cybersecurity, augmented and virtual reality		

Source: Based on (Universities of the future, 2019).

necessary for the Industry 4.0-based labour market workforce identified within this project. Most of these skills are the result of intensive digitalisation processes. As in the case of engineering or design and innovation, management processes are also supported by a wide range of digital solutions and systems. Study programmes should be more focused on the development of digital skills, and graduates (e.g., project managers) will have to be more digitally professional to effectively run projects in the era of the Industry 4.0 revolution (Universities of the future, 2019).

Competency-based approach in education is a promising direction for the development of HEIs which have to be flexible in responding to the labour market demands. The shift towards this competency-based approach has to be accompanied by the implementation of new teaching methods which is discussed Section 1.4.

1.4 New learning methods and forms

1.4.1 Stakeholders of educational process

Requirements of the labour market and the attitude of young generation towards education system make the traditional form of higher education offered by HEIs insufficient. New challenges require a new form of acting. These challenges can be considered from different points of view, which can be shortly represented as Who, What, and How.

The first perspective (**Who**) refers to stakeholders, both people and organisations, participating in the educational process. It covers their needs, requirements, capabilities, and motivations – generally all aspects influencing their attitudes towards education. The second perspective (**What**) refers to the problems related to the educational content: scope and form. The process of its development, in most cases is the internal process of a given HEI, but it is under impact of many internal (e.g., capabilities, staff availability) and external (e.g., labour market needs, students' expectations) factors. The third perspective (**How**) represents the way of interaction between Who and What, in particular, describing the newly developed and introduced forms and methods used in the educational process (Figure 1.2).

New learning methods and forms which are developed in a higher education environment reflect the transformation of goals and priorities shared by educational institutions. The role of a contemporary education institution is not mainly to deliver theoretical knowledge but rather to provide an inspiring environment in which learners can improve their problem-solving skills and analytical competences. Problem-solving skills and creativity are listed among the top five skills which will be necessary on the labour market taking into account the perspective of the year 2025 (World Economic Forum, 2020). This approach implies more active role of students in the teaching process and the necessity of adjustment of teacher's role and teaching methods used (Calvão, Ribeiro, & Simões, 2019).

Taking into account skills expected from HEIs graduates (Table 1.2), it is necessary to redesign methods of teaching in order to develop competencies important for the current labour market. New methods should focus on a more interactive way of teaching, and for this purpose new digital technologies can be widely used (see Section 1.5).

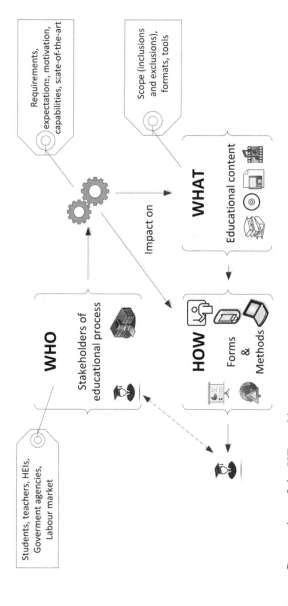

FIGURE 1.2   Perspectives of the HE teaching process.

TABLE 1.2 Skills expected from a student in Education 4.0.

Category of skills	Sample skills
Personal characteristics	Productive, investigative, leader, entrepreneur, adaptable, curious
Technological skills	Producing new information and technologies, using technology effectively, catching up technological developments
Cooperation-communication skills	Teamwork skills, effective communication
Learning skills	Analytical thinking, problem-solving and critical thinking, learning anywhere and anytime

Source: Based on (Himmetoğlu, Ayduğ, & Bayrak, 2020).

1.4.2 Evolution of teaching methods and digitalisation

Although digital technologies bring various opportunities for teaching methods' transformation, some obstacles have to be taken into consideration. One of them refers to the level of resistance among teaching staff to use modern digital technologies. Hence, the challenge faced by higher education in the 21st century does not refer to modern technologies as such but to the ability of teaching staff to use and embed them into the teaching practice (Watty, McKay, & Ngo, 2016). To overcome this obstacle, academics should enhance their understanding of technologies to be able to see what benefits they can bring to the teaching process.

Digital tools that can be used to transform teaching process are based on a variety of ICTs. Digital tools that can support education include the following (Watty et al., 2016):

- intelligent tutoring systems – enabling to profile student work and provide customised instruction and feedback,
- social media technologies – used for collaboration, communication, and effective content delivery,
- click technology – enabling active engagement of students in the learning process (e.g., pooling tools to keep students engaged),
- video learning resources and social media – facilitating content dissemination and open access for students with any type of barriers hindering learning process,
- flipped classroom technologies – used to switch from traditional way of teaching towards blended, flipped approach,
- instant web response tool – directed to develop critical thinking and reflection skills.

Guàrdia et al. (2021) elaborated the list of innovative approaches for the teaching process at higher education institutions. Most of them refer to some aspects of digitalisation and involvement of new ICTs. Even though some trends have been present in the higher education area for a long time, new disruptive technologies boost their usage in teaching. The sample list of these methods includes the following (Guàrdia, Clougher, Anderson, & Maina, 2021):

- adaptive learning – the approach to education where students receive tailored resources, materials, and activities. Artificial Intelligence (AI) can be used to expand the range of possibilities in this area,
- event-based learning – education realised in the frame of planned events in real-life context. Popular activities include Hackathon, Charette (collaborative event for group work on a particular task), Editathon (collaborative event for editing and generating content for digital applications and information repositories), GameJam (collaborative event to develop games and concepts of games), Installfest (collective instalment of a particular software, accompanied sometimes by tutorials and walkthroughs), World Café (discussion event for knowledge sharing based on a specific workflow),
- gamification – uses game elements to increase motivation, enjoyment, and engagement of students in order to improve knowledge retention,
- rhizomatic learning – based on the assumption that learning is a multidimensional process with a complex and chaotic character (teacher as a facilitator of conversation).

Another approach to teaching that supports Education 4.0 principles is the concept of flipped classroom (Smith, Legaki, & Hamari, 2022). In this approach to teaching, knowledge transfer should be realised more individually by students prior to their participation in a class. As a result, class time can be devoted to assist students in the assimilation of what they have accessed and attempted to understand in teaching resources (Farmer, 2018). As ICT technologies facilitate access to educational resources, in case of flipped classroom, students can easily acquire theoretical knowledge at home, whereas on-campus classrooms can provide more opportunities for individual guidance, discussions, practical instructions, and experiments.

Since higher education stakeholders, like students and faculty staff, live in a society where technology gains more importance, evolution of teaching methods should reflect this shift. An important feature of the new teaching methods is interactive character which can be easily achieved through the combination of traditional classroom experience with new ways of knowledge dissemination and provision.

1.4.3 Next generation pedagogy framework

The IDEAS framework developed by Guàrdia et al. (2021) may be treated as the set of guideposts on the path to the next generation pedagogy (Figure 1.3). The intelligent pedagogy concept points at learning analytic tools to provide more adaptive teaching, based on student actual performance. Analysis of individual learning paths can help to identify students with potential problems during study progress. Another important aspect refers to expanded learning activities outside a particular institutional learning platform which provides students with broader learning experiences and ensures higher level of autonomy in the learning process.

Agile pedagogy is another characteristic of the teaching process where the emphasis is put on flexibility and responsiveness to learners' needs. One of the very interesting examples of how to provide this flexibility refers to micro-credentials, which certify learning outcomes of short-term learning activities. This approach has been discussed and developed across European

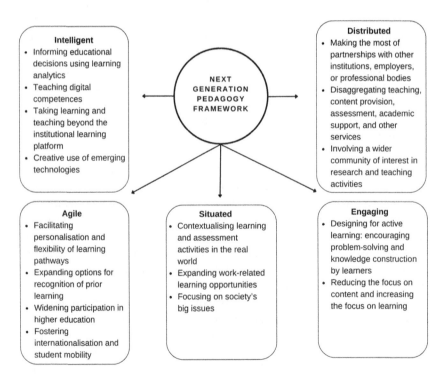

FIGURE 1.3   IDEAS pedagogy framework.

Source: Based on (Guàrdia, Clougher, Anderson, & Maina, 2021).

Higher Education Area with the aim to provide access to education and training to broader population of students, also from disadvantaged groups (The Council of the European Union, 2022).

Situated pedagogy emphasises the importance of the real-world relevance of study curricula and the contextualisation of the learning process which should address students' personal and professional goals. Learning activities should provide opportunities to apply knowledge in practice based on partnership with companies and other organisations.

Distributed teaching underlines the importance of cooperation among various stakeholders, like educational institutions, business partners, or professional bodies. From this perspective, creation of study programmes is based on the prior collaboration between different partners, providing students with more adequate knowledge and skills addressing and responding to the current needs of the labour market.

Engaging pedagogy refers to the shift from the passive content-based approach to methods of teaching where students play a more active role. More responsibility is transferred on students encouraging them to search actively for resources and applying them to the real-life context.

All the above-discussed transformation processes of HEIs and new methods and approaches to education are strongly linked with the growing importance of digital technologies. The impact of digitalisation on the learning process is difficult to overestimate. Various ICTs change the educational landscape, providing tools to replace traditional teaching methods. One of the examples refers to the use of virtual and augmented reality in the classroom in order to create augmented learning experience (eLearning Industry, 2021). The important consequence of the present transformation of education is the emphasis on flexibility based on students' individual needs. To support this, HEIs have to provide more options for educational track students choose, offer flexible schedules, and extend distance learning options.

1.5 Impact of disruptive technologies

1.5.1 Introduction to disruptive technologies

Disruptive technologies bring various opportunities but also challenges to their implementation in organisations (Benner, 2020; Ghawe & Chan, 2022). They offer ways for the improvement of economic efficiency or the quality of life, but also pose new forms of risk by triggering unexpected changes in organisations (Taeihagh, Ramesh, & Howlett, 2021). Disruptive technologies may be analysed from the perspective of the Industry 4.0 revolution. Since Education 4.0 is linked with the Fourth Industrial Revolution,

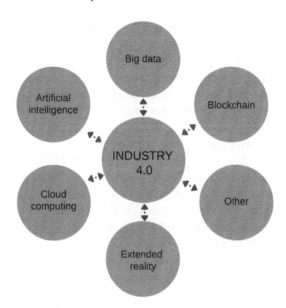

FIGURE 1.4   Disruptive technologies.

some flagship disruptive technologies listed in the context of the 4IR may also be referenced in the case of Education 4.0. These technologies include (Chaka, 2022): blockchain, autonomous robots, artificial intelligence, cloud computing, big data, smart sensors, extended reality (XR) embracing such forms as augmented, mixed and virtual reality, and Internet of Things (Figure 1.4).

Disruptive technologies may be perceived as tools that create possibilities to do things in a way which was not possible in the past. However, also in the case of higher education, implementation of a new disruptive technology does not mean automatic modernisation of existing teaching processes (Christensen, Horn, & Johnson, 2008). Incentives for these technology-based modernisation often come from other institutions which are competitors in the same market. HEIs are nowadays faced by the increasing competitiveness of various non-academic educational initiatives and organisations which are more eager to benefit from new technologies to provide educational content, focusing more on the online approach. Such initiatives may enhance faster implementation of new disruptive technologies in HEIs whose educational offer is based on regular degree programmes. These technologies enhance personalised education based on the identification of students' learning strategies and abilities. Below the main disruptive technologies are discussed with indication on their potential usage of education.

1.5.2 Big data

Big data solutions refer to data sets that exceed the ability of traditional data processing to capture, manage, and process the data. Big data analytics refers to the use of advance analytic techniques on a very large amount of data (IBM, 2023). Organisations, also HEIs, have been generating an increasing amount of data. Analysis of this data can provide a valuable insight into organisational processes and operations.

Big data systems in education are one of the tools that help to eliminate problems related to siloed database systems and insufficient data exchange between various areas of organisational activities. Big data analytics can bring advantages for HEIs, since they produce large amount of data related in particular to study-oriented processes. Educational institutions can use big data solutions to offer innovative teaching (Huda et al., 2016). For example, collecting and analysing large amount of data about students' behaviour allows to elaborate predictions enabling to build learning process in a more individual way (e.g., prognosis on student preferences concerning course or learning materials). Furthermore, big data solutions may be used in recommendation systems which are based on data related to students' learning methods, habits, and interests. These systems can help to solve problems of information overload through recommendation of personalised educational resources (Fu, Tian, & Tang, 2022).

1.5.3 Cloud computing

According to the definition of the American National Institute of Standards and Technology,

> *Cloud computing is a model for enabling ubiquitous, convenient, on-demand network access to a shared pool of configurable computing resources (e.g., networks, servers, storage, applications, and services) that can be rapidly provisioned and released with minimal management effort or service provider interaction.*
>
> *(Mell & Grance, 2011, p. 2)*

Cloud computing has been widely implemented in HEIs, providing tools to share online teaching materials and manage academic assessment and examination. The importance of cloud computing for higher education sector increased dramatically during the COVID-19 pandemic (Noh & Amron, 2021). Applications like Google Classroom, Zoom, Microsoft Teams, and other learning management systems and study-oriented services allowed to organise teaching process based on distance or blended learning approach. They are based on cloud computing services, providing tools to share resources and collaborate on common tasks.

1.5.4 Extended reality

Extended reality is the term embracing both virtual reality (VR) and augmented reality (AR). While in the case of virtual reality, where an immersive virtual environment is created, in augmented reality visual, auditory, or other type of sensory information is overlaid onto the real-world environment. Augmented reality allows user to see both real and virtual objects superimposed on natural view. Hence, one of the main differences between augmented and virtual reality is that the latter creates its own cyber environment whereas the former adds additional digital layer to the real world. Augmented reality can be divided into the following categories (Sinha, 2021): marker-based AR (linked with physical image triggering an augmented experience and additional content), marker-less AR (surrounding environment scanned before placing digital content on a given surface), location-based AR (based on responding to information produced by GPS, accelerometer or digital compasses).

AR has revolutionised the transmission of data. It has some advantages over virtual reality since in case of the latter the user is completely immersed in an artificial environment and shut out from the surroundings (Tan, Chandukala, & Reddy, 2022). Virtual and augmented reality offer new tools for the dissemination of knowledge and facilitate educational content creation which is more intuitive for users (Qushem et al., 2021). Virtual Reality provides methods for creating realistic scenarios which can, in particular, be used for studies like medicine or archaeology. Using AR in education provides tools to create 3D models which improve students' learning experience. AR and VR may clarify abstract and complex content thanks to the visualisation capabilities and interactivity (Dikusar, 2018). AR and VR may be used to explore abstract concepts and study various phenomena in more details (Hernandez-de-Menendez, Díaz, & Morales-Menendez, 2020).

1.5.5 Artificial Intelligence

According to Dikusar (2018), artificial intelligence is one of the two most promising disruptive technologies for education, together with extended reality discussed above. As defined in documents of the European Commission:

> *Artificial Intelligence refers to systems that display intelligent behaviour by analysing their environment and taking actions – with some degree of autonomy – to achieve specific goals. AI-based systems can be purely software-based, acting in the virtual world (e.g., voice assistants, image analysis software, search engines, speech and face recognition systems) or AI can be embedded in hardware devices (e.g. advanced robots, autonomous cars, drones or Internet of Things applications).*
>
> *(European Commission, 2018, p. 1)*

Artificial intelligence may be implemented in supporting digital and web-based educational systems providing tools for the assessment of students' personality traits. Furthermore, it may be used to collect data on student-learning styles or create alerts related to the probability of students' early dropouts (Qushem et al., 2021).

1.5.6 Blockchain

Blockchain as a disruptive technology may play an important role in the transformation of HEIs in the direction towards Education 4.0 (Logofatu, 2017). Its possible implementations in the educational sector, especially in higher education, are broadly discussed in the subsequent chapters. Higher education institutions investigate various ways in which this technology could be implemented for areas like identity management or transcripts of records and diploma management. Since blockchain solutions are based on a distributed data structure with records being replicated in multiple locations and taking into account elimination of the role of a central authority on the top of a ledger, this technology allows to increase the trust among all participants of a blockchain-based system (Alexander et al., 2019). Moreover, blockchain can serve as an interface with other systems based on such disruptive technologies like artificial intelligence, Internet of Things (IoT), big data, which are also being implemented in HEIs (Gutowski, Markiewicz, Niedzielski, & Klein, 2022).

Apart from many conceptual approaches, there are a number of examples of already existing solutions in HEIs where blockchain is used to improve the management of processes. They refer to keeping records of degrees, diplomas, certificates, and credentials in blockchain, providing students with better control over verification and recognition processes. Blockchain can help to prevent fraud in skills recognition on the labour market and streamline recruitment-related processes (Steiu, 2020). Blockchain-based transcript of records listing all educational achievements can not only improve processes on the labour market but also facilitate students' mobility between institutions, for example in the context of the European Union students' mobility programmes.

1.5.7 Other disruptive technologies

Other major disruptive technologies that may be used in higher education sector include Internet of Things and smart sensors or robotics (Choi, Kumar, Yue, & Chan, 2021). These technologies refer more to industry sector, but they may also bring some advantages for education.

Internet of Things concept embraces the solutions where objects, sensors, and other items generate, exchange and consume data based on network connectivity and computing capability with minor human intervention (Rose, Eldridge, & Chapin, 2015). Smart sensors are IoT components that are used to transform real-world variables into digital data. IoT can be used to streamline different operations at HEIs to prepare them better for learning activities. For example, it can support solutions that facilitate tracking students' attendance based on wearable devices; they help to eliminate teacher's obligation on tracking and reporting in this area (Bakla, 2019). IoT can be also useful in managing university infrastructure, for instance through monitoring temperature in classrooms and enabling to create appropriate conditions for learning.

Educational robotics may be used as a teaching tool in higher education. This technology can improve motivation and students' educational performance by providing motivating activities, real experiences, and an attractive learning environment (Sánchez, Martínez, & González, 2019).

Referring to aforementioned technologies (e.g., AR, VR, blockchain), the recent concept of metaverse should be also added to the list of new technological advancements which can be used in education. Metaverse can be defined as

> a persistent and immersive simulated world that is experienced in the first person by large groups of simultaneous users who share a strong sense of mutual presence. It can be fully virtual and self-contained (a virtual metaverse) or it can exist as layers of virtual content overlaid on the real world (an augmented metaverse).
>
> (Rosenberg, 2022)

Metaverse with other technologies like artificial intelligence may offer educational content for students in a more personalised manner and allow a deeper integration of new disruptive technologies in education (Contreras et al., 2022).

Technology which is directly linked with augmented reality and has a potential to transform the way of how people learn is the holographic technology. This technology refers to the usage of lasers, illumination, and light recording to build 3D images. A hologram is produced with photographic projection that records the light scattered from some object and displays it in a way that provides three-dimensional impression. Potential use and benefits of digital holograms for education refer in particular to providing students with more realistic images, creating more appropriate speciation of abstract topics, combining non-alive characters with the real world (Turk & Kapucu Seckin, 2021). Holograms provide methods to perform experiments close to learners without the necessity to sit in one classroom. This technology is already in use in developed countries, and it may be also used by universities to provide education for developing countries, but one of the obstacles of its adoption refers to relatively high costs of the necessary equipment for holographic projection (Habboosh, 2022).

1.6 Conclusions

The landscape of Education 4.0 has a dynamic character determined by transformation processes in a social and economic environment (e.g., Industry 4.0). Increasing demands from new generations entering labour market and raising expectations from employers result in a more and more turbulent environment in which higher education institutions operate. An additional important factor which has an impact on the education sector is the emergence of other organisations not related to formal education. These organisations, offering different programmes and courses, become the competitors for traditional HEIs.

In such circumstances, HEIs have no choice but to change their way of acting and adapt to that situation. To operate efficiently in a competitive market and meet the expectations of both the labour market and new generations, HEIs must not only implement new concepts and methods of teaching, but also alternate the processes of management and administration. All these cannot be done without extensive use of digital technologies.

Modern disruptive technologies like augmented reality, artificial intelligence, and blockchain play an important role in this transformation. They can alternate not only the way of teaching but also enable HEIs to create environment in which every student can be treated individually, according to individual needs, capabilities, and requirements. These new technologies have a great, not fully known, potential which gives HEIs the possibility to meet the expectations of all participants of the education domain.

References

Alexander, B., Ashford-Rowe, K., Barajas-Murph, N., Dobbin, G., Knott, J., McCormack, M., ... Weber, N. (2019). *EDUCAUSE Horizon Report 2019 Higher Education Edition*. Louisville: EDUCAUSE.

Armstrong, M., & Taylor, S. (2014). *Armstrong's Handbook of Human Resources Management Practice*. New York: Kogan Page Ltd.

Attewell, P., & Domina, T. (2011). Educational imposters and fake degrees. *Research in Social Stratification and Mobility, 29*(1), 57–69.

Awaji, B., & Solaiman, E. (2022). Design, implementation, and evaluation of blockchain-based trusted achievement record system for students in higher education. In *Proceedings of the 14th International Conference on Computer Supported Education*, vol. 2 (pp. 225–237).

Bakla, A. (2019). A critical overview of Internet of Things in education. *Mehmet Akif Ersoy Üniversitesi Eğitim Fakültesi Dergisi, 49*, 302–327.

Bauer, S. (2021). Towards competence-oriented higher education: A systematic literature review of the different perspectives on successful exit profiles. *Education + Training, 63*(9), 1376–1390.

Benner, S. (2020, February 13). *Disruptive innovation in higher education.* Retrieved June 24, 2022, from The Blue Review: https://www.boisestate.edu/bluereview/disruptive-innovation-in-higher-education/

Bielińska-Dusza, E., & Gierałt, E. (2021). Selection of tools for motivating employees in a new generation cohort - Generation X, Y, Z. In *Innovation Management and Sustainable Economic Development in the Era of Global Pandemic: Proceedings of the 38th International Business Information Management Association Conference (IBIMA)*, November 23–24, 2021, Seville, Spain (pp. 4945–4956). International Business Information Management Association.

Bonfield, A. C., Salter, M., Longmuir, S., Benson, M., & Adachi, C. (2020). Transformation or evolution? Education 4.0, teaching and learning in the digital age. *Higher Education Pedagogies, 5*(1), 223–246.

Brown, R. (2015). The marketisation of higher education: issues and irony. *New vistas.* Retrieved June 08, 2022, from: https://repository.uwl.ac.uk/id/eprint/3065/1/The%20marketisation%20of%20Higher%20education.pdf

Calvão, A. R., Ribeiro, S., & Simões, A. (2019). Pedagogical practices in higher education: improving students' competences through cross-curricular problem-solving activities. In *EDULEARN19 Proceedings* (pp. 5760–5769).

Chaka, C. (2022). Is Education 4.0 a sufficient innovative, and disruptive educational trend to promote sustainable open education for higher education institutions? A review of literature trends. *Frontiers in Education, 7*, 1–14.

Choi, T., Kumar, S., Yue, X., & Chan, H. (2021). Disruptive technologies and operations management in the Industry 4.0 era and beyond. *Production and Operations Management, 31*(1), 9–31.

Christensen, C. M., Horn, M. B., & Johnson, C. W. (2008). *Disrupting Class: How Disruptive Innovation Will Change the Way the World Learns.* New York: McGraw Hill.

Contreras, G. S., González, A. H., Fernández, M. I., Martínez, C. B., Cepa, J., & Escobar, Z. (2022). The importance of the application of the metaverse in education. *Modern Applied Science, 16*(3), 1–34.

Davis, N. (2016, January 19). *What is the fourth industrial revolution?* Retrieved January 20, 2023, from World Economic Forum: https://www.weforum.org/agenda/2016/01/what-is-the-fourth-industrial-revolution/

Dikusar, A. (2018, August 8). *Disruptive technologies in education sector.* Retrieved July 05, 2022, from XB Software: https://xbsoftware.com/blog/disruptive-technologies-in-education-sector/

Dimitrova, G., Madzhurova, B., Raychev, S., & Stoyanova, D. (2022). Education 4.0 – The change of higher education institutions and the labour market. *Pedagogika-Pedagogy, 94*(4), 515–529.

Dymek, D., Konkol, P., Stal, J., Put, D., & Trąbka, J. (2020). Conceptual model of personal competence integrator based on blockchain technology. *AMCIS 2020 Proceedings*, The Association for Information Systems, Atlanta, pp. 1–10.

eLearning Industry. (2021). *4 Changes that Will Shape the Classroom of the Future: Making Education Fully Technological.* eLearning Industry. Retrieved February 04, 2023, from: https://elearningindustry.com/4-changes-will-shape-classroom-of-the-future-making-education-fully-technological

European Commission. (2018). *Artificial Intelligence for Europe.* Communication from the Commission to the European Parliament, the European Council, the Council, the European Economic and Social Committee and the Committee of the Regions.

European Commission. (2022). *The Digital Economy and Society Index.* European Commission. Retrieved November 23, 2022, from: https://digital-strategy.ec. europa.eu/en/policies/desi

European Union. (2018). Recommendation on key competences for lifelong learning. *Official Journal of the European Union, C 189*(61), 1–6.

Farmer, R. (2018). The what, the how and the why of the flipped classroom. *Innovative Practice in Higher Education, 3*(2), 14–31.

Fisk, P. (2017, January 24). *Education 4.0 … the future of learning will be dramatically different, in school and throughout life.* Retrieved October 15, 2022, from https://www.peterfisk.com/2017/01/future-education-young-everyone-taught-together/

Fu, R., Tian, M., & Tang, Q. (2022). The design of personalized education resource recommendation system under big data. *Computational Intelligence and Neuroscience, 2022*, 1–11.

Ghawe, A. S., & Chan, Y. (2022). Implementing disruptive technologies: What have we learned? *Communications of the Association for Information Systems, 50*(1), 646–689.

Guàrdia, L., Clougher, D., Anderson, T., & Maina, M. (2021). IDEAS for transforming higher education: An overview of ongoing trends and challenges. *International Review of Research in Open and Distributed Learning, 22*(2), 166–184.

Gutowski, P., Markiewicz, J., Niedzielski, P., & Klein, M. (2022). Blockchain in education: The best teaching models. *European Research Studies, 25*(4), 253–266.

Habboosh, M. (2022, January 05). *Education system in the future: The use of hologram technology.* Retrieved January 23, 2023, from Skyline University College. University City of Sharjah: https://www.skylineuniversity.ac.ae/knowledge-update/information-systems/education-system-in-the-future-the-use-of-hologram-technology

Half of UK employers have been victims of degree fraud. (2019). Retrieved January 02, 2023, from Prospects: https://www.prospects.ac.uk/

Hawksworth, J., Berriman, R., & Goel, S. (2018). *Will Robots Really Steal Our Jobs? An International Analysis of the Potential Long Term Impact of Automation.* Price waterhouseCoopers.

HEDD. (2021). *Higher education degree datacheck.* Retrieved November 13, 2022, from https://hedd.ac.uk/

Henle, C., Dineen, B., & Duffy, M. (2019). Assessing intentional resume deception: Development and nomological network of a resume fraud measure. *Journal of Business and Psychology, 34*(1), 87–106.

Hernandez-de-Menendez, M., Díaz, C., & Morales-Menendez, R. (2020). Technologies for the future of learning: state of the art. *International Journal on Interactive Design and Manufacturing, 14*(2), 683–695.

Higher education in a changing and challenging world. (2022, June 2). Retrieved June 07, 2022, from IIEP: http://www.iiep.unesco.org/en/higher-education-changing-and-challenging-world-14177

Himmetoğlu, B., Ayduğ, D., & Bayrak, C. (2020, July). Education 4.0: Defining the teacher, the student, and the school manager aspects of the revolution. *Turkish Online Journal of Distance Education-TOJDE, 21*, 12–28.

Hong, C., & Ma, W. W. (2020). Introduction: Education 4.0: Applied Degree Education and the Future of Work. In *Applied Degree Education and the Future of Work* (pp. 1–13) Singapore: Spinger.

Huda, M., Anshari, M., Almunawar, M. N., Shahrill, M., Tan, A., Jaidin, J. H., & Masri, M. (2016). Innovative teaching in higher education: The big data approach. *Turkish Online Journal of Distance Education-TOJDE*, 15, 1210–1216.

IBM. (2023, January 19). *Big data and analytics support*. Retrieved January 20, 2023, from IBM: ibm.com

Joshi, N. (2022, May 31). Understanding Education 4.0: The machine learning-driven future of learning. *Forbes*. Retrieved February 04, 2023, from: https://www.forbes.com/sites/naveenjoshi/2022/03/31/understanding-education-40-the-machine-learning-driven-future-of-learning/

Judi, H. M., & Sahari, N. (2013). Student centered learning in statistics: Analysis of systematic review. *Procedia - Social and Behavioral Sciences*, *103*, 844–851.

Lathika, K. (2016, June 20). Student centred Learning. *International Journal of Current Research and Modern Education (IJCRME)*, *1*(1), 677–680.

Lee, E., & Hannafin, M. J. (2016). A design framework for enhancing engagement in student-centered learning: own it, learn it, and share it. *Education Tech Research and Development*, *64*(4), 707–734.

Lepiane, C. D., Pereira, F. L., Pieri, G., Martins, D., Martina, J. E., & Rabelo, M. L. (2019). Digital degree certificates for higher education in brazil: A technical policy specification. In *Proceedings of the ACM Symposium on Document Engineering* (pp. 1–10).

Logofatu, B. (2017). The digital technologies - Opportunities and challenges for the 21st century teaching and learning. *Conference Proceedings of "eLearning and Software for Education" (eLSE)*, *14*(1), 159–166. Carol I National Defence University Publishing House.

Machov, R., Korcsmáros, E., Šeben, Z., Fehér, L., & Tóth, Z. (2021). Developing the competences of generation Z with innovative teaching methods in the context of the requirement of labour market by Industry 4.0. *International Journal of Advanced Corporate Learning*, *14*(2), 17–26.

Malik, G., & Venkatraman, A. (2017). "The great divide": skill gap between the employer's expectations and skills possessed by employees. *Industrial and Commercial Training*, *49*(4), 175–182.

Mell, P., & Grance, T. (2011). *The NIST Definition of Cloud Computing*. Gaithersburg: U.S. Department of Commerce, National Institute of Standards and Technology.

Morris, N. P., Ivancheva, M., Coop, T., Mogliacci, R., & Swinnerton, B. (2020). Negotiating growth of online education in higher education. *International Journal of Educational Technology in Higher Education*, *17*, 1–16.

Musselin, C. (2018). New forms of competition in higher education. *Socio-Economic Review*, *16*(3), 657–683.

Noh, N. H., & Amron, M. T. (2021). Exploring cloud computing readiness and acceptance in higher education institution: A PLS-SEM approach. *Asian Journal of University Education*, *17*(4), 367–376.

OECD. (2005). *Programme for International Student Assessment. The Definition and Selection of Key Competencies. Executive Summary*. Paris: Organisation for Economic Co-operation and Development.

OECD. (2017). *Future of Work and Skills*. Organisation for Economic Co-operation and Development.

OECD. (2019). *OECD Skills Strategy Poland: Assessment and Recommendations*. Organisation for Economic Co-operation and Development.

Pérez, L. D., Nebot, A. P., Capmany, A. B., Dima, G., Mula, A., Gonzalez, P., ... Fattore, L. (2020). *National Reports on the Labour Market Soft-Skills*. Brussels: Skills4Employability EU Project.

Pongratz, H. J. (2018). Of crowds and talents: discursive constructions of global online labour. *New Technology, Work and Employment, 33*(1), 58–73.

Pysarevskyi, I., Okhrimenko, I., Bogdan, N., Zharikova, S., Vlashchenko, N., Krasnokutska, I., ... Bloshchynskyi, I. (2022). Digital generation Y and Z in the field of tourism: psychological dimensions of morality. *Postmodern Openings, 13*(4), 448–471.

Qushem, B., Christopoulos, A., Oyelere, S., Ogata, H., & Laakso, M.-J. (2021). Multimodal technologies in precision education: Providing new opportunities or adding more challenges? *Education Sciences, 11*(7), 338.

Robak, E. (2017). Expectations of generation Y connected with shaping the worklife. *Oeconomia Copernicana, 8*(4), 569–584.

Rose, K., Eldridge, S., & Chapin, L. (2015). The internet of things: An overview. *The Internet Society (ISOC), 80*, 1–50.

Rosenberg, L. (2022, January 18). VR vs. AR vs. MR vs. XR: What's the difference? *Big think*. Retrieved January 04, 2023, from: https://bigthink.com/the-future/vr-ar-mr-xr-metaverse/

Sánchez, H., Martínez, L. S., & González, J. D. (2019). Educational robotics as a teaching tool in higher education institutions: A bibliographical analysis. *Journal of Physics: Conference Series, 1391*(1), 1–6.

Schwab, K. (2016). *The Fourth Industrial Revolution*. Cologny/Geneva, Switzerland: World Economic Forum.

Serafin, K. (2016). Kompetencje pracownicze determinantą kreacji wartości kapitału intelektualnego organizacji. *Studia Ekonomiczne. Zeszyty Naukowe Uniwersytetu Ekonomicznego w Katowicach, 283*, 16–28.

Sinha, D. (2021, June 09). *An Overview: Understanding Different Types of Augmented Reality*. Retrieved September 14, 2022, from Analytics Insight.

Smith, A., Legaki, Z., & Hamari, J. (2022). Games and gamification in flipped classrooms: A systematic review. In *Proceedings of the 6th International GamiFIN Conference* (pp. 33–43).

Steiu, M. (2020). Blockchain in education: Opportunities, applications, and challenges. *First Monday, 25*(9). Retrieved November 12, 2022, from: https://firstmonday.org/ojs/index.php/fm/article/view/10654/9726

Stroe, A. C. (2022). Digitalization of Romanian education system: Is Romania ready to embrace Education 4.0? *Informatica Economica, 26*(3), 16–25.

Taeihagh, A., Ramesh, M., & Howlett, M. (2021). Assessing the regulatory challenges of emerging disruptive technologies. *Regulation & Governance, 15*(4), 1009–1019.

Tan, Y.-C., Chandukala, S. R., & Reddy, S. K. (2022). Augmented reality in retail and its impact on sales. *Journal of Marketing, 86*(1), 48–66.

The Council of the European Union. (2022). *Council Recommendation on a European Approach to Micro-Credentials for Lifelong Learning and Employability.* Luxembourg: Council of the European Union.

Ton-Quinlivan, V., & Hackwood, S. (2017, February 10). *Taking Innovation to Scale: Growing Makers for the STEM Economy.* Retrieved October 21, 2022, from The EvoLLLution: https://www.aypf.org/wp-content/uploads/2017/10/Taking-Innovation-to-Scale.pdf

Turk, H., & Kapucu Seckin, M. (2021). Innovative technology applications in science education: Digital holography. *Journal of Education in Science, Environment and Health, 7*(2), 156–170.

Universities of the Future. (2019). *Industry 4.0 Implications for Higher Education Institutions: State of Maturity and Competency Needs.* Retrieved September 01, 2022, from: https://universitiesofthefuture.eu/

Watty, K., McKay, J., & Ngo, L. (2016). Innovators or inhibitors? Accounting faculty resistance to new educational technologies in higher education. *Journal of Accounting Education, 36*, 1–15.

World Economic Forum. (2016). *The future of jobs.* Retrieved February 04, 2023, from: https://www.weforum.org/reports/the-future-of-jobs/

World Economic Forum. (2020). *The Future of Jobs Report 2020.* Cologny: World Economic Forum.

World Economic Forum. (2022). *Catalysing Education 4.0: Investing in the Future of Learning for a Human-Centric Recovery.* Cologny: World Economic Forum.

Xu, M., David, J. M., & Kim, S. H. (2018). The fourth industrial revolution: Opportunities and challenges. *International Journal of Financial Research, 9*(2), 90–95.

2

BLOCKCHAIN AS A DISRUPTIVE TECHNOLOGY IN EDUCATION 4.0

Janusz Stal and Dariusz Put

2.1 Introduction

Industry 4.0 (see Chapter 5) is characterised by, among other things, the use of the Internet and cyber-physical systems in industrial fields. The introduction of increasingly technologically advanced production and organisational processes places new demands on the education sector. As a result, a new paradigm of Education 4.0 has emerged that redefines such concepts as learning, student, teacher, and school, according to the needs of Industry 4.0. Education 4.0 is characterised by open access, student-centred education, introduction of digital technologies to education, seamless learning, lifelong learning, and exploratory and multidisciplinary education (Himmetoğlu, Ayduğ, & Bayrak, 2020). These new challenges posed by Education 4.0 require the use of adequate solutions and tools to support educational processes. One of them may be Distributed Ledger Technology (DLT) and, derived from this concept, blockchain. It can support processes such as storing archives, securing diplomas and transcripts to prevent their forgery, financial transactions, storage of teachers' and students' data, and flexible certificate storage and sharing (Cassandra et al., 2020; Himmetoğlu, Ayduğ, & Bayrak, 2020; Prawiyogi et al., 2021; Rizky, Silen, & Putra, 2021).

Distributed Ledger Technology is a distributed database which allows users to store and access information in a shared mode (Natarajan, Krause, & Gradstein, 2017). This information is distributed among users, who can use it to settle their transfers without the need to rely on a central validation system (Pinna & Ruttenberg, 2016; Rauchs et al., 2018).

DOI: 10.4324/9781003318736-3

Based on DLT, in 1990, blockchain technology (BC) was introduced to protect electronic documents (Haber & Stornetta, 1990). In 2008, Satoshi Nakamoto proposed the Bitcoin cryptocurrency in which the credibility that is traditionally placed in third-party organisations to maintain trusted records is transferred to the blockchain and the cryptographic algorithms it uses (Poston, 2019). Bitcoin was proposed as a peer-to-peer version of electronic cash that allows online payments to be sent directly from one party to another without going through a financial institution (Nakamoto, 2008). The development of this technology, especially the elaboration and implementation of smart contracts and consensus algorithms, has enabled its use in various industries, including education.

The use of blockchain offers a number of advantages (Panicker, Patil, & Kulkarni, 2016): disintermediation (third party is not necessary), freedom in payment for goods and services (anywhere and anytime), decentralisation, control and security (users are in full control of their information and transactions), high-quality data, speeding up transactions, transparency, and reduced transaction costs. Among the most significant disadvantages of blockchain technology, the following can be identified (Panicker, Patil, & Kulkarni, 2016): lack of awareness among users, demand for high standards of technology, the necessity to manage the risks of transitions, the necessity to upgrade regulations and legislations, high initial capital costs, and large energy consumption.

Section 2.2 presents the concept of DLT and describes the related mechanisms used. Then, in Section 2.3, we discuss the determinants that enable the use of DLT. Section 2.4 shows potential paths of reshaping education through the use of blockchain. Final remarks are formulated in Section 2.5.

2.2 Distributed Ledger Technology

2.2.1 The concept

Distributed Ledger Technology enables the transfer of (digital) property relations in decentralised transaction databases or account balance databases, which removes the need for centrally controlled registers. The transaction data is disseminated and confirmed within a distributed network that requires no central authority for registering, sharing, and synchronising transactions on digital assets (Antal et al., 2021; Bouras et al., 2020). DLT is a method of storing records, transactions, contracts, and agreements within and between organisations. It is a distributed database run by nodes in a peer-to-peer (P2P) network and preserved by consensus algorithms. The decentralised nature of DLT enables the security and privacy of data and has the potential for enabling large-scale decentralised data processing (Agbo et al., 2019). This technology also facilitates the maintenance of a global, append-only data structure by a set of mutually untrusted participants in a distributed environment (Antal et al., 2021).

The most notable features of distributed ledgers are immutability, resistance to censorship, decentralised maintenance, and elimination of the need for a centralised trusted third party. There is no need for an entity to be in charge of conflict resolution, and trust between all stakeholders who in general do not trust each other is provided. A distributed ledger is suitable for tracking the ownership of digital assets (Benčić & Žarko, 2018). Although it is a term that is used to describe various technologies, it is commonly thought of as a decentralised dataset architecture which allows the keeping and sharing of records in a synchronised way, while ensuring their integrity through the use of consensus-based validation protocols and cryptographic signatures (Benos et al., 2017; Danzi et al., 2020).

DLT has a potential to enhance transparency and trust, and to enable disintermediation. DLT enables storing new transactions in a distributed, decentralised network after validation by peers. Each transaction is secured by cryptography, verified, immutable, and tamper-proof (Roeck et al., 2020). DLT involves a set of protocols designed to replicate a timestamped and ordered database, named a ledger. The nodes of a DLT network store copies of a common ledger that is kept consistent by means of hash chaining. In a traditional centralised database architecture, information is located, stored, and maintained in a single location and is controlled by a central administrator who ensures its integrity. The data is usually stored in raw form and there is some sort of a security perimeter which protects the database from external attacks (Benos et al., 2017). A distributed ledger is a distributed database in the sense that each node has a synchronised copy of the data, but is different from the traditional distributed database architectures in three important ways (Benos et al., 2017):

1. Decentralisation. The control of the database (read/write access) is decentralised. It is performed by multiple (or all) network participants. There is no need for a central administrator to ensure the integrity of the data or its consistency across nodes. Instead, this is achieved through some consensus mechanism or validation protocol.
2. Reliability in trust-less environments. The consensus mechanism ensures the consistency and integrity of the database even if the parties involved do not fully trust each other.
3. Cryptographic encryption. The ledger uses cryptographic encryption tools to deliver decentralisation and reliability.

DLT can be classified regarding to the types of ledgers into (Natarajan, Krause, & Gradstein, 2017; https://101blockchains.com/what-is-dlt/):

1. **Permissioned**. Permissioned networks are private networks. They are designed to work in a closed ecosystem where the user needs to have access granted through a "Know Your Customer" procedure. The users, once validated, can access the network. Validation nodes are responsible for validating the transactions within the network. The network can also be designed to restrict access to its functionalities. This feature is especially useful for businesses who want to use blockchain but do not want to make their data public.
2. **Permissionless**. Permissionless distributed ledger systems or networks are public networks. Users do not need permission to participate. The system is open to everyone for making transactions, validating blocks, and performing other forms of interaction with the network. There is no limitation on who can use it, irrespective of the location, laws, and other factors that govern how transactions are carried out.
3. **Hybrid**. It combines both permissionless and permissioned networks and offers a network that carries the benefits of both of these forms. Hybrid DLT is a good choice for businesses since their owners may decide which aspects of the system may be public and which ones private.

A distributed ledger has the following properties that make it a suitable candidate for several application domains involving a digital evidence chain (Chowdhury et al., 2019):

- Distributed consensus on the ledger state: Achieving a distributed consensus without being reliant on any trusted third party enables to build and utilise a system where every possible state and interaction is verifiable by any authorised entities.
- Immutability and irreversibility of the ledger state: Achieving a distributed consensus with the participation of a large number of nodes ensures that the ledger state becomes immutable and irreversible.
- Data (transaction) persistence: Data in a distributed ledger is stored in a distributed mode, ensuring its persistency as long as there are participating nodes in the P2P network.
- Data provenance: The data storage process in any distributed ledger is facilitated by transactions. Every transaction needs to be digitally signed using public key cryptography which ensures the authenticity of the source of the data.

Among the most frequently cited challenges concerning DLT application are the following (McLean & Deane-Johns, 2016):

- the need for addressing legal and regulatory issues concerning privacy and security, responsibility, consumer protection, and anti-competitive activities prevention,
- limitation in scalability,
- lack of mainstream understanding of the technology itself and a lack of specialists with technical skills to identify use-cases better,
- the need for collaboration between large groups of users in order to maximise the potential of DLT,
- standardisation,
- interoperability between ledgers to increase the usability of the technology,
- reputational damage to DLT caused by applications which do not work properly.

The DLT concept, which has been developed for many years, has become the basis for creating systems to support various business sectors (see Chapter 2.2.5). However, in order for it to be universally applied, it is necessary to carry out further work, improve its conceptualisation and establish the environment in which it could be implemented.

2.2.2 How DLT works

DLT refers to the recording and sharing of data across multiple data storages (ledgers). Every ledger gathers the same data records and is collectively maintained and controlled by a distributed network of computer servers called nodes (Natarajan, Krause, & Gradstein, 2017). At the centre of DLT is the ledger itself, which consists of consecutive blocks chained together, following a strict set of rules. The ledger is distributed and stored by the nodes of a P2P network where each block is created at a predefined interval in a decentralised mode by means of a consensus algorithm, which guarantees several data integrity-related properties of the ledger (Chowdhury et al., 2019). The P2P network is a fundamental part of DLT and is one of the reasons for its solid security (Sharma, 2018). In a P2P network, the clients do not only employ the system for their own purpose but simultaneously benefit from the operation of the system. In particular, each "peer", often denoted as "node", lends resources from its own capacity such as a network bandwidth, disk storage, or processing power to other participants or miners without a centrally coordinating server. All nodes are considered equal in a P2P network, but each can take different roles at different times (Vokerla et al., 2019).

One of the most relevant issues hindering global-scale DLT adoption is scalability. In order for a transaction to be included in a block, a block must be created. A block is created every time when a consensus is made. The transaction rate is limited by the frequency at which blocks are created, and also by the block size. When the number of nodes in the system is increasing, the frequency of block creation does not increase significantly due to the fact that the consensus mechanism is dynamic so that the block generation time converges to a fixed value (Benčić & Žarko, 2018).

One of the mechanisms to address the performance-related issues is sharding. It involves dividing a large collection of data across several servers, enabling the distributed management for the collection, thereby improving the scalability (Moudoud, Cherkaoui, & Khoukhi, 2021).

2.2.3 Consensus algorithm

One of the fundamental components of any DLT system is the consensus algorithm. It helps to decide which block can be accepted and which should be rejected. There are several types of consensus algorithms. The most popular are Proof of Work (PoW) and Proof of Stake (PoS), and these will be discussed later in this section. The other algorithms are Proof of Activity (PoA) and Practical Byzantine Fault Tolerance (PBFT) (Moudoud, Cherkaoui, & Khoukhi, 2022, Azbeg et al., 2021).

The aim of consensus mechanisms is to ensure consistency of local copies, while limiting the ledger update rate. For instance, in blockchains a bulk of valid transactions can occur from once every few seconds (as in Ethereum) to minutes (in Bitcoin). Moreover, in DLTs, an already included transaction may be reverted (i.e. removed from the ledger) if a consensus is reached on a different and conflicting transaction. Hence, DLTs also introduce the concept of a "finalised transaction", referring to an accepted transaction that will not be reverted with a high probability. The transaction finalisation probability is an increasing function of the time since the transaction was published. This introduces a trade-off between the finalisation certainty and the tolerated transaction validation delay that depends not only on the application but also on the consensus mechanism of the specific DLT (Danzi et al., 2020).

Through a consensus algorithm a distributed ledger is synchronised across multiple nodes. There are many consensus algorithms introduced by DLT platforms that are designed to meet specific goals. Bitcoin introduced the notion of the Proof of Work in which a block creator (miner), to create a block, must solve a cryptographic puzzle by producing a hash which satisfies certain properties. Solving such a cryptographic puzzle requires a considerable amount of computation and, as a result, electricity (Chowdhury et al., 2019). In theory, under the rule of one-CPU-one-vote, an attacker would need to control at least 51% of computing power to alter the ledger. However, under certain circumstances, controlling as little as 30% of computing power might be sufficient to alter the ledger (Benos et al., 2017).

To solve this problem, another consensus method, called Proof of Stake, has been put forward. The core idea of PoS evolves around the concept that the nodes willing to participate in the block creation process must prove that they own a certain number of coins and must lock a certain amount of its currencies, called stake, into an escrow account. The stake acts as a guarantee that they will behave as per the protocol rules. The node which escrows its stake in this manner is known as a stakeholder, forger, or minter in PoS terminology. The minter can lose the stake in case it is found to misbehave. Delegated PoS (DPoS) is a variant of PoS in which a stakeholder delegates the stacking task to another entity (Chowdhury et al., 2019).

The criteria to measure the validators' stake in the system can vary. They can be assessed in terms of internal tokens or off-ledger assets pledged as collateral, or they can be based on the reputation of the validator in the network (if their identity is known). Some PoS processes require voters to place "bets" on the true state of the ledger, thus would-be attackers trying to claim something false would be in a minority with their prediction and lose their bets. Permissioned systems do not have to solve the problem of an untrusted network, and therefore are capable of processing transactions faster and are cheaper to maintain than capital-intensive permissionless systems. On the other hand, permissioned systems are arguably more open to censorship and reversibility (Benos et al., 2017).

PoS has several advantages over PoW. First, it consumes less electricity. Second, attacks on the network are easily penalised as compared to PoW. After an attack on a PoW-driven network, the attacker still owns the hardware used for the attack. In PoS, in contrast, destroying the stake has the same economic effect as dismantling the attacker's mining equipment (Benčić & Žarko, 2018).

During the block generation process, first, a new block is created. Second, the previous block's metadata is added. In the case of permissioned blockchains, permission changes have to be applied in order to avoid unwanted actions performed by users who do not have permission. Next, all transactions will be validated against the consensus rules on the blockchain. In public blockchains, the block generators (i.e. miners) will provide a Proof of Work or Proof of Stake and will be rewarded for their work. In private blockchains, the consensus process can be part of the block generation process. Once the block is constructed, it is submitted to the network and propagated to all the nodes (Ellervee et al., 2017).

The consensus process is performed by each node when a new block has been broadcasted. Each blockchain defines its own "consensus rules", according to the type of the validated blocks and transactions. If validated, the nodes will append the new block to the blockchain; otherwise, it will be rejected (Ellervee et al., 2017).

2.2.4 Smart contracts

An important feature of DLT is that it is not only a database but can also include executable code as part of the ledger to create a so-called *smart contract*. Smart contracts are self-executing, non-modifiable programmes, implemented inside the chain and intended to automatically execute actions according to the terms of a contract (El Houda, Khoukhi, & Hafid, 2018). They can be implemented to help to manage a system or to establish access control inside a network. Smart contracts are the digital equivalent of their paper-based counterparts; they are designed to facilitate the trust between parties using special computer code. This is a protocol intended to facilitate, verify, and enforce the negotiation and performance of a contract digitally. Dynamic execution of smart contracts between peers can be useful for various use cases where real or almost real-time operations and transactions are needed (Cali & Cakir, 2019).

In order to implement smart contracts, more information about the current "state" of the network is required as compared to the Bitcoin blockchain. For example, a smart contract that is used to automatically calculate and pay periodic coupon payments would require information on the current and past states to execute and keep track of the payments. In the context of post-trade processes, the concept of smart contracts goes beyond record keeping and data sharing and may have much deeper implications. For example, the embedding of a pre-specified code in the ledger will allow legal agreements to automatically execute their legal clauses. This could reduce the ability of counterparties to *ex post* negate their contractual obligations which, in turn, could affect other contract parameters, and also lead to smart contracts being used as a means of signalling credibility in cases where it is not easily verifiable otherwise (Benos et al., 2017).

2.2.5 Potential applications of DLT

Although DLT became more widely known through its use in virtual currencies such as Bitcoin, it also has potential applications in other areas. The inherent properties of DLT such as resiliency, integrity, anonymity, decentralisation, and autonomous control have fostered the early adoption of this technology in almost every application domain (Chowdhury et al., 2019). As a distributed database that does not require third parties to store reliable data, DLT can be used to support the activities of a wide variety of sectors (Vokerla et al. 2019). The most important areas of BC applications are discussed below.

Finance. DLT may reduce human errors and simplify the procedure of asset management and also ensure that claims processing is safe and reliable. In particular, for the post-trade cycle, which includes the clearing and settlement of financial transactions, DLT is considered to be promising, with the potential to simplify processes, reduce costs, and increase efficiency and security. Indeed, according to a 2016 report by the European Central Bank (European Central Bank, 2016), the clearing and settlement of securities is a particularly important potential field of application for DLT. The following benefits for the institution adopting a DLT-based trade finance platform are identified (Blidholm & Johnson, 2018; McLean & Deane-Johns, 2016): related to better functioning of the system (automation, including backup, transparency, efficiency, simplicity, speed, paperwork reduction), related to the system's users and its environment (regulatory advantages, cost savings, better customer service), and related to security and safety (fraud prevention, human error reduction, provision of privacy, risk mitigation, cyber threats resilience, confidence enhancement).

Trade. The technology has proven to be particularly useful in transaction services thanks to some of its unique properties, such as immutability and the ability to embed trust in the network. Some commonly perceived advantages of the technology are the cost savings and efficiency improvements it could bring (Blidholm & Johnson, 2018).

Retail services. Goods and services may be traded without any intermediaries, as blockchain can facilitate payment methods, loyalty schemes, and gift cards (Vokerla et al. 2019). In particular, applications of blockchain and Internet of Things (IoT) technologies in the food industry will facilitate the tracing and tracking food throughout its production cycle, covering all entities involved in the agricultural ecosystem (Lin et al., 2018). Such a solution may bring the following benefits: more accurate information, reduction of transaction costs, a better data-driven evaluation of process flow and efficiency, elimination of third parties in transactions, automation of merged monitoring and enforcement, and elimination of the need for intermediation as an information supplier (Roeck et al., 2020).

Transport and tourism. Ride sharing and vehicle leasing can be developed to work with blockchain technologies. Empty hotel rooms can efficiently be tracked and traded through the usage of blockchain-based digital solutions (Vokerla et al. 2019).

Manufacturing and supply chain. Blockchain can be used to accomplish tasks in a supply chain network, to ensure transparency in product supply chains, and to track and trace the product within the nodes while in transport. Throughout a supply chain network, a number of intermediary payments may be involved, for which Bitcoin or another cryptocurrency can be used (Vokerla et al. 2019).

Energy. DLT has a remarkably high potential to provide for the energy domain. More than 300 start-up and spin-off companies initiated various energy-related blockchain use cases. According to the German Energy Agency (https://www.dena.de/en/home/), DLT can improve efficiency of the existing power system operations and markets, further promoting the development of future energy DLT-based use cases. In a comprehensive report by the World Energy Council, the most popular use cases of DLT in the energy sector are categorised as: decentralised and P2P energy trading, labelling, energy provenance and certification, smart metering and billing, charging and payments, and wholesale power trading and settlements (Cali & Cakir, 2019).

Healthcare. Identification of the privacy and security issues related to healthcare big data leads to the proposition of a privacy-preserving blockchain-based healthcare system. In such a system the medical big data can be effectively managed through blockchain (Dwivedi et al., 2019). The evolution of identity management models and the potential opportunities for adopting the decentralised identity management approaches (e.g., DLT) show promising solutions for future eHealth identity systems (Bouras et al., 2020). An example of such a solution can be a self-sovereign identity model which, implemented on top of DLT, enables to move identity access and management towards users and makes individuals independent from any identity providers (Mühle et al., 2018).

Government. Recording and administering benefit payments can be made more efficient and secure, supporting public safety and transport, registration of business, and health regulations (Vokerla et al., 2019).

Intellectual property rights. Blockchain-based solutions may be used to track intellectual property rights and payment for artists. Records of ownership and ensuring royalties can also be created (Vokerla et al., 2019).

Education. Recording and management of skills, competences, and certificates; management of access to learning materials and certificates; and the elimination of document forgery can be supported by blockchain technology (Vokerla et al., 2019).

Smart cities. Blockchain and IoT technology can also be integrated into a smart city ecosystem. Car rentals, healthcare services, location awareness, and related services can be examples of such an integration. DLT-based vehicular public key infrastructure may be used for a faster and more intelligent sharing of services across a smart city ecosystem (Akhtar et al., 2021).

Initially, DLT, and especially blockchain, was identified with cryptocurrencies. With the development of this technology and the emergence of new solutions, it was noted that it can be used to support operations in many industries. Its use can contribute, among other things, to increasing the reliability of transactions, speeding up the execution of certain activities, and reducing the cost of operations. However, its widespread use requires further work related not only to the development of the technology itself, but also to changes in the environment, such as the development of the necessary standards, increased awareness of this technology, and the development of legal regulations.

2.3 Determinants of blockchain technology adoption

Blockchain is becoming increasingly popular in academia and industry thanks to its unique properties (decentralisation, security, reliability, and data integrity) and the elimination of external intermediaries. BC development has been an ongoing process related to three main phases: Blockchain 1.0, 2.0, and 3.0 (Maesa & Mori, 2020). Initially, BC was used as a peer-to-peer ledger to record Bitcoin cryptocurrency transactions (1.0). Applications attributed to Blockchain 2.0 focus on real estate and smart contracts that impose certain conditions and criteria that must be met before being registered on the blockchain. Such a registration takes place without the intervention of third parties. Finally, many applications have been developed in sectors such as government, healthcare, science, and education. This stage of evolution is named Blockchain 3.0 (Raimundo & Rosário, 2021).

It should be noted that numerous factors determine the use of blockchain. Many of them are included in the SWOT analysis of blockchain adoption, which identifies strengths, weaknesses, opportunities and threats, and summarises the advantages and disadvantages of this technology (Gatteschi et al., 2018). The results of the analysis show that the strengths of blockchain technology mainly lie in the transparency, process automation, and lack of intermediaries. The most relevant weaknesses concern scalability, power consumption and performance. The opportunities are mostly related to whether the market would embrace the technology or not. Threats are linked to various external causes. In particular, there is still a risk that the market will distrust this technology and perceive it as insecure or unreliable due to bugs and the volatility of cryptocurrencies. Further, special attention should be paid to legal regulations that could endanger the use of block-chain, as legal and compliance considerations are critical to BC adoption. Organisations need to be aware of the laws and regulations in their specific industry and location and ensure their use of blockchain technology is compliant with them (Fabiano, 2017; Fulmer, 2018).

One issue that is strongly related to the successful implementation of blockchain technology is scalability. Although blockchain has many promising properties, scalability turns out to be challenging when blockchain technology is widely used in real business environments. The ability to handle high volumes of transactions is critical to the adoption of blockchain technology. As the number of users and transactions on a blockchain network increases, scalability becomes a major barrier to blockchain adoption, as this can result in long transaction processing times, which also come with high operational costs. This is particularly important for public blockchain networks that need to process a large number of transactions (Hafid et al., 2020; Xie et al., 2019).

Interoperability is another challenge related to Blockchain adoption. Different blockchain networks and platforms cannot always communicate with each other, which can limit the potential for growth and scalability. Achieving seamless interoperability between blockchains is becoming increasingly important as blockchain technology advances, but the data required to do so is scattered. For blockchain technology to be widely adopted, it must be able to interact and integrate with existing systems. This includes the ability to connect to other blockchains and existing systems such as databases and APIs. The lack of industry-wide standards within the blockchain industry might impede its adoption. Without the commonly accepted standards/agreements on how the technology should be used, different entities may use different solutions, leading to compatibility problems (Belchior et al., 2021).

It should be noted that the implementation of BC is not only a technical challenge, but also involves human aspects such as resistance to change, cultural and organisational barriers, and lack of knowledge about the technology. At the same time, collaboration between different stakeholders is essential for the successful adoption of blockchain technology. This includes collaboration between companies, governments, and academia, as well as collaboration within the blockchain community. There is a need for education and raising awareness about blockchain technology and its benefits, which would help people understand the technology and its potential applications, thus facilitating its adoption (Sas & Khairuddin, 2017).

Other factors that can affect the successful implementation of BC are the regulatory environment, technological infrastructure, and the availability of qualified personnel. In addition, there are also the costs of implementing and maintaining a blockchain system, as well as the ability to integrate with existing systems. In summary, BC adoption will be driven by a combination of perceived benefits, regulatory environment, technological readiness, industry-specific factors, and the willingness of individuals and organisations to embrace the technology.

2.4 Blockchain's potential for reshaping education

2.4.1 Applications of blockchain in education

One of the domains that may benefit from BC is higher education (HE), where the principles of document authenticity, transparency, immutability and trust play a key role. HE can be considered from the point of view of its major stakeholders (Lam & Dongol, 2022): (1) higher education institutions (HEIs), and (2) students. This, in turn, may be the basis for distinguishing two approaches to the implementation of BC in HEIs: institution-centric and student-centric. The primary goal of the former is to facilitate the management and operational activities of HEIs for students' payment management, international collaboration management, and accreditation processes. The student-centric approach gives a student control over their data, simplifying the student activities related to the validation of received documents (Kamišalić et al., 2019).

In order to identify the areas of BC use in HE, it is necessary to analyse the research conducted in the higher education domain. In recent years, a significantly increasing number of publications on BC applications in HE can be observed. A systematic literature review shows that financial management and security issues have been the main research focus since 2015 (Sunny et al., 2022). However, starting from 2020, the main topic of research is the use of blockchain in education. In the domain of BC applications in HE, the following areas can be distinguished (Fedorova & Skobleva, 2020): (1) issue and storage of certificates and diplomas, (2) identification solutions, (3) protection of intellectual property, (4) new network of cooperation between students and their professors, (5) formation of an academic passport (portfolio), (6) payment for studies with a cryptocurrency, (7) accreditation of educational institutions, and (8) administration of the educational process. In addition, the work carried out in academic centres should be taken into account. To this end, Kamišalić et al. (2019) identified 25 use cases in the educational domain. These use cases have been categorised and discussed in the following (names of academic centres where work is conducted are given in brackets):

- **Certificates**: blockchain-based diploma verification; student diploma verification; an open standard for applications that issue and verify blockchain-based certificates; facilitating the creation of a lifelong academic passport (Malta College of Arts, Science and Technology, University of Melbourne, Southern New Hampshire University, Central New Mexico Community College, Ngee Ann Polytechnic, MIT Media Labs, educhain.io platform),

- **Credentials**: verifiable credentials for the completion of a digital currency course; management and control of credits that students gain for completed courses (University of Nicosia, University of Maribor),
- **Intellectual property**: registration of intellectual property assets; copyright registration service used for images; intellectual property rights for artists (bernstein.io platform, binded.com platform, Zhejiang University, Shenzhen University, Chinese Academy of Sciences),
- **Dissemination**: invention process; determining the uniqueness of an idea and providing a possibility to claim own ideas; open publishing platform that supports the peer review process (University of Pittsburgh),
- **Payments**: accepting payment with Bitcoin (King's College, University of Nicosia, Simon Fraser University, University of Cumbria),
- **Learning environment**: learning platform for cryptocurrency courses; online education platform offering a gamified learning experience and cryptocurrency-based scholarships; platform connecting learners and educators (Extra Credit platform, BitDegree platform, Woolf University platform).

However, it is worth noting that although the number of blockchain-based applications in the HE domain is increasing, only a few of them have been launched to the public. The main areas of BC adoption in the HE domain concern primarily certificate management, protecting learning objects and copyright management, fees and credits transfer, and supporting lifelong learning (Alammary et al., 2019). Each category addresses an issue related to trust, privacy, or security within the educational environment. The main areas of BC applications in the educational processes in HE are depicted in Figure 2.1 and are discussed in the following paragraphs.

The university education process begins with the enrolment at the university. Then, the student takes part in lectures and classes, where they gain experience, knowledge and skills. After graduation, a new phase in the life of the young person begins when they enter the labour market.

One of the key aspects related to university education concerns the payments of tuition fees, which are required in most countries. Due to the significant costs of studies, they are usually financed with loans. Both the payment of tuition fees and the subsequent repayment of the loan can be based on the use of smart contracts to fulfil the contract between a student and a university. The repayment process is linked to the students' performance, salary, and

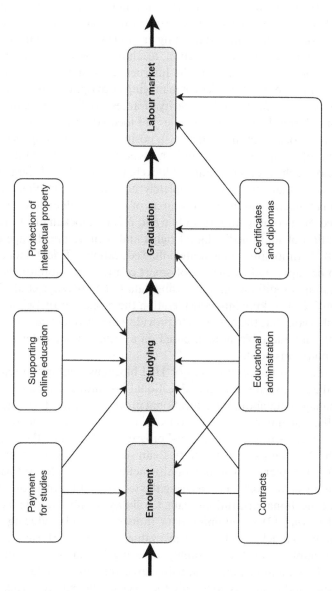

FIGURE 2.1   The use of blockchain in the educational process at HEIs.

other factors. A blockchain-based student loan management system can reduce the processing time, documentation overhead, and intermediary costs (Sunny et al., 2022).

The COVID-19 pandemic has shown that online education starts to play a key role. Even though the pandemic has passed in many countries, numerous elements of remote or hybrid learning are still available at many universities. With regard to distance education, teaching resources are stored in a digital form and made available on the Internet. This entails the protection of intellectual property, in particular managing copyright to digital educational resources, and ensuring the security of access to digital data and their distribution. Currently, numerous studies are focused on managing remote learning using blockchain that can bring a positive impact on improving the management of distance learning and on assessing its quality (Min & Bin, 2022). One of such studies contains a blockchain-based digital rights management system that includes a completely new network architecture for sharing and managing multimedia resources of distance education. The system is based on a combination of public and private blockchains to realise the registration of multimedia digital rights and their secure storage (Guo et al., 2020). Additionally, to facilitate online education, efficient data distribution can be supported by the use of smart contracts to monitor the process of creating, modifying, and accessing data (Ubaka-Okoye et al., 2020) (see Section 2.2.4). Taking into consideration the properties of BC, it seems that the technology has the potential to provide a highly open, decentralised, transparent, and auditable system, based on a secure online database, that e-learning platforms need.

One of the most important areas of HEI blockchain adoption refers to educational administration. Every educational institution is obliged to collect and manage data about the educational process, student data, and data related to the teaching process. The collected data can be used for statistical purposes, as well as to predict students' progress or determine their desired career path. BC, thanks to its properties, can support such document management (see Chapter 5). The potential benefits of using BC in this area include (Sunny et al., 2022): (1) ensuring the security and protection of students' and educational institutions' data, (2) ability to effectively define data access restrictions, (3) maintaining data transparency, (4) reducing costs, and (5) ability to quickly and effectively evaluate student performance. It is also worth emphasising the possibility of using BC in the area of data science and in maintaining and processing large amounts of data.

Certificates and diplomas constitute the basic documents confirming the completion of studies, most often issued in a paper form. However, it can be expected that with the development of information technology, such documents will be issued in a digital form. This raises the problem of storage, access, ensuring the credibility of such documents in the context of graduates' professional career (Ma & Fang, 2020). It is possible to use BC technology to validate and share documents confirming the participation in the educational process (Gräther et al., 2018). Decentralisation and immutability of stored documents and the existence of a verification service that allows third parties to verify the authenticity of documents are considerable advantages of using BC in HE. Shared documents can be present online in an immutable form for the labour market players and be protected against manipulation of the existing certification system (Rama Reddy et al., 2021). It should be also emphasised that a blockchain-based certificate management system can be managed without the help of third parties (Sunny et al., 2022). More information on practical applications can be found in Chapter 7.

It is also worth mentioning that recent years have brought significant development of technologies that are successfully used in the education sector, e.g. artificial intelligence, virtual reality, and machine learning. Numerous studies show the benefits of integrating available technologies into HE (Shah et al., 2021). For example, the combination of BC and machine learning makes it possible to predict student progress, which can lead to predictions of future professional roles for students after graduation. The result may enhance the credibility of diplomas and certificates confirming graduation.

Summing up, BC could bring significant benefits to education, including high security, low cost, enhancing students' assessment, better control of data access, enhancing accountability and transparency, identity authentication, enhancing trust, improving efficiency of students' records management, supporting learners' career decisions, and enhancing learners' interactivity (Alammary et al., 2019). In addition, research efforts should be directed towards building new knowledge to improve sustainable innovation and smart contracts for both students and universities (Raimundo & Rosário, 2021).

2.4.2 Challenges in adopting blockchain in education

The ability to protect sensitive data and the approach to organisational processes pose technical and organisational challenges to blockchain applications in higher education. Despite the unquestionable benefits of BC (e.g., decentralisation, data sharing, currency digitisation), a large body of research also points to the existing limitations and challenges of using this technology in education (Cunha et al., 2021). Universities should take those limitations into account when considering the use of blockchain technology.

In particular, two important aspects should be taken into account when adopting BC in HE. The first aspect is technical limitations, including

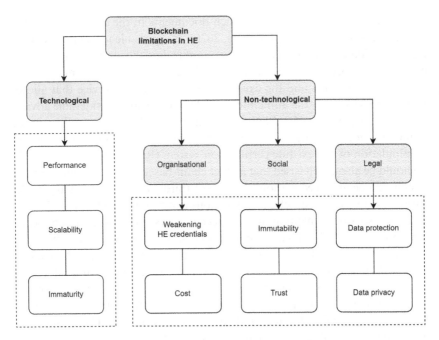

FIGURE 2.2 Blockchain limitations in the higher education (HE) domain.

Proof of Work, i.e. a consensus mechanism for verifying new blocks (see Section 2.3). The larger is the size of the blockchain, the larger and more expensive is its proof of work. The second aspect concerning the use of BC is related to the lack of compliance with the philosophy of the sustainable development of education (Park, 2021). At present, the use of BC in educa-tion is more at an experimental stage than a real solution to many of the problems faced by education. As Figure 2.2 shows, it has to overcome a number of obstacles caused by technological and non-technological factors (Saputra, Ochtaffia, & Apriani, 2023).

Numerous technology-related factors should be taken into account (Sunny et al., 2022). First, the length of the blockchain. When it becomes too long, the performance of the entire network can be reduced. Another challenge is the large amount of traffic in the system, as transactions are maintained for many nodes, many users, large numbers of blocks, and many devices. After that, an issue to consider is security. Privacy and security are ensured by the digital identity of the private key. If this private key is stolen or lost, all resources associated with the private key may be lost. Factors related to technology also include scalability issues arising from increasing the number of nodes (relatively slow speed of blockchain transactions may impose bottlenecks when it comes to scaling blockchain applications in the education domain), and the increasing storage needs while reducing the network (Hafid et al., 2020; Xie et al., 2019). It is also worth emphasising that blockchain is an innovative technology and thus might be considered immature. The relative immaturity of BC may hamper the success rate of using blockchain in education (Alammary et al., 2019; Steiu, 2020). Many other factors surrounding the use of BC in education stem from general limitations of BC adoption (see Section 2.3). In addition, many technical problems for the use of blockchain in education have not yet been solved. One of them is the Proof of Work consensus mechanism, which performs poorly in terms of the number of transactions per second, has additional costs, and is difficult to use in schools (Vukolić, 2016).

Apart from technological limitations, numerous non-technological challenges have to be overcome when implementing blockchain in education (Steiu, 2020). One of them relates to organisational issues. It is worth noting that the use of BC technology disrupts the current universities' monopoly on formal accreditation (Haugsbakken & Langseth, 2019) and, at the same time, is weakening university credentials (Alammary et al., 2019). The use of BC will result in universities having to cede some of their autonomy to a self-organising and autonomous algorithm or a decentralised digital technology, the scope and consequences of which we do not fully understand. Therefore, it is important to consider how the use of BC affects the automation, access, and processing of university data. In addition, the influence of BC on the bureaucracy and the cost of functioning of universities should be taken into account. This particularly includes the environmental cost associated with the amount of electricity needed to run complex code on multiple computers. Finally, stakeholders' confidence in the new technology is also important. Apart from that, the costs of implementing a BC-based system should be considered. They can be high because there is no common platform or standard for implementing blockchain technology in different fields. Using BC forces the use of high-speed, high-bandwidth Internet connections. The total cost of setting up such a system can be so high that most institutions may not be able to afford it.

As for the social issues, it should be noted that some of the advantages of BC in education can be viewed as disadvantages. In particular, using BC in education would integrate students' education data into blockchain ledgers. The immutability of blockchain technology would act as a double-edged sword, preventing educational records from being altered for legitimate reasons for some students (Chen et al., 2018). However, this problem can be overcome as described in Chapter 7, where an example of a practical solution has been discussed. Finally, a lack of trust in the technology and knowledge of how to harness the potential of blockchain use in education can result in slow market acceptance.

The legal aspects form the third category of limitations. These include the General Data Protection Regulation, which may impose restrictions on the transfer of personal data. In addition, the definition of personal data remains vague even in legislation. It is also worth highlighting the issues regarding privacy and security, which means that assuring privacy while providing security on the blockchain can be very difficult to achieve.

Other technology-independent factors include the lack of qualified personnel who are familiar with blockchain technology and issues of the access rights to educational data or their analysis results. It is also necessary to take into account the attitude of educational institutions to the use of BC, especially with regard to the decentralisation of the implemented solutions, the issue of questioning the prospects of using blockchain technology in education, or the weak regulatory policies for the use of blockchain in education (Zhou et al., 2020).

2.5 Conclusions

Blockchain is a decentralised peer-to-peer network and the distributed ledger accessible to all nodes. Since 2008, Bitcoin and blockchain are the two most important developments in information systems. Many applications use blockchain to perform tasks in a trusted environment without requiring a central authority. For this purpose, Distributed Ledger Technology is used, where the transaction data is disseminated and confirmed within a distributed network that does not require a central authority to register, share, and synchronise transactions on digital assets.

This technology is widely known in relation to cryptocurrencies; however, numerous studies indicate its potential applications also in the following areas: financial sector, commercial sector, retail services, transport and tourism, manufacturing and supply chain, energy sector, healthcare, government, intellectual property rights, smart cities, and education. However, the use of blockchain comes with numerous limitations resulting from the characteristics of this technology. One of them, strongly related to the successful implementation of blockchain technology, is scalability, which poses a challenge when blockchain technology is widely adopted in real business environments. With the increase in the number of transactions, scalability becomes a major obstacle to blockchain adoption, leading to an increase in the time and cost of transactions.

One of the potential uses of BC is higher education. Numerous studies are being conducted on the use of BC to manage issued documents and diplomas, intellectual property rights, tuition fee payments, and supportive learning environments that connect learners and teachers. However, we should be aware of numerous challenges if blockchain is to be used in education, not only in terms of the technology used (performance, scalability, immaturity) but also with respect to organisational, social, and legal considerations.

Summing up, while blockchain technology has the potential to bring significant benefits to the education sector, more research and development is needed to fully realise its potential. This also depends on the willingness of educational institutions, educators, and students to embrace the technology. Finally, a regulatory environment fostering the use of blockchain in education should be worked out.

References

Agbo, B., Qin, Y., & Hill, R. (2019). Research Directions on Big IoT Data Processing Using Distributed Ledger Technology: A Position Paper. In *IoTBDS. Proceedings of the 4th International Conference on Internet of Things, Big Data and Security (IoTBDS 2019)* (pp. 385–391).

Akhtar, M. M., Rizvi, D. R., Ahad, M. A., Kanhere, S. S., Amjad, M., & Coviello, G. (2021). Efficient data communication using distributed ledger technology and iota-enabled internet of things for a future machine-to-machine economy. *Sensors, 21*(13), 4354.

Alammary, A., Alhazmi, S., Almasri, M., & Gillani, S. (2019). Blockchain-based applications in education: A systematic review. *Applied Sciences, 9*(12), 2400.

Antal, C., Cioara, T., Anghel, I., Antal, M., & Salomie, I. (2021). Distributed ledger technology review and decentralized applications development guidelines. *Future Internet, 13*(3), 62.

Azbeg, K., Ouchetto, O., Jai Andaloussi, S., & Fetjah, L. (2021). An Overview of Blockchain Consensus Algorithms: Comparison, Challenges and Future Directions. In Saeed, F., Al-Hadhrami, T., Mohammed, F., Mohammed, E. (eds.) *Advances on Smart and Soft Computing. Advances on Smart and Soft Computing*, vol. *1188* (pp. 357–369). Singapore: Springer.

Belchior, R., Vasconcelos, A., Guerreiro, S., & Correia, M. (2021). A survey on blockchain interoperability: Past, present, and future trends. *ACM Computing Surveys (CSUR), 54*(8), 1–41.

Benčić, F. M., & Žarko, I. P. (2018). Distributed Ledger Technology: Blockchain Compared to Directed Acyclic Graph. In *2018 EEE 38th International Conference on Distributed Computing Systems (ICDCS)* (pp. 1569–1570). IEEE.

Benos, E., Garratt, R., & Gurrola-Perez, P. (2017). *The economics of distributed ledger technology for securities settlement.* (Working Paper No. 670). Available at SSRN 3023779.

Blidholm, G., & Johnson, M. (2018). *The Adoption of Distributed Ledger Technology in Trade and Export Finance Operations of Swedish Banks.* ME200X: Degree Project in Industrial Economics and Management. Retrieved January 30, 2023, from https://www.diva-portal.org/smash/get/diva2:1277987/FULLTEXT01.pdf

Bouras, M. A., Lu, Q., Zhang, F., Wan, Y., Zhang, T., & Ning, H. (2020). Distributed ledger technology for eHealth identity privacy: state of the art and future perspective. *Sensors, 20*(2), 483.

Cali, U., & Cakir, O. (2019). Energy policy instruments for distributed ledger technology empowered peer-to-peer local energy markets. *IEEE Access*, *7*, 82888–82900.

Cassandra, C., Widjaja, H., Prabowo, H., Fernando, E., & Chandra, Y. (2020). A Blockchain Technology-Based for University Teaching and Learning Processes. In *2020 International Conference on Information Management and Technology (ICIMTech)*, pp. 244–247.

Chen, G., Xu, B., Lu, M., & Chen, N. S. (2018). Exploring blockchain technology and its potential applications for education. *Smart Learning Environments*, *5*(1), 1–10.

Chowdhury, M. J., Ferdous, M. S., Biswas, K., Chowdhury, N., Kayes, A. S., Alazab, M., & Watters, P. A. (2019). A comparative analysis of distributed ledger technology platforms. *IEEE Access*, *7*, 167930–167943.

Cunha, P. R. D., Soja, P., & Themistocleous, M. (2021). Blockchain for development: a guiding framework. *Information Technology for Development*, *27*(3), 417–438.

Danzi, P., Kalør, A. E., Sørensen, R. B., Hagelskjær, A. K., Nguyen, L. D., Stefanović, Č., & Popovski, P. (2020). Communication aspects of the integration of wireless IoT devices with distributed ledger technology. *IEEE Network*, *34*, 47–53.

Dwivedi, A. D., Srivastava, G., Dhar, S., Singh, R. (2019). A decentralized privacy-preserving healthcare blockchain for IoT. *Sensors*, *19*, 326.

El Houda, Z. A., Khoukhi, L., & Hafid, A. (2018, December). Chainsecure-A Scalable and Proactive Solution for Protecting Blockchain Applications Using SDN. In *2018 IEEE Global Communications Conference (GLOBECOM)* (pp. 1–6). IEEE.

Ellervee, A., Matulevicius, R., & Mayer, N. (2017, November). A Comprehensive Reference Model for Blockchain-based Distributed Ledger Technology. In *ER Forum/Demos* (pp. 306–319).

European Central Bank. (2016). *Annual Report*. Retrieved January 30, 2023, from: https://www.ecb.europa.eu/pub/pdf/annrep/ar2016en.pdf

Fabiano, N. (2017, June). Internet of Things and Blockchain: Legal Issues and Privacy. The Challenge for a Privacy Standard. In *2017 IEEE International Conference on Internet of Things (iThings) and IEEE Green Computing and Communications (GreenCom) and IEEE Cyber, Physical and Social Computing (CPSCom) and IEEE Smart Data (SmartData)* (pp. 727–734). IEEE.

Fedorova, E. P., & Skobleva, E. I. (2020). Application of blockchain technology in higher education. *European Journal of Contemporary Education*, *9*(3), 552–571.

Fulmer, N. (2018). Exploring the legal issues of blockchain applications. *Akron Law Review*, *52*(1), 161–192.

Gatteschi, V., Lamberti, F., Demartini, C., Pranteda, C. & Santamaría, V. (2018). Blockchain and smart contracts for insurance: Is the technology mature enough? *Future Internet*, *10*(2), 20.

Gräther, W., Kolvenbach, S., Ruland, R., Schütte, J., Torres, C., & Wendland, F. (2018). Blockchain for Education: Lifelong Learning Passport. In *Proceedings of 1st ERCIM Blockchain Workshop 2018. European Society for Socially Embedded Technologies (EUSSET)*, vol. 2 (pp. 15–16).

Guo, J., Li, C., Zhang, G., Sun, Y., & Bie, R. (2020). Blockchain-enabled digital rights management for multimedia resources of online education. *Multimedia Tools and Applications*, *79*(15), 9735–9755.

Haber, S., & Stornetta, W. S. (1990, August). How to Time-Stamp a Digital Document. In *Conference on the Theory and Application of Cryptography* (pp. 437–455). Springer, Berlin, Heidelberg.

Hafid, A., Hafid, A. S., & Samih, M. (2020). Scaling blockchains: A comprehensive survey. *IEEE Access, 8*, 125244–125262.

Haugsbakken, H., & Langseth, I. (2019). The blockchain challenge for higher education institutions. *European Journal of Education, 2*(3), 41–46.

Himmetoğlu, B., Ayduğ, D., & Bayrak, C. (2020). Education 4.0: defining the teacher, the student, and the school manager aspects of the revolution. Turkish Online Journal of Distance Education. IODL-Special Issue Article 2. July 2020. 12–28.

Kamišalić, A., Turkanović, M., Mrdović, S., & Heričko, M. (2019). A Preliminary Review of Blockchain-Based Solutions in Higher Education. In *International Workshop on Learning Technology for Education in Cloud* (pp. 114–124). Springer, Cham.

Lam, T. Y., & Dongol, B. (2022). A blockchain-enabled e-learning platform. *Interactive Learning Environments, 30*(7), 1229–1251.

Lin, J., Shen, Z., Zhang, A., & Chai, Y. (2018, July). Blockchain and IoT Based Food Traceability for Smart Agriculture. In *Proceedings of the 3rd International Conference on Crowd Science and Engineering* (pp. 1–6). Association for Computing Machinery, Singapore.

Ma, Y., & Fang, Y. (2020). Current status, issues, and challenges of blockchain applications in education. *International Journal of Emerging Technologies in Learning (IJET), 15*(12), 20–31.

Maesa, D. D. F., & Mori, P. (2020). Blockchain 3.0 applications survey. *Journal of Parallel and Distributed Computing, 138*, 99–114.

McLean, S., & Deane-Johns, S. (2016). Demystifying blockchain and distributed ledger technology–hype or hero? *Computer Law Review International, 17*(4), 97–102.

Min, L., & Bin, G. (2022). Online teaching research in universities based on blockchain. *Education and Information Technologies, 27*, 6459–6482.

Moudoud, H., Cherkaoui, S., & Khoukhi, L. (2021). Towards a Scalable and Trustworthy Blockchain: IOT Use Case. In *2021 IEEE International Conference on Communications (ICC)* (pp. 1–6).

Moudoud, H., Cherkaoui, S., & Khoukhi, L. (2022). *An Overview of Blockchain and 5G Networks. Computational Intelligence in Recent Communication Networks* (pp. 1–20). Retrieved January 30, 2023, from: https://www.researchgate.net/publication/358164500_An_Overview_of_Blockchain_and_5G_Networks

Mühle, A., Grüner, A., Gayvoronskaya, T., & Meinel, C. (2018). A survey on essential components of a self-sovereign identity. *Computer Science Review, 30*, 80–86.

Nakamoto, S. (2008). *Bitcoin: A Peer-to-Peer Electronic Cash System.* Retrieved January 30, 2023, from: https://assets.pubpub.org/d8wct41f/31611263538139.pdf

Natarajan, H., Krause, S., & Gradstein, H. (2017). *Distributed Ledger Technology and Blockchain.* Washington: World Bank Group.

Panicker, S., Patil, V., & Kulkarni, D. (2016). An overview of blockchain architecture and it's applications. *International Journal of Innovative Research in Science, Engineering and Technology, 5*(11), 1111–1125.

Park, J. (2021). Promises and challenges of Blockchain in education. *Smart Learning Environments, 8*(1), 1–13.

Pinna, A. & Ruttenberg, W. (2016). *Distributed Ledger Technologies in Securities Post-Trading Revolution or Evolution?* ECB Occasional Paper No. 172. Retrieved January 30, 2023, from: https://www.ecb.europa.eu/pub/pdf/scpops/ecbop172.en.pdf

Poston, H. L. (2019). A brief introduction to blockchain concepts: Understand the principles of blockchain technology and the security considerations of using a decentralized network. *GhostVolt*. Retrieved January 30, 2023, from https://a.co/d/dDU8dVO

Prawiyogi, A. G., Aini, Q., Santoso, N. P. L., Lutfiani, N., & Juniar, H. L. J. (2021). Blockchain education concept 4.0: Student-centered ilearning blockchain framework. *JTP-Jurnal Teknologi Pendidikan, 23*(2), 129–145.

Raimundo, R., & Rosário, A. (2021). Blockchain system in the higher education. *European Journal of Investigation in Health, Psychology and Education, 11*(1), 276–293.

Rama Reddy, T., Prasad Reddy, P. V. G. D., Srinivas, R., Raghavendran, C. V., Lalitha, R. V. S., & Annapurna, B. (2021). Proposing a reliable method of securing and verifying the credentials of graduates through blockchain. *EURASIP Journal on Information Security, 2021*(1), 1–9.

Rauchs, M., Glidden, A., Gordon, B., Pieters, G. C., Recanatini, M., Rostand, F., Vagneur, K., & Zhang, B. (2018). *Distributed Ledger Technology Systems: A Conceptual Framework*. Cambridge: Judge Business School. University of Cambridge.

Rizky, A., Silen, S., & Putra, D. A. (2021). The role of blockchain technology in facing revolution education 4.0. *BEST Journal (Biology Education, Science and Technology), 4*(1), 77–85.

Roeck, D., Sternberg, H., & Hofmann, E. (2020). Distributed ledger technology in supply chains: A transaction cost perspective. *International Journal of Production Research, 58*(7), 2124–2141.

Saputra, M. A. W., Ochtaffia, D., & Apriani, D. (2023). Blockchain applications in education affecting challenges and problems in digital. *Blockchain Frontier Technology, 2*(2), 15–23.

Sas, C., & Khairuddin, I. E. (2017). Design for Trust: An Exploration of the Challenges and Opportunities of Bitcoin Users. In *Proceedings of the 2017 CHI Conference on Human Factors in Computing Systems* (pp. 6499–6510).

Shah, D., Patel, D., Adesara, J., Hingu, P., & Shah, M. (2021). Exploiting the capabilities of blockchain and machine learning in education. *Augmented Human Research, 6*(1), 1–14.

Sharma, T. K. (2018). *How Does Blockchain Use Public Key Cryptography?* Retrieved January 30, 2023, from: https://www.blockchain-council.org/blockchain/how-does-blockchain-use-public-key-cryptography

Steiu, M. F. (2020). Blockchain in education: Opportunities, applications, and challenges. *First Monday, 25*(9). Retrieved January 30, 2023, from https://journals.uic.edu/ojs/index.php/fm/article/view/10654

Sunny, F., Hájek, P., Munk, M., Abedin, M., Satu, Md. S., Efat, Md. I. A., & Islam, Md. J. (2022). A Systematic Review of Blockchain Applications. *IEEE Access, 10*, 59155–59177.

Ubaka-Okoye, M. N., Azeta, A. A., Oni, A. A., Okagbue, H. I., Nicholas-Omoregbe, O. S., & Chidozie, F. (2020). Blockchain framework for securing e-learning system. *International Journal of Advanced Trends in Computer Science and Engineering*, *9*(3), 2933–2940.

Vokerla, R. R., Shanmugam, B., Azam, S., Karim, A., De Boer, F., Jonkman, M., & Faisal, F. (2019, March). An Overview of Blockchain Applications and Attacks. In *2019 International Conference on Vision towards Emerging Trends in Communication and Networking (ViTECoN)* (pp. 1–6). IEEE.

Vukolić, M. (2016). The quest for scalable blockchain fabric: Proof-of-work vs. BFT replication. In Open Problems in Network Security: IFIP WG 11.4 International Workshop, iNetSec 2015, Zurich, Switzerland, October 29, 2015, Revised Selected Papers. Springer International Publishing. 112–125.

Xie, J., Yu, F. R., Huang, T., Xie, R., Liu, J., & Liu, Y. (2019). A survey on the scalability of blockchain systems. *IEEE Network*, *33*(5), 166–173.

Zhou, L., Lu, R., & Wang, J. (2020, August). Development status, trends and challenges in the field of "Blockchain and Education". *Journal of Physics: Conference Series*, *1621*(1), 012112. IOP Publishing.

3

SUPPORTING THE MANAGEMENT OF EDUCATIONAL INSTITUTIONS USING BLOCKCHAIN

Jan Trąbka and Mariusz Grabowski

3.1 Introduction

Blockchain technology, thanks to attributes such as self-sovereignty, trust, transparency and provenance, immutability, disintermediation, and collaboration (Grech & Camilleri, 2017, p. 8), is perceived by many as a tool that will disrupt the way how business activities are conducted today in various industries and domains. Indeed, thanks to such features as persistency of record-keeping, decentralised and distributed nature, as well as introducing business logic in the form of smart contracts (see Chapter 2), it enables the creation of solutions that are novel to today's organisational practices. Blockchain helps to reengineer organisational processes from both internal and external perspectives. The first perspective finds its application, especially in the case of organisations that are distributed geographically, with particular attention paid to transborder structures (Lacity, Moloney, & Ross, 2018), the second allows to create value networks between cooperating parties (Laurier, 2019).

Blockchain technology may be used as a strategic weapon that helps to gain a competitive advantage (Kant, 2021). This statement is justified especially in the realms of resource-based view of the firm (Barney, 1991) associated with the resources, competencies and distinctive capabilities school of strategic thinking. According to this theory, a company that has access to commonly available resources needs to connect them by competent employees to produce distinctive capabilities. As blockchain may be perceived as a commonly available resource (public, permissionless blockchains) or proprietary resource (consortium-based or private-permissioned blockchains) (see Chapter 2), it may produce distinctive capabilities for the organisation.

DOI: 10.4324/9781003318736-4

The potential for creating a competitive advantage for a given company or a consortium of organisations is especially present in the case of permissioned blockchain. Nevertheless, it may also be admitted that organisations which will decide to enter the blockchain market using a publicly available blockchain implementation, i.e. Bitcoin or Ethereum, thanks to the first mover advantages, may also strengthen its strategic position. According to Kant (2021), organisations must not avoid risk-taking within this context. There are many examples of companies that have lost their strategic position or even shrunk by not assimilating a disruptive innovation. Examples include Kodak which underestimated digital photography (a technology it invented) (Mui, 2012), and Digital Equipment Corporation as it did not respond correctly to the personal computer revolution (Christensen & Overdorf, 2000).

Blockchain-based solutions implemented in the higher education domain, even if being in the initial phase of adoption, reveal a high potential for future progress (Grech & Camilleri, 2017). The prospective areas of blockchain implementations in higher education institutions (HEIs) include (Grech & Camilleri, 2017): (1) issuing students' diplomas and other certificates, storing educational records and eliminating paperwork, (2) providing a possibility of verifying the certificates without the necessity of contacting the issuer, (3) enabling transparent access to HEIs accreditation results, (4) permitting the student-oriented ownership of educational records, and (5) facilitating the use of cryptocurrencies for paying tuition fees (see Chapters 4 and 6).

This chapter describes the use of blockchain in HEI organisational processes: (1) at the strategic level illustrated by the assimilation of a disruptive technology while defining the organisation's process architecture and (2) at the tactical level, in the implementation of specific internal and external (inter-organisational) processes. In so doing, Section 3.2 presents HEIs as organisations in which the processes are managed in a systematic manner, and discusses recommendations for the HEI Business Process Management (BPM) teams on how to improve processes using blockchain and smart contracts. The external perspective where HEIs participate in inter-organisational processes is characterised in Section 3.3. Next, the process of documenting and distributing qualifications in the educational ecosystem on a global scale is presented. Section 3.4 also discusses the idea of streamlining HEI accreditation processes. Section 3.5 presents the discussion of the ways in which blockchain may reshape the management of educational institutions, and Section 3.6 gives the conclusions concerning the development of HEI management systems based on blockchain.

3.2 Business process management in educational institutions

3.2.1 Introduction to the process approach

The process approach is one of the most important perspectives used in management theory and practice. It was initiated in the 1990s by the works of Davenport (1993), Davenport and Short (1990) and Hammer and Champy (1993), who placed the "process" as a focal point of organisational management. The processes themselves are "chains of events, activities, and decisions that ultimately add value to the organisation and its customers" (Dumas, La Rosa, Mendling, & Reijers, 2018, p. 1). This definition became the basis for creating new management methods. Such methods include Business Process Re-engineering (BPR) (Hammer & Champy, 1993), Lean Management (Marchwiński, Shook, & Schroeder, 2010), Total Quality Management (TQM) (Dahlgaard, Kristesen, & Kanji, 2000), and Business Process Management (BPM) (Jeston & Nelis, 2008).

The effectiveness of the process approach has been repeatedly confirmed by numerous studies published over several decades (e.g., McCormack & Johnson, 2001; Kohlbacher, 2010). Studies on the effectiveness of the business process approach were conducted not only in the developed but also in the less developed economies of Central and Eastern Europe (Skrinjar, Stemberger, & Hernaus, 2007; Gębczańska & Bujak, 2017).

The key factor for the introduction of the process approach is the use of IT/IS (Information Technologies/Information Systems). For processes to function properly within an organisation, uniform sources of information about resources (e.g., customers, products, goods, and/or people) are required. Scholars recognised information resource identification as a key requirement for effective and efficient implementation of successful organisational change (Davenport, 1993). To facilitate the process orientation, integrated systems have been implemented in organisations since the 1970s. These systems evolved into Material Requirement Planning (MRP)/Enterprise Resource Planning (ERP), which are integrated, multi-module systems that cover key areas of an enterprise: procurement, production, sales, and finance. ERP systems provide their users access to shared data, while allowing them to perform assigned tasks in business processes in which they participate.

Another category of systems that meet the requirements of the process approach are workflow management systems (WfMS). WfMS enable the distribution of tasks and information between users in an organisation according to defined paths (process models). The first step in implementing WfMS is to model and redesign processes which will then be controlled or partially performed by the system. The ability to define process models and execute them by users within an organisation, with the possibility of their subsequent redesign, has become an advantage over ERP systems. Therefore, WfMS are a natural complementary component to ERP. As WfMSs became more sophisticated and better integrated with other enterprise systems, they became known as Business Process Management Systems (BPMS) (Dumas, La Rosa, Mendling, & Reijers, 2018).

3.2.2 Business process orientation in educational institutions

BPM studies, including those cited in Section 3.2.1, do not refer to the application of the process approach in educational institutions (including HEIs). Indeed, in this type of institutions, the concept of efficiency is interpreted differently (educational institutions are not focused on maximising the profit for owners) and has less importance. However, several aspects of HEI functioning such as operational costs, quality of customer service, or inter-functional conflicts require process-oriented management.

HEIs carry out various processes, their primary client is the student, and the value they deliver is knowledge and skills. From that perspective HEIs implement three main process areas:

- Educational cycle processes that provide the students with service from the moment of enrolment to the final award of the diploma: This area includes the processes of social and medical care or access to educational resources.
- Research processes that provide researchers with access to all resources used in scientific inquiry: These ensure that the management of grants and research projects, international mobility, organisation of conferences and other scientific events are properly accomplished.
- Management and administrative processes which provide the HEI with strategic and tactical decisions for the operations of all organisational units: These processes also include handling external contacts (public relations), quality management, and knowledge management. Administrative processes ensure the continuous functioning of the HEI as an institution with various assets.

Figure 3.1 presents the main HEIs processes along with the related information systems infrastructure and their stakeholders. Stakeholders participate in the relevant groups of main processes and use dedicated information systems. The process approach requires the integration of information systems throughout the organisation; therefore. the figure shows the "integration" relationship, indicating the directions of data exchange.

HEIs need to provide integrated and uniform data about students, employees, suppliers, and equipment. At the same time, HEI information

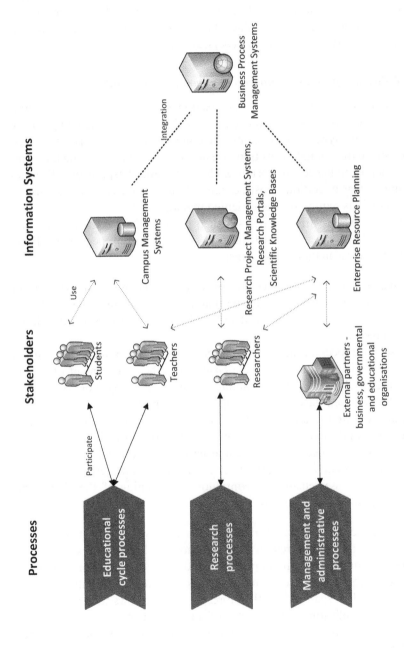

FIGURE 3.1 HEIs main processes and IS infrastructure.

systems should be process-aware and provide digital support for the three main organisational process areas. Like business organisations, HEIs also use integrated ERP systems. Processes specific to educational units are carried out by Campus Management Systems (CAMS), supporting students' entire educational lifecycle, from application to ex-matriculation (Sprenger, Klages, & Breitner, 2010). As process-oriented organisations, HEIs increasingly implement BPMS, allowing users to create process models themselves and supervise them using process engines. An important attribute of BPMS is the ability to interact with processes through web and mobile interfaces. The implementation of the above-mentioned systems not only supports, but often forces universities to use a process approach (Bührig, Ebeling, Hoyer, & Breitner, 2014).

3.2.3 Business process management lifecycle

Business process management (1) builds on the philosophy of continuous improvement proposed by TQM (see Section 3.2.1), (2) embraces the principles and techniques of operational management and Lean Management, and (3) combines the above attributes with the functionalities offered by modern IT to optimally align business processes with the organisation's performance goals (Dumas, La Rosa, Mendling, & Reijers, 2018). BPM helps organisations improve efficiency through business processes optimisation. According to Elzinga et al. (1995, p. 121), BPM is "a systematic, structured approach to analyse, improve, control, and manage processes with the aim of improving the quality of products and services". Business process management deals with the design, execution, monitoring, and improvement of processes (Mendling et al., 2018). BPM is also intended to align the business processes with strategic objectives and customers' needs and requires a change in a company's orientation from functional to process-centred (Lee & Dale, 1998).

The BPM lifecycle is an essential framework of BPM adoption. We can perceive BPM as a continuous cycle consisting of the following phases (Dumas, La Rosa, Mendling, & Reijers, 2018):

• Process identification: In this phase, the organisational areas that require changes are defined based on reported business problems and opportunities for improvement. The identification phase is the answer to the questions of which processes need to be changed, where these processes start, where they end, and which processes they interact with. In this phase, the process architecture is created.

- Process discovery (also called AS-IS process modelling): In this phase, it is necessary to answer the question of how the processes which will be subject to change currently operate. Detailed models of processes are created. AS-IS process modelling describes the current flows of processes, without their improvement. These process models should reflect what is the organisational stakeholders' understanding of the work being done. In this phase, the BPM team uses many tools of data collection, such as surveys, interviews, workshops, analysis of procedures, and instructions.
- Process analysis: In this phase, business problems in the modelled processes are identified and methods of their improvement are indicated. A very important element of the analysis is process evaluation and/or indication of process performance measures, also called process performance metrics. These metrics provide a basis for determining which parameters of the process are considered "bad", which level of metrics should be considered as the target, and at which metric values the process can be described as "good". Process measures are classified into cost, quality, and time-related (Lee & Dale, 1998). The analysis should lead to the identification of the reasons due to which the observed process metrics have unsatisfactory values.
- Process redesign (also called process improvement): In this phase, process variants are created that consider organisational and technical ways to remove the identified business problems and achieve the process metrics expected in the BPM project. The analysis of possible variants should consider, on the one hand, the desired improvement of metrics, and, on the other hand, the costs of the variants' implementation. The output of this phase is typically a TO-BE process model.
- Process implementation: In this phase, the changes needed to be introduced within the organisation are prepared. In consequence, the optimised processes can replace the currently used ones. The implementation includes two aspects: organisational change and process automation. The first aspect is particularly risky, as employees are reluctant to change the processes they are involved in. The second aspect concerns the implementation of optimised processes in the entire organisational ecosystem. This applies to Process-aware Information Systems such as ERP, WfMS, CAMS (in the case of HEIs) and BPMS. The implementation phase ends with the launch of the optimised processes.
- Process monitoring and controlling: In this phase, the implemented processes are measured. It is examined whether the designated process performance metrics are consistent with the assumptions made in the initial phases of the cycle. When required goals and metrics are not met, another full "corrective BPM cycle" is triggered.

3.2.4 Blockchain recommendations for BPM lifecycle

Blockchain, thanks to its attributes such as trust, transparency and immutability, is both a great challenge and opportunity for organisations managed in accordance with the BPM approach. Process redesign should take into account not only the persistency of record-keeping, the decentralised and distributed nature of blockchain, but also the possibility of creating algorithms and procedures (thanks to smart contracts that can reflect internal and external process control). Smart contracts may be considered as media tors in intra-organisational processes. Based on prior studies (vom Brocke, Mendling, & Weber, 2018; Mendling et al., 2018; Rosemann & vom Brocke, 2015), recommendations for the use of blockchain technology at each stage of the BPM life cycle are proposed (Figure 3.2).

The following are the recommendations proposed in the work of vom Brocke, Mendling, and Weber (2018) supplemented by our propositions of adjustments to the HEIs conditions:

- Recommendation 1 – Identification. In the first stage of the BPM lifecycle, strategic observation of high-level HEI process areas is carried out. Strategic observation is performed within the context of process areas' weaknesses and directions for their improvement. Technologies that can radically improve the efficiency of the analysed processes, such as blockchain, should be considered. Process variants using blockchain to support their flows are analysed in terms of their strengths, weaknesses, opportunities, and threats. Benchmarking with different HEIs can play an important role in this stage.
- Recommendation 2 – Discovery. Blockchain technology defines new challenges for process discovery techniques: the information may be fragmented and encrypted, accounts and keys can change frequently, and process data may be stored partly on-chain and partly off-chain. This fragmentation might require a repeated alignment of information from all parties operating on the blockchain. When modelling the process and creating a data model, their compliance with block structures in the network should be considered.
- Recommendation 3 – Analysis. In this phase, the problems and their causes in the modelled processes are identified. Records of processes executed on the blockchain yield valuable information that can help to assess the duration and frequency of paths, parties involved, and dependencies between unencrypted data items. The HEI's BPM team should use this blockchain-stored information in the analysis.
- Recommendation 4 – Redesign. In this phase, process variants are created, considering organisational and technical means for the improvement of

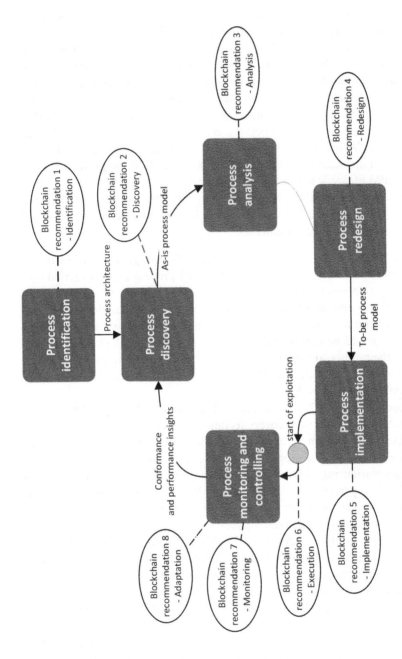

FIGURE 3.2 Blockchain in the BPM Lifecycle.

Source: Based on (Dumas, La Rosa, Mendling, & Reijers, 2018).

indicated organisational problems and achieving desired process metrics. The HEI's BPM team should answer the question of where blockchain can be applied for optimising existing interactions and where new interaction patterns can be established (without the mediation of a trusted central party). At this point, it should also be considered which process variant will be optimal for the HEI, taking into account the costs of using blockchain.

- Recommendation 5 – Implementation. In this phase, the technical and organisational resources needed to implement the redesigned processes are prepared. Blockchain-based business process engineering requires new tools, e.g., modelling languages, software patterns and quality assurance mechanisms. An important engineering challenge is the definition of abstractions, including modelling primitives like Business Process Model and Notation (BPMN) extensions, libraries, connectors, and tailored execution engines (Object Management Group, 2011).

- Recommendation 6 – Execution. In this phase, the most important element is ensuring the synchronisation between transactions in the blockchain, smart contracts, and processes performed in local BPMS, CAMS or ERP systems. An important issue in this regard is the involvement of systems providers or integrators in creating components (interfaces) to be linked with blockchain. An example of such an integrator might be the Sphereon platform (https://sphereon.com) which creates solutions that combine blockchain and smart contracts technology with popular BPMS systems: Microsoft Sharepoint (https://www.microsoft.com) and Alfresco (http://alfresco.com).

- Recommendation 7 – Monitoring. In this phase, data on the executed process instances are collected. Monitoring can be carried out on an ongoing basis in the form of alerts or by analysing historical data collected in the BPMS process engines. Key elements in this regard are the process evaluation metrics defined in the analysis phase, which should be evaluated periodically. When blockchain is used as an intermediary in an inter-organisational process, the BPM team should monitor and compare data on the blockchain with local off-chain data. In this phase, techniques and tools described as Process Mining may be used (van der Aalst, 2016). Process mining is a technique designed to model and improve real processes by extracting readily available knowledge from the event logs of information systems.

- Recommendation 8 – Adaptation. In this phase, there is a reaction to unacceptable values of the process evaluation metrics or to changes in the process execution environment. When implementing processes based on blockchain and smart contracts, the BPM team should ensure compliance of the changed process models with their interactions recorded in smart contracts.

Blockchain is a technology that might improve processes in various areas of an organisation. An increasing number of organisations, including HEIs, have been improving their processes in an organised, cyclical, and consistent way, using BPM methods. All the recommendations, presented above, should help BPM teams to include blockchain technology in process management initiatives.

3.2.5 Using blockchain to process tenders for HEIs

According to Viriyasitavat et al. (2020, p. 1737): "BPM systems in Industry 4.0 are required to digitize and automate business process flows and to support transparent collaboration between service providers". Collaboration processes (often referred to as B2B processes) require trust. This problem is clearly visible in the supply chain where the manufacturer, broker, freight forwarder, supplier, and customer work together (Michalski, Kirill, & Montes Botella, 2014). The subsequent steps performed by the cooperating parties are determined by the actions of other participants. In practice, it is often impossible to check whether a given activity has been performed in accordance with the contract. Such a cooperation process contains places where dishonest actions of one party may expose others to losses while stopping the entire supply chain. We can call such cases untrusted business processes. Therefore, a need for a trusted, external, and impartial coordinator (mediator) of the entire B2B process exists (Weber, Xu, Riveret, Governatori, & Mendling, 2016).

At HEIs, we can encounter untrusted business processes in inventory management. Purchasing processes, especially in public educational institutions, are usually preceded by tendering procedures. The institution must admit an unlimited number of bidders and the best bid is selected based on equal treatment, fair competition, and transparent economic criteria. Purchasing Departments announce tenders and collect offers that are to be kept secret until the tender is settled. Disclosure of the content of the submitted offer by a supplier to another supplier would result in the possibility of issuing competitive conditions and winning the tender. The tender conditions themselves may contain parameters that are confidential to bidders until the tender is resolved. At this point a suspicion may arise that the Purchasing Department may disclose this parameter to other bidders in advance so that they can adjust the bids and win the tender. The tendering process carried out in the traditional way is therefore an untrusted process. Figure 3.3 presents the tendering process at HEIs modelled in BPMN notation.

There are two participants in the modelled process: the supplier and the HEI Purchasing Department. The process begins with the announcement of the terms of the tender. The supplier prepares and submits an offer which must be archived in the Purchasing Department. The offer is deposited until

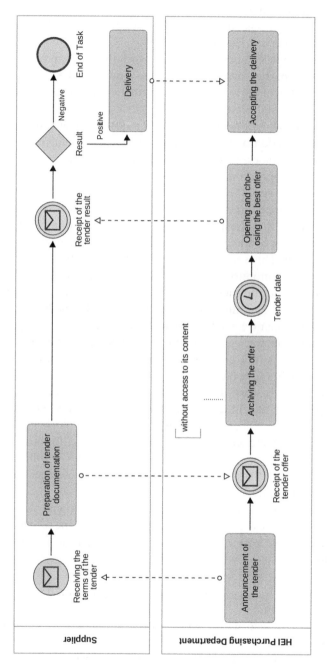

FIGURE 3.3 Process of handling tenders at HEIs.

the indicated date of tender settlement, when the Purchasing Department opens all submitted offers, compares them, and decides on the selection of the best one. Tender decisions are sent to all suppliers who submitted offers. The selected supplier carries out the delivery.

The process modelled above is burdened with the problem of the lack of trust between the parties involved in the transactions. In the case of tenders, there is a possibility of early access to submitted offers and disclosing information to unfairly preferred suppliers. In the case of traditional deliveries carried out by many intermediaries, there is a possibility of false confirmations of the completion of transaction stages or false confirmations of the payment. Applying blockchain technology can be a solution to the problem of mistrust. The proposition to use blockchain in relation to many cooperative processes in the supply chain was presented by Weber et al. (2016). The authors have developed an approach of mapping a business process to a peer-to-peer execution infrastructure that stores transactions in the blockchain and uses smart contracts to check conditions and trigger the next steps of the transaction. This solution has three benefits. Firstly, by storing data in the blockchain, a monitoring function is provided. It integrates an automatic and invariant transaction history. Secondly, smart contracts (see Chapter 2) are used as a direct implementation of the mediator's process control logic. Automatic mediators ensure trusted, i.e. without the participation of the human factor, execution of conditional steps in the business process. Thirdly, an audit trail, created and stored on the blockchain, is obtained for complete collaborative business processes.

At this point, it is worth to pay attention to smart contracts and their launching platform, the Ethereum blockchain, which was selected in the solution described by Weber et al. (2016). The Ethereum blockchain offers a built-in Turing complete scripting language called Solidity for programming smart contracts. At the same time, Ethereum provides a full Ethereum Virtual Machine (EVM) run time that is used to execute Solidity scripts across all network nodes.

Taking into account the above-described considerations, Weber et al. (2016) proposed a blockchain-based system which solves the problem of distrust in collaborative business processes. It is based on the following main components:

- BPMN model – It reflects a process in the supply chain described using dedicated notation,
- Translator – It transforms the process specification in BPMN into a smart contract algorithm written in the Solidity language,
- Factory contract – In this element actual participants are assigned the roles they will perform in the process. The factory contract contains all

the information needed to create a process instance. It includes instantiation methods and two types of artefacts:

- interface specification for each role (e.g., buyer, producer, and shipper) in the collaborative process to be broken down into appropriate triggers,
- process instance contract that is deployed on the blockchain when the process is created.

- Interfaces or triggers - These connect the process running on the blockchain and the external world. Since smart contracts cannot directly interact with the world outside of the blockchain, the trigger stores sensitive information and runs on a full blockchain node, tracking the execution context and state of running business processes. When needed, the trigger invokes an external application programming interface (API), receives API calls from external components, and updates the state of the blockchain process based on external observations.

In order to apply the described solution to the tendering process for HEI, modelled in the first part of the section, it is necessary to create the environment presented in Figure 3.4, where the elements are mapped onto the

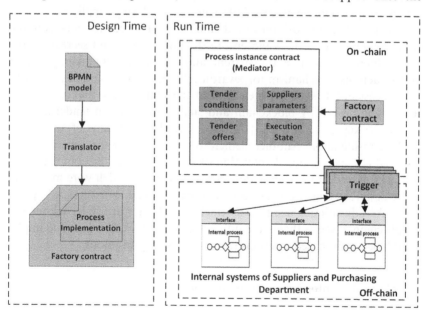

FIGURE 3.4 Process of handling tenders at HEIs realised on the blockchain.

Note: BPMN – Business Process Model and Notation.

Source: Based on (Weber, Xu, Riveret, Governatori, & Mendling, 2016; Weber, Xu, Riveret, Governatori, & Mendling, 2016).

tendering process phases, i.e. the component configuration phase (Design Time), and the performing phase (Run Time).

A HEI tendering process based on blockchain might be executed as follows. After announcing the terms of the tender by the Purchasing Department, the potential suppliers would place their offers on the blockchain. The following sets of parameters, which formulate the Process instance contract (Mediator), would be stored on the blockchain: Tender conditions, Suppliers' parameters, Tender offers, and Execution state. The Mediator (Process instance contract) is a smart contract that executes a process (single instance) for a single supplier. The Factory contract would code tender control mechanisms and all tender parameters – quantity, value, and time periods. Factory contract code would be made available to all bidders. The Trigger would be responsible for placing bids and transferring information throughout the bid to individual internal vendor processes. The Factory contract would control the access rights to bids over the duration of the tender. At the moment of resolving the tender, the Factory contract would compare the parameters of all submitted bids and, in accordance with the programmed algorithm, would indicate the best offer. The Trigger would then transfer the tender results from the Mediator to the HEI's Purchasing Department and all the suppliers who participated in the process (both winning and losing suppliers).

The described proposition would eliminate untrusted elements from the entire tender process. It would ensure the invariability and secrecy of the bids submitted and is a transparent and automatic (eliminating biased human actions) mechanism for awarding tenders. The solution applies to one process in HEIs, being an element of the supply chain that can be successfully improved by blockchain and smart contracts. In tendering processes, the key element is trust in respecting the conditions of secrecy of tender consideration. Another element of delivery processes where trust is essential is the conditional activation of payments after the completion of the tasks agreed in the transaction. Smart contracts, which were mediators in the described tender process, can also be used to perform financial operations. As educational institutions (including HEIs) are links within the supply chain, it seems that in the future they will gradually adopt and implement blockchain-based solutions from business organisations.

3.3 Managing inter-organisational processes

3.3.1 Introduction to inter-organisational processes

Today's organisations cooperate by forming virtual supply and value chains (Salvini, Hofstede, Verdouw, Rijswijk, & Klerkx, 2022; Steyn & Semolic, 2018). This creates a high demand for providing the interoperability of their internal systems (Rajaguru & Jekanyika, 2013). Such a requirement is sometimes met through the platforms offered by value chain integrators or is organised individually by players within the supply/value chain (Schmidt, Veile, Müller, & Voigt, 2022). Coordinating the activities within such networks requires centralised control. Usually, this is performed through the platform provider or an organisation that is considered a supply/value chain leader. The central authority's role is, among other things, to guarantee that all transactions within the network are trustworthy and verifiable. This task is however sometimes difficult to perform as "supply chains usually lack trust, transparency, and documentation" (Ciccio et al., 2018, p. 57).

The Industry 4.0 trends indicate that the number of cooperating organisations is increasing constantly (McKinsey & Company, 2022). The technological innovations such as the Internet of Things, Artificial Intelligence, and Big Data allow to effectively and efficiently manage the information provided by a much higher number of business players than before (Chen, 2020). Providing a centralised control for managing such an ecosystem is, however, problematic due to the high volume and complexity of data.

3.3.2 Adding value to higher education organisational processes

Blockchain applications in the supply chain context mainly involve the manufacturing and distributing companies interested in the verification of the quality and origin of the materials, components, and products supplied within the upstream part of the chain in which they participate. For instance, the work by Ciccio et al. (2018) describes a blockchain application in the pharmaceutical industry using a consortium-based, permissioned type of blockchain. The authors have specified the model utilising Caterpillar (López-Pintado, García-Bañuelos, Dumas, Weber, & Ponomarev, 2019) – a business process management solution operating on the Ethereum blockchain and using smart contracts. The system is built on the premises of a globally recognised standard in the healthcare industry – GS1 (GS1, 2013). The authors plan to extend their application to other platforms, including IBM Blueworks Live with the Hyperledger blockchain.

HEIs are rather not involved in typical supply/value chains as they do not process physical resources into the finished goods. We may, however, refer to a university's product as an alumnus. In this case, we may imagine the supply/value chain concept from the HEIs' perspective as transforming the resources (students) through different stages of education, by equipping them with skills and knowledge (and thus add value in each link of the chain), beginning from primary school, and finishing at the Ph.D. level. Although the implementation of the above-given idea is rather the matter of the future, one of the first examples of the conceptualisation of the value chain model in education is presented in (Karamitsos, Papadaki, Themisto-cleous, & Ncube, 2022). The authors demonstrate how value can be added through blockchain application to the certification issuance process. They indicate one of the ways in which blockchain can contribute to the value proposition offered by HEIs to their final customers, i.e. students.

Nowadays, while talking about inter-organisational processes in the HEI ecosystem, we refer to the cooperation between various stakeholders, including students, staff, other HEIs, accreditation institutions, employers, as well as society and/or national economy (Saurbier, 2021). The main precondition for this information exchange is the standardisation which provides interoperability (Zhao & Xia, 2014). The first important step in this direction was introducing Internet and web-based protocols, which allowed to access IS through web-based interfaces. Universities provide such an access for their stakeholders by the means of e-learning platforms, campus management systems (see Section 3.2.2), university study administrative systems and workflow systems, to mention the most important.

Blockchain technology, however, enables a step forward to be made. As a distributed solution, it unifies various network users into one ecosystem (Geroni, 2021). It allows for the exchange of information between parties in an immutable, verifiable, and trustworthy manner. It is, therefore, a good candidate for creating inter-organisational systems for educational institutions, providing the possibility of information exchange whose credibility and verifiability are of particular importance. The examples of such information are diploma certificates, course completion certificates, and records that prove obtaining specific qualifications.

When designing a blockchain-based system for information exchange, we have to keep in mind that storing the information in the publicly available solutions, e.g., Ethereum (which is a very popular platform thanks to the possibility of smart contracts execution) is expensive (Golosova & Romanovs, 2018). For this reason, a possible solution to this problem is to store on the blockchain as little information as possible (i.e. hashes and certificates – see Chapter 4) and link them with the remaining information stored in internal information systems of a particular organisation.

3.3.3 Sample blockchain implementations in the higher education domain

3.3.3.1 QualiChain

QualiChain (https://qualichain-project.eu) (Decentralised Qualifications' Verification and Management for Learner Empowerment, Education Reengineering and Public Sector Transformation) is a European Union's Horizon

2020 financed piloting and evaluation project aimed at creating a decentralised platform for storing and evaluation of education and employment qualifications (Kontzinos et al., 2019). The main goal of the project is to create, pilot, and evaluate "a distributed platform targeting the storage, service, and verification of academic and employment qualifications" (Kontzinos et al., 2019, p. 93). It aims to analyse various technologies (i.e. blockchain, algorithmic techniques and computational intelligence) and their capability of reshaping the domain of public education. The project encompasses a broader socio-economic perspective, assuming that public education may cooperate with private education, the labour market, and public sector administration.

The project scope includes various dimensions, i.e. technical, political, socio-economic, legal, and cultural. It also indicates the impact of the combination of used technologies on potential benefits and risks associated with the project implementation (QualiChain, n.d.). As far as blockchain technology is concerned, the benefits are as follows (Politou et al., 2019): (1) using online certificates to improve the learning accreditation and recruitment processes, (2) introducing a distributed learning environment, (3) providing secure, traceable, and transparent verification benefiting all stakeholders (learners, education institutions, educators, and employers), (4) eliminating mediators, providing self-sovereignty and identity management with the General Data Protection Regulation (GDPR), and (5) tracking transactions in a transparent and immutable manner. The project indicates some risks of blockchain technology which mainly refer to: (1) scalability problems, (2) infancy stage of development, and (3) exposing to uncertain security issues.

There are four pilot scenarios already implemented in four key areas, i.e. Lifelong Learning, Smart Curriculum Design, Staffing the Public Sector, and Recruitment and Competency Management Services. The project is developed by 12 partner institutions, from various countries (Greece, Germany, Portugal, and the United Kingdom) that represent universities, research and innovation agencies as well as public administration organisations.

3.3.3.2 EBSI

The European Blockchain Services Infrastructure (EBSI) (https://ec.europa. eu/digital-building-blocks/wikis/display/ebsi/) is a project of the European Commission and the European Blockchain Partnership (EBP) aimed at creating an open blockchain platform for the implementation of various cross-border services. The main objective of the project is to empower public administrations and unify their ecosystems to verify information in a trustworthy way. The European Blockchain Partnership is focused on diminishing the blockchain fragmentation and encouraging EU member countries to closely collaborate on the development of public administration services in an interoperable, standardised, and coherent way (European Commission, n.d.-a). EBP provides expertise in the subject of blockchain deployment and assures that proposed solutions will be compliant with EU regulations and have transparent governance structures and models.

EBSI have formulated four potential areas for blockchain implementations, called "Use cases" in the project terminology. They include Self-Sovereign Identity, Diploma, Social security, and Document traceability. Although EBSI is dedicated to all potential services offered by institutions from EU countries, it also launched a pilot project dedicated solely to the educational domain within the Early Adopters Programme, entitled "Piloting on EBSI in the education sector: the multi-university pilot" (European Commission, n.d.-b). It has identified the following actors within the accreditation ecosystem of HEIs: Trusted Accreditation Organisation (Government entity), Issuer (HEI), Holder (Student), Wallet provider, and Verifier (HEI/Employer). This concept has been an inspiration for the accreditation ecosystem described further in this chapter.

3.3.3.3 EduCTX

QualiChain and EBSI belong to the category of inter-organisational projects constituting a general-purpose solution that may be utilised to implement specific blockchains enabling education-oriented organisational processes. The Blockchain-Based Higher Education Credit Platform (EduCTX) (http://eductx.org) (Turkanović, Hölbl, Košič, Heričko, & Kamišalić, 2018) is a specific IS deployment platform aimed to facilitate the European Credit Transfer and Accumulation System (ECTS) between HEIs. Each student is granted a blockchain wallet where all ECTS credits issued by various HEIs are collected. The initial version of the system was implemented as an open-source solution, based on the Delegated Proof of Stake consensus algorithm and the ARK Blockchain platform (https://ark.io). One of the goals of ARK Blockchain is to enable the interoperability of other blockchain implementations. ECTS credits are the equivalent of the cryptocurrencies used in other blockchain-based environments. As the ARK Blockchain platform does not implement smart contracts (see Chapter 2), it was necessary to disable "selling" gained ECTS by one student to another. We can imagine a situation when a particular student takes a course and passes it, and then transfers the gained ECTS credits to another student who declares this as their own achievement. The authors have proposed a solution based on multi-signature mechanisms – a well-known cryptography concept enabling various parties to jointly sign a transaction. In the case of EduCTX, there are two signees:

the HEI and the student. This makes the credit transfer done solely by a student impossible as two signatures are necessary. The authors have proposed a modification of the initial implementation by moving to the Ethereum blockchain (Hölbl et al., 2018). In this case they could replace the multi-signature mechanisms with business logic expressed in smart contracts, which puts the constraints on the valid network transactions.

The system was first implemented in the University of Maribor, Slovenia. Then other universities joined the network, i.e. Brno University of Technology, The Czech Republic, FH Bielefeld University of Applied Sciences, Germany, and the Faculty of Electrical Engineering of the University of Sarajevo, Bosnia and Herzegovina. The limited number of participating institutions puts the future of EduCTX in doubt, as a critical success factor of such inter-organisational systems is obtaining a satisfactory network effect.

3.4 Facilitating accreditation of educational institutions

3.4.1 Motivation and stakeholders of the accreditation process

The 21st century has introduced substantial changes into higher education systems. These are associated with progressing globalisation, economic development, technological progress, rising costs, and decreases in governmental subsidisation (Saurbier, 2021). Today's commonly used buzz word expressing the above-mentioned factors is "Industry 4.0" in general and "Education 4.0" in particular.

The higher education ecosystem over the years has evolved from a university-centred model, initiated in medieval Europe, to a student-centred paradigm observed today (see Chapter 4). The latter is characterised by the following attributes: (1) substantial increase in the number of HEIs, (2) substantial increase in the number of students, and (3) constantly increasing demand for a qualified workforce (Kontzinos et al., 2019).

The most important outcome of the HEIs' functioning is the quality of the delivered results. This concerns two essential HEI activities, which are teaching and research. In the past, what guaranteed the credibility of outcomes for the stakeholders (i.e. students, employers, grant providers), was the university's name. Even today, the prestige of the university is perceived as a safeguard for quality. The students and employers do not look for additional certificates of quality in the case of the universities that are on the top of rankings such as the THE (Times Higher Education World University Ranking) (Times, 2022). However, in the case of other, less prestigious HEIs, an additional proof of quality is demanded, as we can observe the trend of deteriorating value of college education (Saurbier, 2021) and the cases of committing fraud by some HEIs (de Souza-Daw & Ross, 2021) or students (Ronnie & Goodman, 2019).

The above-mentioned concerns are being solved through accreditation. Accreditation can be defined as: "the fact of being officially recognized, accepted, or approved of, or the act of officially recognizing, accepting, or approving of something" (Cambridge Dictionary, 2022). It is performed as a process that is based on "self-regulation and continuous improvement based on periodic reviews under the guidance of a recognized accrediting agency" (Manimala, Wasdani, & Vijaygopal, 2020, p. 10). We can, therefore, look at the accreditation as a safeguard for quality and compliance with the referred standards. Its process and outcomes may be associated with TQM (Section 3.2.1) (Fernandes & Singh, 2022) and integration of approaches expressed in stakeholder, systems, ethical, and consumer theory (Saurbier, 2021). On the example of the United States, Saurbier (2021) has identified the following education ecosystem stakeholders: institutions, students, employers, faculty, community, accreditation institutions, higher education industry, government, national economy, and society.

The accreditation process is performed either by accrediting institutions – which is related to organisations (HEIs), or by HEIs and professional training organisations – which is related to individuals (students). In all cases, accreditation is a guarantee that a given entity conforms with identified quality and legal standards.

We can distinguish two kinds of accreditation institutions (Manimala, Wasdani, & Vijaygopal, 2020):

- State accreditation institutions – These are established by a given country or state. They audit accredited institutions for compliance (agreement with legal regulations) and quality requirements. In the case of HEIs, the area of accreditation is usually divided into teaching and research. In Poland there are two institutions: the Polish Accreditation Committee (PAC) (for teaching) and the Science Evaluation Committee (for research). Accreditation performed by state accreditation institutions is obligatory.
- Domain accreditation institutions – These are usually globally recognised bodies that are specialising in a given domain or discipline. These institutions usually audit accredited institutions in the areas of teaching and research. The examples for the business education discipline include AACSB (Association to Advance Collegiate Schools of Business), AMBA (Association of MBAs), and EQUIS (EFMD Quality Improvement System). Business schools that have accreditations from all these institutions jointly belong to the elite group of HEIs that can boast having the so-called "Triple Accreditation". The accreditations performed by domain accreditations are voluntary.

The individuals (students) are accredited by the HEIs and professional training organisations. Accreditations by HEIs include mother universities and visiting universities during exchange programmes (e.g., Erasmus). Both mother HEIs and visiting ones grant certificates of completed courses, e.g. ECTS credits. The diplomas for finished studies are granted by mother institutions. The diplomas for the completion of professional trainings are granted by professional training organisations. The concept of accreditation stakeholders presented in this chapter was inspired by Saurbier (2021) and the European Commission (n.d.-b) and is presented in Table 3.1. The final list of stakeholders, however, was modified comparing with the propositions discussed in the above-mentioned works since (1) they are limited only to the stakeholders that are actors in the accreditation process (modification of the concept proposed by Saurbier (2021)) and (2) they are not limited to EU countries but are open to the global audience, as some stakeholders do not originate from the EU, e.g., domain accreditation institutions (modification of the concept proposed by European Commission (n.d.-b)). The stakeholders of the higher education accreditation have various roles in the process. They might be issuers, receivers, or viewers of granted accreditation certificates.

3.4.2 Accreditation process

The accreditation of HEIs is performed according to the procedure defined by a relevant accreditation institution. In the case of the PAC, which performs accreditation of the majors offered by Polish HEIs, both public and private, the procedure consists of eight steps (Polish Accreditation Committee, 2022):

- preparation of a self-assessment report by the university,
- on-site visit by an evaluation team,
- preparation of the report by the evaluation team,
- submitting the evaluation team's report to the HEI,
- presentation of the HEI's position in response to the report,
- preparation of an opinion by the evaluation team and formulating the HEI's response to the report,
- decision – a resolution of the PAC Presidium,
- publication of the report, the resolution of the PAC Presidium, and the university's statement.

The institutional accreditation process should focus on the programme outcomes and educational goals rather than on the educational process. It should encourage innovation, be diagnostic (not prescriptive), recognise

TABLE 3.1 Higher education accreditation stakeholders.

Stakeholders	Roles	Description
Students	Receiver/Viewer	Students are receivers of certificates (diplomas, ECTS). Certificates are issued by their mother HEI or by other HEIs that they visited during exchange programmes (e.g. Erasmus). Students may also view the certificates of given HEIs issued by the accreditation institutions (state and domain).
Employers	Viewer	Employers are viewers of the certificates of potential employees and universities. Employers also may view the certificates of given HEIs issued by the accreditation institutions (state and domain).
Higher education institutions	Viewer/Issuer/ Receiver	HEIs are the viewers of the certificates issued by other HEIs related to their students. They are also the issuers of the certificates of study completion (diplomas) to their own students and of course completion (ECTS) to both own and visiting students. HEIs are also receivers of certifications from state and domain accreditation institutions.
Professional training organisations	Issuer/Viewer	Professional training organisations issue certificates of the professional courses completed by the students. These trainings may also be recognised by HEIs and required by employers due to the recent changes in the educational ecosystem.
State accreditation institutions	Issuer/Viewer	State accreditation institutions are responsible for issuing obligatory certifications for HEIs' educational and research activities. They are obliged to check whether a given HEI is compliant with state legal regulations and satisfies the quality outcomes for educational and research processes. The certifications granted are usually valid for a certain period. State accreditation institutions may also act as viewers for some certifications and use this information for planning future audit activities.
Domain accreditation institutions	Issuer/Viewer	Domain accreditation institutions issue certificates in relation to a given discipline in which a particular HEI is functioning. These types of accreditation institutions are usually globally recognised. The certifications that are granted are usually valid for a certain period. Domain accreditation institutions may also act as viewers for some certifications granted by other accreditation institutions.

Source: Based on (Saurbier, 2021) and (European Commission, n.d.-b).

institutional diversity, avoid isolated evaluations, minimise the burden of accreditation, consult the audited institution, and give greater weight to academic than professional matters. It should also analyse the current context of a given institution (Manimala, Wasdani, & Vijaygopal, 2020).

Individual accreditation is less procedural than institutional. The certificate is granted either by a teacher or a professional training organisation (in the case of a course or training), or by a HEI (in the case of the entire degree). The standards for accreditation are written in a course syllabus or study regulations.

The main problem of the existing accreditation system is the verifiability of the certificates, which is particularly evident in the case of individual accreditation but is also visible in the case of institutions. As the volume of false certificates constantly increases (Ronnie & Goodman, 2019) we need to find a solution to eliminate this trend. Another problem stems from the fact that the accreditation system is fragmented and not easily available for all stakeholders. Both problems may be solved through a blockchain-based accreditation system.

3.4.3 The proposition of a blockchain-based accreditation system

There are already several solutions related to the accreditation process (see Section 3.3.3). They, however, either do not arouse sufficient interest (EduCTX) or express a potential for future applications rather than an implemented solution (QualiChain and EBSI). The question whether they will succeed is rather open. Blockchain for education is still a concept that awaits the gaining of maturity, and new ideas are welcome.

The investigation of the scholarly literature related to "blockchain higher education accreditation" through the keyword search in the Scopus bibliographic database has indicated that the "blockchain" keyword is directly impacted by another keyword – "smart contracts". This may indicate that a public blockchain type, i.e. Ethereum, might be commonly used in this realm, as it implements the concept of smart contracts through the Solidity programming language (as mentioned in Section 3.2.5). The example of moving EduCTX from the ARK Blockchain platform and multi-signature verification to Ethereum and smart contract-based business logic (Section 3.3.3) seems to support this statement.

Figure 3.5 presents a proposition of a blockchain-based accreditation system. For accreditation purposes it must be a permissioned solution to control the credibility of the blockchain stakeholders, and it is based on the public Ethereum blockchain. In this case, an access-control layer is built into the permissionless Ethereum blockchain (Neville, 2022). The stakeholders

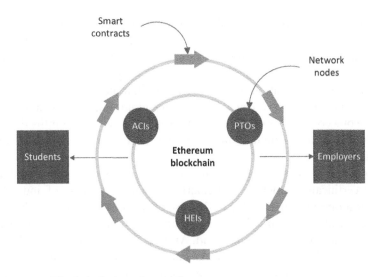

FIGURE 3.5 Blockchain-based accreditation system.

Note: ACIs – Accreditation Institutions, PTOs – Proffessional Training Organisations, HEIs – Higher Education Institutions.

that are issuers of certificates, i.e. HEIs, professional training organisations, and accreditation institutions (both national and domain specific) (Table 3.1) represent the network nodes, and each one stores a copy of all network transactions (represented by circles in the picture). These stakeholders can also view the certificates they are interested in, as it is described in Table 3.1.

An example of a smart contract (arrows) in the system can be the way in which a given certificate is issued to a student. When a student completes all required courses (the requirements for a smart contract), the certificate is automatically assigned to this student (smart contract is executed) with no actions taken from the side of HEIs employees.

The ultimate stakeholders of the solution are the certificate viewers, i.e. students and employers (represented by squares in the picture). They interact with the network using blockchain wallets. Employers are considered as the final consumers of the accreditation process products, i.e. students' qualifications (Saurbier, 2021).

The advantages of the proposed solution include a broad perspective on the accreditation process that comprises not only HEIs as the issuers of certificates but also professional training organisations. This complies with the necessity of recognising professional training demanded nowadays by employers. The next advantage is the fact that the proposed solution is dedicated to the global audience and may include HEIs and accreditation institutions from different parts of the world. Finally, blockchain would provide access to the published certificates which would be trustworthy, immutable, verifiable, and offered transparently to all stakeholders.

The limitation of the system mainly stems from the fact that it might share the fate of other blockchain deployments that have neither gained a network effect nor public approval (see Section 3.3.3). The other shortcoming is related to the fact that an Ethereum-based blockchain solution may incur relatively high costs of the processed transactions (Golosova & Romanovs, 2018).

3.5 Reshaping management of the educational processes

The framework proposed by Hart and Milstein (2003) inspired us to discuss the problem of transforming the management of educational processes inside and outside educational institutions (Figure 3.6). It helps to position a given organisation according to two factors. The horizontal axis reflects the organisation's capacity to orient its processes for either internal or external orientation, while the vertical one reflects the desire to gain short-term

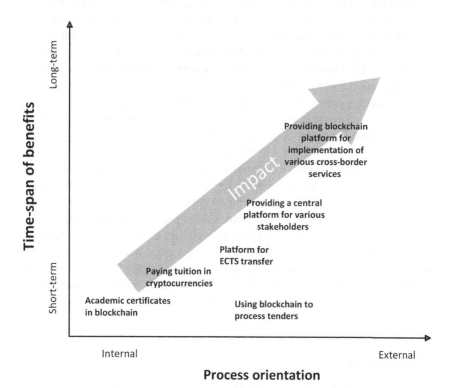

FIGURE 3.6   Blockchain impact on the management of HEIs.

gains versus long-term benefits. As we progress from the internal, short-term orientation towards external, long-term orientation, blockchain applications might have higher impact on the management of an organisation (including HEIs). The impact arrow starts in the internal organisation, short-term gains section, and rises towards external organisational processes focused on long-term benefits. Its direction indicates the transformation of the blockchain applications from those that are based on simple organisational processes towards the ones concentrating on complex networks of external stakeholders.

Initially, an organisation may concentrate on internal processes in the short-term benefit perspective. Then it may follow the direction of going up (long-term investments), right (external processes) or both directions (long-term investments and external processes). The last case is related to the most complex applications having the potential of bringing the highest benefits to the organisation (or participating organisations). The selected existing and potential blockchain applications in the education sector are shown within the proposed framework in Figure 3.6.

The leader in the field of blockchain applications in education is the University of Nicosia (UNIC), Cyprus (UNIC, n.d.) (see Chapters 6 and 7 for more details). UNIC uses blockchain to facilitate its management processes, such as storing certificates on the blockchain and receiving tuition fees in cryptocurrency. These processes may be considered to be rather internal, as they integrate the organisation in a downstream way with the final customers, i.e. students, who are not active players in the value chain. They also have a rather short-term focus on benefits. It is, however, worth noting that the above-given examples appear to be the most advanced blockchain applications in the education domain today.

The other applications, like those mentioned in the current chapter, i.e. using blockchain to process tenders (Section 3.2.5), providing a platform for ECTS transfer (EduCTX), providing a central platform for various stakeholders (QualiChain), and offering blockchain platform for the implementation of various cross-border services (EBSI), are either in a conceptual or infant phase. They, however, if successful, may occupy more advanced (i.e. more long-term benefits and external processes oriented) positions in the proposed framework, since these applications either integrate upstream in the value chain (tenders) or are aspiring to create a less (EduCTX) or more complex (QualiChain, EBSI accreditation) ecosystem.

3.6 Conclusions

This chapter is aimed at describing the role of blockchain in managing HEIs from both internal and external perspectives. It was indicated that process orientation, in general, and the use of BPM methodology, in particular, are essential prerequisites for effective and efficient blockchain implementation aimed at the automation of processes and document workflows in educational institutions or in the networks of educational organisations. We believe that the proposed adjustment of the BPM lifecycle by including blockchain recommendations can enrich blockchain-based organisational change in HEIs. While the concept of BPM and the value chain is not frequently applied to the education sector, it has been argued that this concept may change the education industry in the future.

Existing and potential applications of blockchain in the higher education sector, i.e. accreditation of both HEIs and students (e.g., granting ECTS and certificates) as well as blockchain-based public tender process are rather in their infancy stage. Critical success factors that will determine blockchain's applicability to the education sector are related to overcoming various barriers. The most important factor, in our opinion, is reaching the critical mass, reflected in the involvement of a significant number of HEIs and selecting the common and open blockchain implementation based on smart contracts. An example from the past which supports the above-given statement was the necessity of adopting one, open network protocol in the form of TCP/IP by the users of the Internet. This was done gradually and collectively by all stakeholders, even though other, competing technologies already existed. As blockchain is called the next disruptive technology of the same or even greater significance as the Internet (Karamitsos, Papadaki, Themistocleous, & Ncube, 2022), such a comparison seems to be justified.

References

Barney, J. (1991). Firm resources and sustained competitive advantage. *Journal of Management, 17*(1), 99–120.

Bührig, J., Ebeling, B., Hoyer, S., & Breitner, M. H. (2014). Process-oriented standard software – An impulse for sustainable business process management at higher education institutions? In *Proceedings Multikonferenz Wirtschaftsinformatik 2014 (MKWI)* (pp. 558–570). Paderborn, Germany.

Cambridge Dictionary. (2022). *Cambridge Dictionary*. Retrieved May 23, 2022, from: https://dictionary.cambridge.org/pl/dictionary/english/accreditation

Chen, Y. (2020). IoT, cloud, big data and AI in interdisciplinary domains. *Simulation Modelling Practice and Theory, 102*(102070), 1–5.

Christensen, C. M., & Overdorf, M. (2000). Meeting the challenge of disruptive change. *Harvard Business Review, 78*(2), 66–76.

Ciccio, C. D., Felix, D., Haas, D., Lilek, D., Riel, F., Rumpl, A., & Uhlig, P. (2018). Blockchain-Based Traceability of Inter-Organisational Business Processes. In B. Shishkov (Ed.), *BMSD 2018, LNBIP 319* (pp. 56–68). Cham, Switzerland: Springer International Publishing AG, part of Springer Nature B.

Dahlgaard, J., Kristesen, K., & Kanji, G. (2000). *Podstawy zarządzania jakością.* Warszawa: PWN.

Davenport, T. H. (1993). *Process Innovation: Reengineering Work Through Information Technology.* Boston: Harvard Business School Press.

Davenport, T. H., & Short, J. E. (1990). The new industrial engineering: Information technology and business process redesign. *MIT Sloan Management Review, 31*(4), 11–27.

de Souza-Daw, T., & Ross, R. (2021). Fraud in higher education: A system for detection and prevention. *Journal of Engineering, Design and Technology* (ahead-of-print). DOI: 10.1108/JEDT-12-2020-0504

Dumas, M., La Rosa, M., Mendling, J., & Reijers, H. (2018). *Fundamentals of Business Process Management.* Berlin: Springer.

Elzinga, D., Horak, T., Chung-Yee, L., & Bruner, C. (1995). Business process management: Survey and methodology. *IEEE Transactions on Engineering Management, 24*(2), 119–128.

European Commission. (n.d.-a). *Digital Europe: eIDAS Enablers/News.* Retrieved Jan. 12, 2023 from: https://ec.europa.eu/digital-building-blocks/wikis/display/BLOG/2021/10/04/University+pilot+proves+value+of+a+European+Blockchain

European Commission. (n.d.-b). *Shaping Europe's Digital Future.* Retrieved Jan. 12, 2023 from https://digital-strategy.ec.europa.eu/en/policies/blockchain-partnership

Fernandes, J. O., & Singh, B. (2022). Accreditation and ranking of higher education institutions (HEIs): Review, observations and recommendations for the Indian higher education system. *The TQM Journal, 34*(5), 1013–1038.

Geroni, D. (2021, 08 10). *101 Blockchain.* Retrieved Jan. 3, 2023 from: https://101blockchains.com/blockchain-ecosystem/

Gębczańska, A., & Bujak, A. (2017). Assessment of the degree of process approach implementation in Polish businesses. *The TQM Journal, 29*(1), 118–132.

Golosova, J., & Romanovs, A. (2018). The advantages and disadvantages of the blockchain technology. In *2018 IEEE 6th Workshop on Advances in Information* (pp. 1–6). Electronic and Electrical Engineering (AIEEE).

Grech, A., & Camilleri, A. (2017). Blockchain in Education. In A. Inamorato dos Santos (Ed.), *Publications Office of the European Union, EUR 28778 EN.* Luxembourg: Publications Office of the European Union.

GS1. (2013). *GS1: Global Traceability Standard for Healthcare.* Retrieved Jan. 29, 2022 from: https://www.gs1.ee/doc/download/GS1_Global_Traceability_Standard_Healthcare.pdf

Hammer, M. H., & Champy, J. (1993). *Reengineering the Corporation: A Manifesto for Business Evolution.* New York: Harper Business.

Hart, S. L., & Milstein, M. B. (2003). Creating sustainable value. *Academy of Management Executive, 17*(2), 56–69.

Hölbl, M., Turkanović, M., Kamišalić Latifić, A., Heričko, M., Podgorelec, B., Rek, P., & Hrgarek, L. (2018). *EduCTX: A Decentralized System for Managing Micro-Credentials, Based on Smart Contracts and the Ethereum Blockchain Platform.* Primošten: DAAD Workshop.

Jeston, J., & Nelis, J. (2008). *Business Process Management.* London: Routledge.

Kant, N. (2021). Blockchain: A strategic resource to attain and sustain competitive advantage. *International Journal of Innovation Science, 13*(4), 520–538.

Karamitsos, I., Papadaki, M., Themistocleous, M., & Ncube, C. (2022). Blockchain as a service (BCaaS): A value modeling approach in the education business model. *Journal of Software Engineering and Applications*, *15*, 165–182.

Kohlbacher, M. (2010). The effects of process orientation: A literature review. *Business Process Management Journal*, *16*(1), 135–152.

Kontzinos, C., Markaki, O., Kokkinakos, P., Karakolis, V., Skalidakis, S., & Psarras, J. (2019). University process optimisation through smart curriculum design and blockchain-based student accreditation. In *18th International Conference on WWW/Internet*. Cagliari, Italy.

Lacity, M., Moloney, K., & Ross, J. W. (2018). *Blockchain at BNP Parias: The Power of Co-Creation*. CISR, WP No. 428.

Laurier, W. (2019). Blockchain value networks. In *IEEE Social Implications of Technology (SIT) and Information Management (SITIM)* (pp. 1–6).

Lee, R. G., & Dale, B. G. (1998). Business process management: A review and evaluation. *Business Process Management Journal*, *4*(3), 214–225.

López-Pintado, O., García-Bañuelos, L., Dumas, M., Weber, I., & Ponomarev, A. (2019). Caterpillar: A business process execution engine on the ethereum blockchain. *Software: Practice and Experience*, *49*(7), 1162–1193.

Manimala, M. J., Wasdani, K. P., & Vijaygopal, A. (2020). Facilitation and Regulation of educational institutions: The role of accreditation. *Vikalpa: The Journal for Decision Makers*, *45*(1), 7–24.

Marchwiński, C., Shook, J., & Schroeder, A. (2010). *Leksykon Lean. Ilustrowany słownik pojęć z zakresu Lean Management. Wrocław: Wydawnictwo Lean Enterprise Institute Polska, 2010, s. 3*. Wrocław: Wydawnictwo Lean Enterprise Institute Polska.

McCormack, K. P., & Johnson, W. C. (2001). *Business Process Orientation – Gaining the E-Business Competitive Advantage*. Washington, DC: St. Lucie Press.

McKinsey & Company. (2022, 06). *Transforming Advanced Manufacturing through Industry 4.0*. Retrieved Nov. 18, 2022, from: https://www.mckinsey.com/capabilities/operations/our-insights/transforming-advanced-manufacturing-through-industry-4-0

Mendling, J., Weber, I., van der Aalst, W., vom Brocke, J., Cabanillas, C., Daniel, F., … la Rosa, M. (2018). Blockchains for business process management - Challenges and opportunities. *ACM Transactions on Management Information Systems*, *9*(1), 1–16.

Michalski, M., Kirill, M., & Montes Botella, J. (2014). Trust and it innovation in asymmetric environments of the supply chain management process. *Journal of Computer Information Systems*, *54*(3), 10–24.

Mui, C. (2012). *How Kodak Failed*. Retrieved Oct. 21, 2022 from: https://www.forbes.com/sites/chunkamui/2012/01/18/how-kodak-failed/?sh=7f48d9f66f27

Neville, C. (2022). *Enterprise Ethereum Alliance Permissioned Blockchains Specification v3*. Retrieved Dec. 18, 2022 from: https://entethalliance.github.io/client-spec/chainspec.html

Object Management Group. (2011). *About The Business Process Model and Notation Specification Version 2.0*. Retrieved Jun. 5, 2022, from: https://www.omg.org/spec/BPMN/2.0/About-BPMN/

Polish Accreditation Committee. (2022). *Polish Accreditation Committee*. Retrieved May 22, 2022 from https://www.pka.edu.pl/en/home-page/

Politou, N., Kontzinos, C., Ergazakis, K., Karakolis, V., Kokkinakos, P., Melo, R., ...Zarafidis, P. (2019, 06 03). *D2.1 Landscape Analysis, QualiChain Concept and Potential Investigation Report*. Retrieved Dec. 18, 2022 from: https://qualichain-project.eu/deliverables/

QualiChain. (n.d.). *About*. Retrieved Jan. 12, 2023 from: https://qualichain-project.eu/about/

Rajaguru, R. M., & Jekanyika, M. (2013). Effects of inter-organizational compatibility on supply chain capabilities: Exploring the mediating role of inter-organizational information systems (IOIS) integration. *Idustrial Marketing Management*, *42*(4), 620–632.

Ronnie, L., & Goodman, S. (2019, 02 5). *Fake Qualifications are on the Rise. How universities can manage the risk*. Retrieved Dec. 18, 2022 from: https://theconversation.com/fake-qualifications-are-on-the-rise-how-universities-can-manage-the-risk-109962

Rosemann, M., & vom Brocke, J. (2015). Six Core Elements of Business Process. In M. Rosemann, & J. vom Brocke (Eds.), *Handbook on Business Process Management: Introduction, Methods, and Information Systems (International Handbooks on Information Systems)* (pp. 105–122). Berlin: Springer.

Salvini, G., Hofstede, G. J., Verdouw, C. N., Rijswijk, K., & Klerkx, L. (2022). Enhancing digital transformation towards virtual supply chains: a simulation game for Dutch floriculture. *Production Planning and Control*, *33*(13), 1252–1269.

Saurbier, A. (2021). Modelling the stakeholder environment and decision process in the U.S. higher education system. *Business, Management and Economics Engineering*, *19*(1), 131–149.

Schmidt, M. C., Veile, J. W., Müller, J. M., & Voigt, K. I. (2022). Industry 4.0 implementation in the supply chain: A review on the evolution of buyer-supplier relationships. *International Journal of Production Research*, 1–18. DOI: 10.1080/00207543.2022.2120923

Skrinjar, R., Stemberger, M., & Hernaus, T. (2007). The impact of business process orientation on organizational performace. In *Proceedings of the 2007 Informing Science and IT Education Joint Conference* (pp. 171–185). Ljubljana.

Sprenger, J., Klages, J., & Breitner, M. H. (2010). Cost-benefit analysis for the selection, migration, and operation of a campus management system. *Business & Information Systems Engineering*, *2*, 219–231.

Steyn, P., & Semolic, B. (2018). Designing Industry 4.0 virtual networks of partners value chains. *PM World Journal*, *7*(5), 1–27.

Times. (2022). *Times Higher Education*. Retrieved Sep. 15, 2022 from: https://www.timeshighereducation.com/world-university-rankings

Turkanović, M., Hölbl, M., Košič, K., Heričko, M., & Kamišalić, A. (2018). EduCTX: A blockchain-based higher education credit platform. *IEEE Access*, *6*, 5112–5127.

UNIC. (n.d.). *Leading Blockchain Education and Research Since 2013*. Retrieved Dec. 18, 2022, from: https://www.unic.ac.cy/blockchain/

van der Aalst, W. (2016). *Process Mining – Data Science in Action*. Berlin, Heidelberg: Springer-Verlag.

Viriyasitavat, W., Da Xu, L., Bi, Z., & Sapsomboon, A. (2020). Blockchain-based business process management (BPM) framework for service composition in Industry 4.0. *Journal of Intelligent Manufacturing*, *31*, 1737–1748.

vom Brocke, J., Mendling, J., & Weber, I. (2018). *Blockchain & Business Process Management. Part 1 the BPM Lifecycle.* BPTrends (pp. 1–9). Retrieved Sep. 15, 2022 from https://www.bptrends.com/class-notes-blockchain-business-process-management-part-1-the-bpm-lifecycle/

Weber, I., Xu, X., Riveret, R., Governatori, G., & Mendling, J. (2016). Untrusted Business Process Monitoring and Execution Using Blockchain. In M. La Rosa, P. Loos, & O. Pastor (Eds.), *Business Process Management. BPM 2016. Lecture Notes in Computer Science*, vol. 9850. Cham: Springer.

Zhao, K., & Xia, M. (2014). Forming Interoperability Through Interorganizational Systems Standards. *Journal of Management Information Systems, 30*(4), 269–298.

4

MANAGEMENT OF STUDENT-CENTRED LEARNING WITH BLOCKCHAIN

Mariusz Grabowski and Paweł Konkol

4.1 Introduction

Over the past centuries, education in general, and higher education, in particular, has evolved from the paradigm in which the educational institutions and teachers were at the centre of the educational process. This was reflected in the concept of a master-apprentice relationship, in which the master, who occupied the dominant position, was recognised as a "treasury" of knowledge and skills and was responsible for passing them on to the students. Today, this form of education is shifting to the model in which the emphasis is put on students. They have a dominating position in a teaching–learning relationship and are individually responsible for their own education. This model is known as the student-centred learning model (Brush & Saye, 2000; Overby, 2011; Wright, 2011).

Student-centred learning may be characterised as bringing "the classroom and students to life. The teacher is considered a 'guide on the side', assisting and guiding students to meet the goals that have been made by the students and the teacher" (Overby, 2011, p. 109). The important factors of student-centred learning are acquisition and enhancement of higher-order competencies such as critical thinking and problem-solving (Brush & Saye, 2000). It also emphasises the teamwork in small groups. This type of grouping, when conducted in diverse (in terms of ethnicity, disabilities, and gender) and comfortable environments, allows for exchanging the ideas introduced by group members, strengthens their critical thinking, improves communicational skills, and increases self-esteem (Overby, 2011). It also supports self-management, monitoring, and evaluation of the educational process by learners (Brush & Saye, 2000).

DOI: 10.4324/9781003318736-5

Furthermore, in the student-centred learning the evaluation of the learning outcomes is of great importance. It should not concentrate solely on obtaining the grades but needs to promote learning *per se*. Therefore, the course objectives need to be precisely defined and students ought to be directed to manage the whole process. The teacher should ask critical questions in a constructive way and give the opportunities to validate the achieved outcomes in practice (Wright, 2011).

The student-centred learning demands establishing a conducive space, referenced within the pedagogy literature as an inspiring and/or supportive learning environment (Thompson & Wheeler, 2008; Della Ventura, 2017; Campbell, 2020). A supportive or inspiring learning environment consists of three dimensions: physical, intellectual, and emotional (Thompson & Wheeler, 2008). The first dimension covers such functions of the teaching room as furniture and its arrangement, lightening, presentation equipment, and other aids including whiteboards and flipcharts. The second includes educational standards, students' and teachers' expectations, defined objectives and learning strategies, as well as methods of assessment. The third consists of individual feeling of safety and social participation, mutual support, and respect as well as other vital elements of the emotional dimension such as in-class discipline and individual motivations for the whole didactic process (Thompson & Wheeler, 2008).

In student-centred learning, students have become responsible for managing their learning paths through active and flexible curriculum design. They may accomplish this task by selecting appropriate electives or short, competency-based courses and thus shape the skills and knowledge necessary in the field in which they want to specialise (Rau, 2021).

The student-centred higher education paradigm has entered an accelerated phase through Information and Communication Technologies (ICT). ICT facilitate the transition from traditional to virtual (i.e. digital) learning environments that commonly implement the concept of social constructivist pedagogy, in which "people actively construct new knowledge as they interact with their environments" (Moodle, 2018). The main factor that recently accelerated this shift was the COVID-19 pandemic. Higher education institutions (HEIs) have been forced to create in a very short time the technological infrastructure and organisational procedures enabling emergency of remote teaching and learning (Vollbrecht, Porter-Stransky, & Lackey-Cornelison, 2020). The acquired experience has enriched students and teachers with the tools and skills necessary to use digital learning environments in an individual and interactive way. At present, we can assume that students and educators are used to digital ways of teaching and learning. The question is not whether these tools and methods are appropriate, but how to use them effectively and efficiently.

By drawing an analogy between the student-centred learning paradigm and the concept of relationship marketing (Gronroos, 1994; Steinhoff, Arli, Weaven, & Kozlenkova, 2019), we may use five Is as proposed by Peppers and Rogers (1997) and Peppers et al. (1999). The five Is describe the attributes of relationship marketing in the context of the Internet. These attributes are the following:

• Identification – a student knows the teacher and teacher knows the student. This is not just superficial knowing of each other, but a relationship focused on a win–win strategy.
• Individualisation – the learning path, tools and methods are tailored to the student's needs, capabilities, and expectations.
• Interaction – the learning process is based on mutual communication, where student also has the dialogue initiative.
• Integration – a course in which a student participates in is embedded into the entire learning path, shaping the curriculum.
• Integrity – a learning contract between the student and the teacher is based on ethical and transparent principles.

In our opinion, the next step that can add value to the student-centred learning concept facilitated by ICT capabilities will be by application of blockchain (see Chapter 2), which is by some considered as a more influential technological improvement than Internet (Karamitsos, Papadaki, Themistocleous, & Ncube, 2022). By the same token, the *EDUCAUSE Horizon Report: 2019 Higher Education Edition* (Alexander et al., 2019; Grech & Camilleri, 2017) has indicated blockchain as an important factor in educational technology for higher education in a timespan of four to five years.

According to Swan (2015), blockchain has evolved from stage 1.0, characterised by development of cryptocurrencies, through stage 2.0 focusing on cash transactions, (i.e. stocks, bonds, loans, property) utilising smart contacts, into stage 3.0, adding value to business processes in such domains like government, health, science, culture, and art. The application of blockchain in education belongs to the third category. It is worth mentioning that Cunha et al. (2021, p. 418) distinguish additional stage 4.0 characterised by improved scalability, increased interoperability, and integration of blockchain applications with existing business solutions and IT infrastructures, as well as with other advanced technologies (e.g., Artificial Intelligence and Internet of Things).

Although current implementations of blockchain in educational sector are rather rare, there are several deployments that are presented in the scholarly literature (Grech & Camilleri, 2017; Chen, Xu, Lu, & Chen, 2018; Sharples & Domingue, 2016). In the current state of development, blockchain in education is primarily used for issuing certificates, degrees, and academic records, and paying tuitions with cryptocurrencies (see Chapters 6 and 7). However, the potential for using blockchain technology in educational sector is not limited only to above-mentioned applications. The remaining part of this chapter is devoted to three possible areas of blockchain applications in the educational sector that are developed together with student-centred learning concept, i.e. supporting distributed learning, facilitating lifelong learning, and accessing educational content. The chapter is summarised by concluding remarks.

4.2 Supporting distributed learning

4.2.1 Introduction to distributed learning

Distributed learning, also called *spaced learning*, is not precisely defined within the literature. Victor and Hart (2016) indicate that in general terms, distributed learning is characterised as an instructional model of learning that includes blended and multimedia components, and in most cases, it is referred to the physical distribution of learners. In distributed learning "the material to be learned is distributed over a long period of time so that the learner must integrate the various separated parts of material into a unique entity" (Kirkley, 2012, p. 1020). Hence, a learning process is more efficient when the time between the knowledge acquisition and retrieval is relatively long.

Distributed learning is currently supported by *distributed technologies* and technology-based *distributed learning environments*. Distributed technologies in education utilise computational environments to virtually combine students and teachers allowing for face-to-face collaboration, enriched by computer mediation (analysis, search and recording of interactions) (Psotka, 2012). Distributed technologies implement the concept of supportive or inspiring digital learning environments which may be perceived as tools that link the interactive capabilities supported by networking, computing, and multimedia with learning-centred paradigm (Kirkley, 2012). The concept of distributed learning environments has been highly explored in the United States Department of Defense, which has resulted in adding "advanced" adjective to the original concept. The main goal of advanced distributed learning is to allow for access to high-quality education on demand, anytime and anywhere (Fletcher, 2012).

Summing up, the "distributed" label in the distributed learning concept may be understood in the following dimensions:

- the learning process is distributed over *time* – which supports an assumption that the long-term memory is improved when the learning is done through the "chunks" of information (Kirkley, 2012),

- the learning process is distributed over *space* – which allows for more inclusive access to education through the means of digital methods of interaction and collaboration (Fletcher, 2012),
- the learning process is distributed over the different *media*, i.e. types of content delivered – which supports the argument that efficient learning process demands a rich communication channel, as indicated by Media Richness Theory (Daft & Lengel, 1986).

Distribution learning may also incorporate a variety of learning methods, i.e. blended learning (Ifenthaler, 2012) supported by various technology solutions (Psotka, 2012). The above-mentioned dimensions of distributed learning define a frame of reference for a description of selected blockchain applications in this chapter.

4.2.2 Distance education

The concept of distributed learning is rooted in the idea of *distance education*. Its origins are dated to the beginning of the 18th century, where the corresponding school model was introduced (Harting & Erthal, 2005). However, some scholars indicate that the instructional correspondence form of teaching was originated by Apostle Paul in his letters written in the 1st century to the members of Christian churches, located in the Roman Empire (Wheeler, 2012). Over the years, distance education development was rather the matter of an evolution than revolution (Harting & Erthal, 2005).

The technological and organisational progress allowed to gradually utilise increasingly advanced ways of content delivery and interaction, including telegraph, telephone, mass media, and the Internet. The latter has highly intensified the presence of distant education in the didactic offer of many institutions, including academia, and business. In this respect, the world's first university that started to teach exclusively in the distance form was established in the United Kingdom – The Open University (https://www.open.ac.uk). Currently, especially after the COVID-19 pandemic, it is difficult to imagine any university that has not introduced at least one form of distance education (Dymek, Grabowski, & Paliwoda-Pękosz, 2022).

Distance education occurs when a teacher and students are separated in terms of physical distance (Harting & Erthal, 2005). The separation of parties is an essential qualifier of distance education, and it leads to the need of considering some additional aspects, e.g., virtual presence (do students are really present during virtual classes) and performance (do students achieve the expected educational results) (Picciano, 2002).

Distance education gives various opportunities that are unavailable in traditional face-to-face classes. These include (Willis, 1992; Al-Khatir Al-Arimi, 2014):

- reaching a wider student audience,
- allowing the participation of people that are unable to attend on-campus classes (including individuals with disabilities),
- involving outside speakers,
- providing flexibility, convenience, and adaptability for learners,
- facilitating a two-way communication between teachers and learners,
- including diverse social, cultural, ethnic, and economic student backgrounds.

Distance education can be related to *distance learning* which may be considered as a synonym of distance education. It is characterised as an activity which

> is location and time independent, encouraging students to assume the responsibility for their own learning. In many cases, the teacher is more remote and less accessible than the learning materials, acting as another learning resource rather than as a central component in the learning process.
>
> *(Wheeler, 2012, p. 1019)*

In distance learning, the learning materials may be acquired by students in a "pull" mode as contrary to a "push" mode utilised in traditional learning. Students are granted more freedom in selecting the materials for studying in terms of order and depth, especially when they are offered in web-based layouts (Wheeler, 2012).

Another concept related to distance education is *blended learning* or *hybrid learning*. It combines a face-to-face way of interaction with technology-based instructions. The depth of a "blended" dimension may be characterised as a combination of (Ifenthaler, 2012):

- different IT-based technologies,
- different pedagogical theories,
- instructional technology helping students to obtain required skills and competencies.

The concepts of distributed learning, distance learning, and blended/hybrid learning, are interrelated in various dimensions (including ICT) and should be approached in a holistic way. For an effective and efficient implementation of learning strategies in these times, it is essential to find synergies between them to obtain desired benefits.

4.2.3 Blockchain support

As the Fourth Industrial Revolution progresses (Skilton & Hovsepian, 2018), the demand for a qualified workforce suitable for new sectors of economy has been intensified. This forces employees to quickly adjust their skills and competencies to an increasing demand. Therefore, the requirement for educational offer in the area focused on competency development rather than on general knowledge has grown. Contemporary workers must continuously update their skills in a short module-oriented learning path rather than participating in a completely new and complex curriculum. This trend is referenced within the educational domain as micro-credentials (The Council of the European Union, 2022). Micro-credentials reflect short, tailored competency-based courses, enabling flexible acquisition of skills and knowledge, necessary to fill the gap in employees' skills in the fast-changing economy. It is worth noting that they are not intended to replace traditional forms of education (The Council of the European Union, 2022). The micro-credentials concept highlights and supports the idea of distributed learning (the *time* dimension), as well as the notion of lifelong learning, described in Section 4.3.

When implementing the concept of micro-credentials in a distributed learning environment, the question arises: How to store grades and the confirmation of the successful learning completion, especially when more complex learning paths are concerned? The Council of the European Union recommendation indicates that learning paths should be expressed in the concept of *stacks* across different systems. Micro-credentials should be designed in a modular way and be able to be stacked into the records that are available to each learner. The recommendation also indicates that a learning system should be portable, i.e. owned, stored, and easily shared by a credential holder, using secure digital wallets which comply with General Data Protection Regulation (GDPR). The infrastructure for data storage should be implemented using open standards and ensure interoperability and data authenticity (The Council of the European Union, 2022).

The confirmation of learning outcomes may be stored in a form of digital badges or certificates. A digital badge is "a representation of an accomplishment, interest or affiliation that is visual, available online, and contains metadata including links that help explain the context, meaning, process and result of an activity" (Gibson, Ostashewski, Flintoff, Grant, & Knight, 2015, p. 404). Digital badges are intended to certify short learning portions and therefore are aimed to support the micro-credentials concept. A digital certificate proves accomplishment of the learning session that is usually completed with an exam (Leaser, 2016).

Blockchain technology (BC) is a good candidate for storing and sharing the micro-credentials' digital badges and certificate-related information with the stakeholders of an educational process (Han et al., 2018). It fulfils all the requirements suggested by The Council of the European Union (2022) and allows for the following (Grech & Camilleri, 2017):

- giving a possibility of building "stacks" of micro-credentials through digital ledger relationships. These stacks are immutable, verifiable, transparent, and decentralised and thus secure,
- providing the ownerships of the records to the user,
- implementing of secure digital wallets,
- building blockchain projects based on open standards,
- supporting various areas of GDPR compliance.

Using blockchain for storing digital certificates on course completion may also be used in the case of students that take part in exchange programmes, e.g., Erasmus+ (https://erasmus-plus.ec.europa.eu). Such records may be accessed and verified by various stakeholders of the whole process including students and partner institutions. In this context, blockchain facilitates the *space* dimension of distributed learning (The Council of the European Union, 2022).

The last dimension of distributed learning (i.e. *media*), in our opinion is the least promising area of blockchain applications. This results mainly from the fact that media files containing educational materials are usually "heavy" as far as the amount of data involved is concerned. Taking into account high costs of blockchain transactions (Golosova & Romanovs, 2018) and, in consequence, costly in-chain data storage as well as its relatively low scalability, storing multimedia in blockchain is not appropriate. It is also questionable what the benefits of such storage will be. It should be noted that storing media in the blockchain resembles the concept of NFT (Non-Fungible Token), i.e. tokens representing files that have an embedded attribute of originality (see Section 4.3.3). In this case, the blockchain only stores information about the owner (who owns what), but the entire media file is stored outside of the blockchain (off-chain), using such technologies as IPFS (InterPlanetary File System) (see Section 4.4.3) which allows to store data in a distributed, peer-to-peer network. In the case of IPFS the file that is stored outside of blockchain is resistant to tampering (IPFS, n.d.). Summing up, the use of BC in the media dimension of distributed learning is mainly related to copyright and authorship issues. The discussion of distribution of educational content is provided in Section 4.4.

In our opinion BC applications in the context of distributed and distance learning are good candidates for future enhancement of higher education institutions (HEIs) didactic processes. In this respect, some scholars indicated that BC may be used in the organisational strategic planning and, therefore, be considered as a factor allowing to gain a competitive advantage by educational institutions (Kant & Anjali, 2020).

4.3 Facilitating lifelong learning

4.3.1 Introduction to lifelong learning

Lifelong learning may be perceived as the voluntary, self-motivated education that is focused on personal and professional development (Ates & Alsal, 2012). One of the reasons behind the growing popularity of this approach is the rapid economic development fostered by the implementation of new digital technologies, which results in a growing demand for new skills and competencies and dynamic adjustment of employers' profiles (see Chapter 5).

According to estimations of the American Brookings Institution, in the case of some occupations like office administration, production, transportation, and food preparation, which seem to be more vulnerable to automation, the level of risk of task being potentially automatable exceeds 70% (Mark, Maxim, & Whiton, 2019). Hence, the responsibility of the higher education sector is to broaden the offer of reskilling with more flexible learning paths. In order to achieve this goal, HEIs should not put all their attention to regular full degree programmes but offer much more flexibility in terms of learning paths.

The general goal of lifelong learning is focused on continuing professional development (CPD), which refers to intentional maintenance and development of skills and competencies for better performance in a job-related context. The goal of CPD is to ensure that the knowledge and skills of employees are up to date and appropriate for the labour market requirements (Friedman, 2013). In other words, continuing professional development can be seen as the main goal and perspective behind lifelong learning. CPD can be realised in formal (e.g., workshops, seminars) or informal (e.g., work-based training, mentoring) education. CPD may be also based on self-directed study. The problem that may be often encountered by lifelong learners is how to verify courses which have external certification, given the fact that they may vary significantly in terms of forms and course providers, ranging from conferences, courses, internships, and other kinds of non-regular teaching activities. Continuing professional development is difficult to manage and deliver because it is usually fragmented. As a result, tracking of CPD is difficult and often insufficient.

Benefits and opportunities brought by the lifelong learning approach for individuals refer to fostering the ability to acquire and absorb information, enhancement of creativity or adaption to new conditions and learning from past mistakes (Mohamed & Kinyo, 2020). Building a professional career through lifelong learning refers to various aspects like work-based learning possibilities or online courses. Diversity of learning paths refers also to micro-credentials (see Section 4.2.3) which may be perceived as one of the tools to support lifelong learning provision, especially in low-income countries (Msweli, Twinomurinzi, & Ismail, 2022).

4.3.2 Lifelong learning challenges

Lifelong learning brings various challenges to HEIs that want to embark on its adoption. The challenges relate mainly to diploma and certificates management and verification or integration of data between different institutions.

Diploma, certificates, and individual learning records as a proof of lifelong learning attendance and course completion have an important role in the career development of professionals. Since lifelong learning embraces various forms of learning paths, the range of possible diploma, certificates and other types of documents issued as a confirmation is also very broad. They must be managed in a reliable and reputable system. In their traditional paper form, lifelong learning certificates, besides some advantages (e.g., still widespread use in recruitment process or easy process of issuing), present various problems, especially those related to verification of their content (Gräther et al., 2018). On the other hand, management of digital certificates is complicated from the technological perspective and their registration has to be based on common standards to provide a possibility for verification. Hence, an important aspect of lifelong learning refers to tracking and managing of lifelong records. It does not only refer to transcripts or certificates as typical documents but also to some more diversified, specific data, presenting how learning and teaching process were conducted.

In order to conduct a more in-depth analysis of students' performance in lifelong learning, which, by definition, is realised in different institutions, there is a need for educational institutions to use systems which integrate data from different stages related to a student's learning path. These systems have to support data exchange between institutions which allows for a wider, deeper and more personalised analysis. However, as lifelong learning data are very often stored in separate databases, this causes serious problems with integration and consolidation of data (Office of Educational Technology, 2021). This becomes a problem when there is a need to exchange an employees' data between different institutions in the form of transparent portfolio, proving skills, competencies and experience gained at various educational providers.

In addition to difficulties related to the broad diversity of lifelong learning documents, another challenge relates to the need of a simple mechanism of certificate and diploma verification. Documents can be checked in a long process, which requires contacting individual companies, schools, and universities, but this process generates additional costs and is time consuming. Moreover, this traditional way of verification is complicated because of personal data protection legislation, which brings various obstacles for both sides of the process (the institution that needs verification and the institution that can provide this verification).

4.3.3 Blockchain-related solutions in lifelong learning

One of the benefits of using BC in lifelong learning concerns tokenisation. Tokenisation refers to the process in which sensitive data is replaced with unique identification symbols that keep all essential information, ensuring at the same time that the data security is not compromised (Grech & Camilleri, 2017). Non-Fungible Tokens (NFTs) are an example of tokens which have a form of digital assets representing real world objects and various types of assets, from piece of art, music, financial instruments to real estates. It is a special unique cryptographic record associated with an asset (Cornelius, 2021). NFT can be perceived as a unit of digital information (token) which may be kept on blockchain (Chochan, 2021). They serve as a proof of ownership rights. BC enable to exchange or trade tokens without any intermediaries (Schwarz, 2022).

In lifelong learning, blockchain-based tokens may be used to track the progress of students and encourage them to continue at other levels. One of the problems with lifelong learning refers to the low-level completion rates of online learning activities. This may be caused by the fact that this type of learning does not offer enough incentives for a course completion and continuation (Garbade, 2018). This is particularly true in the case of courses and training programmes that are free and do not provide any type of certification. Tokenisation based on blockchain may facilitate improvements in this area. As lifelong learning participants will collect tokens for different educational activities, especially those taking place outside the classroom, it will be easier to foster their motivation for further learning (MIT Labs, 2022). It should be emphasised that the use of tokens as rewards are not limited to students for their achievements. NFTs may be also used to verify teachers' work. For example, the Preply is a language learning platform that uses NFTs to reward teachers for their contribution to students' achievements and experience (Vilchis, 2022).

Another area in which blockchain and tokens may be used in lifelong learning is the facilitation of collaboration between students and their academic mentors. Mentors can use BC for the validation and reinforcement of student learning (Tapscot & Kaplan, 2019). This positive reinforcement may be based on tokens used for completing tasks and certain steps of a learning path, which in turn will result in greater student involvement and engagement. Tokens can serve as tools for students and mentors to monitor progress in an educational process. Another promising area refers to building recommendations for further learning steps for students based on their previous achievements and skills possessed (Mikroyannidis, 2022).

Taking into account a fast and intensive growth of the lifelong learning sector, some considerations occur that are related to the quality of courses and credibility of their providers. Here blockchain can also be used to store verified records on course accreditation providing more transparency in this area (Rosewarne, 2020). An example solution could be the initiative of the Continuing Professional Development Standards Office, an organisation based in the United Kingdom which has the partnership with Gradbase, the first company from the United Kingdom which offers blockchain-based digitalisation of professional education participation. The CPD Standards Office offers methods for issuing formal CPD Delegate Attendance Certificates on blockchain through a free online service. Certificates can be quickly verified by scanning a QR code. An employer can easily verify certificates presented by the employee, eliminating the need for traditional paper documents (The CPD Standards Office, n.d.).

The European Union funded QualiChain project, referenced in Chapter 3, examined how decentralised platforms can be used for storing, sharing, and verifying qualifications acquired through education and employment (Mikroyannidis, 2022). The QualiChain platform is planned to store personal ePortfolios of lifelong learners. They obtain Smart Badges from teaching or training entities upon completion of certain courses or their parts (Figure 4.1). These badges are stored on blockchain to guarantee credibility and transparency. Smart Badges combine information about skills that learners gained. As students continue to collect badges, the QualiChain platform is designed to provide tools to assist students with individual recommendations about possible paths of further education, which is also based on the analysis of current skills needed on the labour market. Based on these recommendations learners can take more adequate decisions on their further professional development.

As far as the legal issues related to the personal data protection are concerned, storing individual educational information and credentials in distributed ledgers like blockchain may lead to non-compliance with the GDPR regulation. The first problem relates to the GDPR requirement stating that

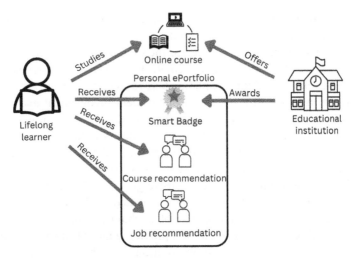

FIGURE 4.1 The QualiChain project use case.

Source: Based on (Mikroyannidis, 2022).

there is one natural or legal person (data controller) who can be addressed on data protection issues and must comply with GDPR regulations (Steiu, 2020). However, in the case of blockchain, its decentralised nature causes problems in determining how this data controller can be precisely identified, which results in some level of threats to data protection of individuals. Another issue related to GDPR concerns the necessity of providing data holder with an opportunity to modify or erase their personal data which, in the case of blockchain, is very difficult as one of the main goals of this technology is to provide data immutability and trust. In other words, in some situations, immutability which generally should be perceived as one of the blockchain's strengths, appears as one of its weaknesses (Godyn, Kedziora, Ren, Liu, & Song, 2022).

Blockchain-based system may be also used to improve integration of data between various institutions where students attended courses included in their learning paths. Blockchain-based system may be used for this purpose as it would allow to transfer individual learning records between institutions in a transparent and credible format (Ocheja, Flanagan, Ueda, & Ogata, 2019). Blockchain of Learning Logs (BOLL), the system designed by Ocheja et al. (2019), is planned to maintain hashes in a digital form related to learning activities and use smart contracts as a tool to manage access rights to this digital content. BOLL provides data analytics platforms with access to learning logs from different institutions based on a student's consent.

Learning logs contain credible, verifiable evidence of learning activities completed by students (Ogata et al., 2011). The BOLL system addresses the issue of personal control and privacy of information based on lifelong learning logs. Learners and education institutions possess the role of signatories on smart contracts designed (see Chapter 2) to protect lifelong learning records on the blockchain (Ocheja, Flanagan, Ueda, & Ogata, 2019).

It should be mentioned that prospective implementations of blockchain-based solutions for lifelong learning are linked with some limitations and obstacles. Taking into account a dynamic growth of the lifelong learning sector, the amount of data, resources, documents, and certificates will increase to such a scale that it might be difficult to manage them using BC, with its limitations regarding scalability. Another problem refers to smart contracts implementations in lifelong learning. Smart contracts, described in more details in Chapter 2, refer to a set of self-executing programmes stored on blockchain that run when certain foreseen conditions are met. Low efficiency of the serial execution methods used in this technology might be problematic for the lifelong learning sector that generates increasing amount of data (Li, Wang, Qian, & Liu, 2020).

Building blockchain-based lifelong learning portfolios or passports accompanying employees on the labour market will facilitate verification of individual's competencies, skills, and related credentials. Considering that lifelong learning refers very often to non-degree, short and diversified ways of teaching and training, this challenge related to credibility and verification is fundamental to improve employees' position on the labour market and facilitate recruitment process for companies. From this perspective, blockchain-based solutions may be a response to the needs of both employees and employers.

4.4 Accessing educational content

4.4.1 Introduction to accessing educational content

Collaboration in sharing educational resources is necessary to provide a broad access to education. It also contributes to the creation of learning materials of higher quality. For some institutions, the reason behind sharing educational resources may be based on altruism, whereas by others this can be perceived simply as a kind of an indirect marketing method to gain competitive advantage (Hylén, 2021). Although many resources are offered as an open-course content based on a copyright exemption, other offer more limited access based on royalty sharing between contributors (Chou, Lin, Nakaguchi, & Ishida, 2022).

Creation and distribution of digital educational resources is particularly important for higher education institutions that operate in various locations and campuses located in different regions and countries. Even though HEIs maintain large collections of digital content, there is a need for improved methods and tools of dissemination, especially in the case of smaller institutions without advanced resource sharing systems. Because of these obstacles, students often experience difficulties with access to resources needed for their studies. On the other hand, when making educational resources available for a wider audience, content creators and academics often express concern on how to share their resources without a risk of losing ownership rights (Hylén, 2021).

The traditional approach to resource sharing refers to universities' websites, e-learning databases and digital libraries managed at an institutional level. However, in the Internet era, there are many more options. HEIs should work on the development of resource sharing between institutions towards offering more opportunities for students and eliminating unnecessary redundancy and duplication of teaching materials (Shen, 2021). This is the domain when blockchain solutions may be implemented, encouraging institutions and authors to share resources, and securing intellectual property rights and mutual trust.

A quick and convenient access to teaching materials is crucial for ensuring better provision of education at all levels. This is particularly true in the case of developing countries where costs of textbooks and other teaching resources are one of the main obstacles for continuing education. In order to share teaching resources, institutions and authors have to maintain an appropriate level of control on how and by whom they will be used, keeping in mind not to put too many restrictions on teaching resources. This is necessary to encourage education content creators to participate more actively in education resources sharing. These resources in present education environments are often distributed based on free access, as open educational resources are accessed online by learners in the public domain under an open licence (Tlili et al., 2021). Open educational resources eliminate the need for building learning process exclusively on expensive resources and enable the switch to a wider set of teaching materials. The United Nations Educational, Scientific and Cultural Organization (UNESCO) documents underline that free open educational resources are a prerequisite to provide global learners, especially from developing countries, with access to education (UNESCO, 2015). Many learners and students are not able to continue education because of problems related to high costs or low availability of educational resources.

Open educational resources do not necessarily refer to textbooks but embrace other various forms like podcasts, videos and other types of materials. They bring various benefits and advantages for educational institutions which include (Hilton, 2016):

- expanded access to learning (students' access resources at any time and in a repeated manner),
- scalability (easy and low-cost distribution of open educational resources),
- augmentation of class materials (resources easily used as supplementary materials in the case of deficit in teaching resources),
- enhancement of regular course content (information presented in multiple formats),
- quick circulation (information disseminated quickly),
- showcasing of innovation and talent (dissemination of research and innovation for the wide audience),
- ties for alumni (resources helping to maintain contacts with alumni),
- continually improved resources (fast improvement and modification of resources content).

With regard to open educational materials, BC may be used to group various HEIs which decide to form a network with the aim to facilitate the management and maintenance of open educational resources (Nammari, 2019). HEIs, as nodes of such a blockchain-based solution, would be authorised to verify, and evaluate the resources registered in the system. The system would use the advantages of BC to provide reliable tracking of system's user activities. The public digital key would be used to identify users, together with any resource content submitted to the network, providing tools to ensure its authenticity, and protecting intellectual property. Advantages of using blockchain as a technology for the management of resources and their proper verification and validation include (Nammari, 2019):

- checking quality of open educational resources managed by the network may be based on the consensus mechanism (see Chapter 2) agreed upon by the network nodes (e.g., higher education institutions),
- the basis of consensus mechanism built on common quality criteria shared between network nodes,
- authenticity of resources and protection of intellectual property rights based on a blockchain-based digital key system which provides users with digital keys to access resources,
- editing and adaptation of resources content, managed by the network stored in the blockchain records of transactions reflecting all changes and modifications.

Accessing of educational content is directly linked with intellectual property rights that are discussed in the next section.

4.4.2 Intellectual property rights in sharing educational resources

From the general perspective of distribution of educational resources and their usage tracking, the following aspects should be taken into consideration (Stankovich, 2021):

- blockchain can assist with management of intellectual property rights and technology transfer or commercialisation practices,
- blockchain may be used as the registry of intellectual property rights where the holders of these rights may keep digital certificates of their rights and apply a blockchain platform to collect royalties using smart contracts,
- blockchain can serve as the general proof and catalogue, storing creative and original work and facilitating tracing of its use.

For example, Chou et al. (2022) designed the TMchain system, which can be used for management of copyright-restricted learning resources. The system applies BC to solve the problem of the authorship-related issues referring to the usage of educational resources created by various authors. Blockchain is used to store information about authorship of learning materials and implements smart contracts used by teachers who give permission to use their materials. A TMchain blockchain-based register stores records with data on the usage of educational resources and utilises word processing software to register editing activities concerning reusing of teaching resources. The data about authorship and contribution to further content editing of an educational resource is stored on blockchain. Resources are not kept on blockchain, which facilitates the scalability and lowers the costs of the entire solution. They can be stored in IPFS as an external system (see Section 4.4.3). TMchain allows to calculate contribution distribution of various resource creators and manage authorship records of updated resources. A smart contract functionality included in the system allows management of materials developed by different teachers. Teachers joining a smart contract give their consent to use the resources they have created and register authorship distribution information. Such a smart contract produces transactions of authorship of an original educational resource or, in the case of resources based on other materials, combined authorships, and information about contribution distribution.

Blockchain technology can enhance collaboration between faculties on the educational content creation (How Blockchain Can Improve Higher Education, 2020). Since blockchain-based solutions can be helpful in transparent tracing of how the resources are used, they will enable the efficient management of copyrights fees and author reimbursement policies.

Dissemination of educational materials usually involves some level of fear and concern about the risk of plagiarism. In the case of resources stored in blockchain-based databases it is easier to provide adequate level of security. As attempts to use and adapt the resources can be registered and traced in a permissioned blockchain (see Chapter 2), this gives a powerful tool for authors to investigate usage of their work output. These tracing capabilities are also important as some educational institutions may disappear from the educational market or authors can change institution they work for (McGreal, 2021).

Blockchain may be also used in the management of study curricula and progressive dissemination of educational materials. A popular approach is to determine students' access to subsequent teaching resources upon the completion of prior tasks and activities. This is the stage where Distributed Ledger Technology may be useful. Smart contracts may be implemented in the first step to verify completion of various tasks, then to open access to further assignments and resources. Since BC can support keeping track on how learning materials are used, it can provide mechanism to reward content creators based on the usage of their materials (Lemoie & Soares, 2020). One of the challenges when analysing the shared access to educational resources based on blockchain refers to the fact that blockchain is not the best solution to store large amount of data (Chen, Lv, & Song, 2019). In order to mitigate this problem, a combined solution based on blockchain and IPFS was developed. It is presented in the next section.

4.4.3 Solutions based on blockchain and InterPlanetary File System

To overcome the problem of the large number of learning resources stored in various university databases which are not shared, Meng and Zhang (2020) proposed a method of the university resource sharing based on blockchain and IPFS. The method includes usage of smart contract and digital signature for the purpose of identity authentication of a higher education institution and setting up the alliance chain of universities. In such an approach, learning resources can be stored on IPFS whereas hash addresses of these resources and corresponding basic information may be kept on blockchain (see Figure 4.2). This will increase the security of the proposed solution and significantly decrease the cost of storage.

IPFS is based on content addressing which allows to identify resources which can be fetched from the closest sources (Triebstok, 2018). Content addressing is based on Distributed Hash Table which allows to locate a file in the storage system. This content-based addressing indicates that in order to

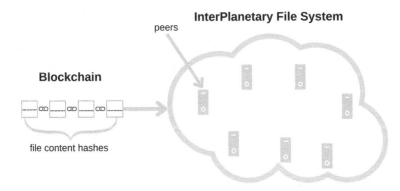

InterPlanetary File System

peers

Blockchain

file content hashes

FIGURE 4.2   Blockchain and IPFS.

access a resource we do not necessarily need to know its location since we track the content based on its hash fingerprint. Resources like documents, movies, audio files (or parts of them) are stored on devices of the users of this decentralised system who can keep all data or its portion. Users of such a network can share a resource using its content address, so the other nodes in the network can fetch it from various locations based on the Distributed Hash Table.

The IPFS network takes care of automatic deletion of duplicates and provides the history of versions based on cryptographic hashes allocated for each file uploaded to IPFS. The nodes of the IPFS network can create and upload new content, at the same time they can retrieve content and data already kept in the network. Using IPFS enables deduplication of information stored in the system (Akineymi, 2021). Consequently, if several users were to upload the same file on the IPFS, the file will be created only once (Moralis Academy, 2021).

An example of a content sharing system using blockchain and IPFS may be a public discussion platform on mental health – InnerLight (Xu et al., 2021). In this system data like text, images, links are kept in IPFS nodes. This solution allows to build a community whose members can create and exchange articles on specific topics. InnerLight uses cryptocurrency micropayments as incentives for participants interacting with the system in such a way that authors can obtain virtual money for the content they have created, whereas readers may receive cryptocurrency for their comments posted in the forum.

4.5 Conclusions

One of the challenges to fast-paced transformation of higher education institutions is how the management of learning processes is organised based on new technologies. Blockchain may be seen as a promising technology helping to implement the student-centred learning concept. The value added by blockchain is the improvement of processes by providing more transparency and trust, especially considering relations with external stakeholders on the labour market.

Although to some extent blockchain may be seen as a non-fully matured technology, for instance from the perspective of relatively limited use in the educational sector, there are areas in which it can be implemented as a supportive technological tool. These primarily include improvements in the management of learning processes, i.e. distributed and lifelong learning as well as access to educational content.

Distributed learning requires a much more advanced level of flexibility in how teaching materials are disseminated and accessed. Although blockchain opens new ways for administration in this area and brings more trust for intellectual property rights management, some limitations still have to be considered, referring for instance to its scalability and immutability which, in some circumstances, can pose obstacles. Possible future solutions may refer to combining blockchain with other technology like IPFS, broadening its usage in the education sector.

Other challenges to blockchain applications refer for instance to lifelong learning. These include the lack of standards, scalability, cost, fulfilling all GDPR requirements (i.e. one owner of data and/or a possibility of deleting the data), choosing between the type of blockchain to be used (i.e. public vs. private, permissioned vs. permissionless), and creating one common and coherent implementation that can gain a critical mass.

It is worth noting that the shift towards more flexible and transparent learning management systems is a response to the requirements of Industry 4.0, as the labour market requires fast and reliable methods of skills recognition. Considering all advantages and disadvantages of blockchain technology, in our opinion the former overweight the latter, and BC is one of the disruptive technologies that may foster this transition process.

References

Akineymi, I. (2021). *Decentralized Data Storage Using IPFS and React: A Tutorial with Examples*. Retrieved Jan. 10, 2023, from: https://blog.logrocket.com/decentralized-data-storage-using-ipfs-and-react-a-tutorial-with-examples/

Alexander, B., Ashford-Rowe, K., Barajas-Murphy, N., Dobbin, G., Knott, J., McCormack, M., … Weber, N. (2019). *EDUCAUSE Horizon Report: 2019 Higher Education Edition*. Louisville, CO: EDUCAUSE.

Al-Khatir Al-Arimi, A. M. (2014). Distance Learning. *Procedia – Social and Behavioral Sciences, 152*, 82–88.

Ates, H., & Alsal, K. (2012). The importance of lifelong learning has been increasing. *Procedia – Social and Behavioral Sciences, 46*, 4092–4096.

Brush, T., & Saye, J. (2000). Implementation and evaluation of a student-centered learning unit: A case study. *Educational Technology Research and Development*, *48*(3), 79–100.

Campbell, M. (2020). Teaching in an inspiring learning space: An investigation of the extent to which one school's innovative learning environment has impacted on teachers' pedagogy and practice. *Research Papers in Education*, *35*(2), 185–204.

Chen, G., Xu, B., Lu, M., & Chen, N.-S. (2018). Exploring blockchain technology and its potential applications for education. *Smart Learning Environments*, *5*(1), 1–10.

Chen, J., Lv, Z., & Song, H. (2019). Design of personnel big data management system based on blockchain. *Future Generation Computer Systems*, *101*, 1122–1129.

Chochan, U. (2021). *Non-Fungible Tokens: Blockchains, Scarcity, and Value*. Retrieved Nov. 21, 2022, from: https://ssrn.com/abstract=3822743

Chou, H., Lin, D., Nakaguchi, T., & Ishida, T. (2022). TMchain: A blockchain-based collaboration. *Journal of Information Processing*, *30*, 343–351.

Cornelius, K. (2021). Betraying blockchain: accountability, transparency and document standards for non-fungible tokens (NFTS). *Information*, *12*(9), 358.

Cunha, P. R., Soja, P., & Themistocleous, M. (2021). Blockchain for development: A guiding framework. *Information Technology for Development*, *27*(3), 417–438.

Daft, R. L., & Lengel, R. H. (1986). Organizational information requirements, media richness and structural design. *Management Science*, *32*(5), 554–571.

Della Ventura, M. (2017). Creating inspiring learning environments by means of digital technologies: A case study of the effectiveness of Whatsapp in music education. *EAI Endorsed Transactions on e-Learning*, *4*(14), 1–9.

Dymek, D., Grabowski, M., & Paliwoda-Pękosz, G. (2022). Impact of COVID-19 pandemic on students' online behavioral pattern. *Journal of e-Learning and Higher Education*, *2*, 1–16.

Fletcher, J. D. (2012). Advanced Distributed Learning. In N. M. Seel (Ed.), *Encyclopedia of the Sciences of Learning* (pp. 151–153). Boston, MA: Springer.

Friedman, A. (2013). *Continuing Professional Development: Lifelong Learning of Millions*. London: Routledge.

Garbade, M. (2018). *How Project-Based Learning and Blockchain Can Improve the Professional Development Industry*. Retrieved July 11, 2022 from: https://hacker noon.com/

Gibson, D., Ostashewski, N., Flintoff, K., Grant, S., & Knight, E. (2015). Digital badges in education. *Education and Information Technologies*, *20*, 403–410.

Godyn, M., Kedziora, M., Ren, Y., Liu, Y., & Song, H. (2022). Analysis of solutions for a blockchain compliance with GDPR. *Scientific Reports*, *12*(1), 1–11.

Golosova, J., & Romanovs, A. (2018). The Advantages and Disadvantages of the Blockchain Technology. In *IEEE 6th Workshop on Advances in Information* (pp. 1–6). Electronic and Electrical Engineering (AIEEE).

Grech, A., & Camilleri, A. (2017). Blockchain in Education. In *Publications Office of the European Union, EUR 28778 EN*, A. Inamorato dos Santos (Ed.), Luxembourg: Publications Office of the European Union.

Gronroos, C. (1994). From marketing mix to relationship marketing: Towards a paradigm shift in marketing. *Management Decision*, *32*(2), 4–20.

Gräther, W., Kolvenbach, S., Ruland, R., Schütte, J., Torres, C., & Wendland, F. (2018). Blockchain for Education: Lifelong Learning Passport. In *Proceedings of*

1st ERCIM Blockchain Workshop 2018. European Society for Socially Embedded Technologies (EUSSET).

Han, M., Li, Z., He, J., Wu, D., Xie, Y., & Baba, A. (2018). A Novel Blockchain-based Education Records Verification Solution. In *Proceedings of the 19th Annual SIG Conference on Information Technology Education* (pp. 178–183).

Harting, K., & Erthal, M. J. (2005). History of distance learning. *Learning and Performance Journal, 23*(1), 35–44.

Hilton, J. (2016). Open educational resources and college textbook choices: A review of research on efficacy and perceptions. *Education Tech Research and Development, 64*(4), 573–590.

How Blockchain Can Improve Higher Education (2020). Retrieved May 12, 2022 from: https://pixelplex.io/blog/how-blockchain-can-improve-higher-education/

Hylén, J. (2021). *Open Educational Resources: Opportunities and Challenges*. Paris: OECD's Centre for Educational Research and Innovation.

Ifenthaler, D. (2012). Blended Learning. In N. M. Seel (Ed.), *Encyclopedia of the Sciences of Learning* (pp. 463–465). Boston, MA: Springer.

IPFS. (n.d.). *IPFS*. Retrieved Dec. 8, 2022, from: https://ipfs.tech/#how

Kant, N., & Anjali, K. (2020). Can blockchain be a strategic resource for ODL?: A study. *Asian Association of Open Universities Journal, 15*(3), 395–410.

Karamitsos, I., Papadaki, M., Themistocleous, M., & Ncube, C. (2022). Blockchain as a service (BCaaS): A value modeling approach in the education business model. *Journal of Software Engineering and Applications, 15*, 165–182.

Kirkley, J. (2012). Distributed Learning. In N. M. Seel (Ed.), *Encyclopedia of the Sciences of Learning* (pp. 1020–1021). Boston, MA: Springer.

Leaser, D. (2016). *Open Badges vs. Certifications: Is There a Battle Brewing in the IT Credential Market?* Retrieved Jan. 8, 2023, from: https://www.ibm.com/blogs/ibm-training/open-badges-vs-certifications-is-there-a-battle-brewing-in-the-it-credential-market/

Lemoie, K., & Soares, L. (2020). *Connected Impact. Unlocking Education and Workforce*. Washington: American Council on Education.

Li, X., Wang, F., Qian, X., & Liu, X. (2020). Technical challenges & countermeasures of blockchain technology application in lifelong education. *Advances in Educational Technology and Psychology, 4*, 48–51.

Mark, M., Maxim, R., & Whiton, J. (2019). *Automation and Artificial Intelligence: How Machines are Affecting People and Places*. Washington: The Brookings Institution.

McGreal, R. (2021). *How Blockchain Could Help the World Meet the UN's Global Goals in Higher Education*. Retrieved Sep. 19, 2022 from https://world.edu/how-blockchain-could-help-the-world-meet-the-uns-global-goals-in-higher-education/

Meng, N., & Zhang, S. (2020). University Education Resource Sharing Based on Blockchain and IPFS. *International Conference on Big Data Analytics for Cyber-Physical System in Smart City* (pp. 1808–1813). Singapore: Springer.

Mikroyannidis, A. (2022). Work-in-Progress: Piloting Smart Blockchain Badges for Lifelong Learning. In M. E. Auer, H. Hortsch, O. Michler, & T. Köhler (Eds.), *Mobility for Smart Cities and Regional Development – Challenges for Higher Education* (pp. 746–753). Cham: Springer.

MIT Labs. (2022). *Tokenization of Degrees and Educational Certificates*. Retrieved Jul. 11, 2022, from: https://mitsoftware.com/

Mohamed, S., & Kinyo, L. (2020). Constructivist theory as a foundation for the utilization of digital technology in the lifelong learning process. *Turkish Online Journal of Distance Education, 21*(4), 90–109.

Moodle. (2018). *Moodle.* Retrieved Dec 12, 2022, from: https://docs.moodle.org/401/en/Philosophy

Moralis Academy. (2021). *InterPlanetary File System Explained – What is IPFS?* Retrieved Jan. 20, 2023, from: https://academy.moralis.io/blog/interplanetary-file-system-explained-what-is-ipfs

Msweli, N. T., Twinomurinzi, H., & Ismail, M. (2022). The international case for microcredentials for life-wide and life-long learning: A systematic literature review. *Interdisciplinary Journal of Information, Knowledge, and Management, 17*, 151–190.

Nammari, B. (2019, February 07). *Open Educational Resource & Blockchain.* Retrieved Jun. 30, 2022, from: https://www.linkedin.com/pulse/open-educational-resource-blockchain-brian-nammari

Ocheja, P., Flanagan, B., Ueda, H., & Ogata, H. (2019). Managing lifelong learning records through blockchain. *Research and Practice in Technology Enhanced Learning, 14*(4), 1–19. doi:10.1186/s41039-019-0097-0

Office of Educational Technology. (2021). *The Lifelong Learner: How Blockchain Solutions Can Facilitate Data.* Retrieved Jun. 28, 2022, from: https://tech.ed.gov/files/2021/02/blockchain-lifelong-learner.pdf

Ogata, H., Li, M., Hou, B., Uosaki, N., El-Bishouty, M., & Yano, Y. (2011). SCROLL: supporting to share and reuse ubiquitous learning log in the context of language learning. *Research and Practice in Technology Enhanced Learning, 6*(2), 69–82.

Overby, K. (2011). Student-centered learning. *ESSAI, 9*(32), 109–112.

Peppers, D., & Rogers, M. (1997). *Enterprise One-to-One: Tools for Building Unbreakable Customer Relationships in the Interactive Age.* London: Piatkus.

Peppers, D., Rogers, M., & Dorf, B. (1999). Is your company ready for one-to-one marketing? *Harvard Business Review, 77*(1), 151–160.

Picciano, A. G. (2002). Beyond student perceptions: issues of interaction, presence, and performance in an online course. *Journal of Asynchronous Learning Network, 6*(1), 21–40.

Psotka, J. (2012). Distributed Technologies. In N. M. Seel (Ed.), *Encyclopedia of the Sciences of Learning* (pp. 1021–1023). Boston, MA: Springer.

Rau, H. (2021). Moving towards mass-customization in higher education. *Business Education Innovation Journal, 13*(1), 94–99.

Rosewarne, A. (2020). Blockchain is powering E-learning – But beware the charlatans. *Millgens.* Retrieved Jun. 29, 2022, from: https://millgens.com/blockchain/blockchain-e-learning/

Schwarz, M. (2022). Blockchain-based tokenisation: Status and implications of early design decisions. *Journal of Securities Operations & Custody, 14*(2), 171–182.

Sharples, M., & Domingue, J. (2016). The Blockchain and Kudos: A Distributed System for Educational Record, Reputation and Reward. In K. S. Verbert (Ed.), *EC-TEL 2016, Adaptive and Adaptable Learning., Lecture Notes in Computer Science. 9891* (pp. 490–496). Cham: Springer.

Shen, D. (2021). Research on the sharing mode of educational information resources in colleges and universities based on the Blockchain and new energy. *Energy Reports, 7*(7), 458–467.

Skilton, M., & Hovsepian, F. (2018). *The 4th Industrial Revolution. Responding to the Impact of Artificial Intelligence on Business.* Cham: Palgrave Macmillan ipublished by Springer Nature.

Stankovich, M. (2021). *Is Intellectual Property Ready for Blockchain?* Retrieved Sep. 19, 2022, from: https://dai-global-digital.com/is-intellectual-property-ready-for-blockchain.html

Steinhoff, L., Arli, D., Weaven, S., & Kozlenkova, I. V. (2019). Online relationship marketing. *Journal of the Academy of Marketing Science, 47*(3), 369–393.

Steiu, M.-F. (2020). Blockchain in education: Opportunities, applications, and challenges. *First Monday, 25*(9). https://firstmonday.org/ojs/index.php/fm/article/view/10654

Swan, M. (2015). *Blockchain: Blueprint for a New Economy.* Sebastopol, CA: O'Reilly Media.

Tapscot, D., & Kaplan, A. (2019). *Blockchain Revolution in Education and Lifelong Learning.* Blockchain Research Institute. Retrieved Aug. 16, 2022, from: https://www.ibm.com/downloads/cas/93DDVAKE

The Council of the European Union. (2022, June 27). European approach to micro-credentials for lifelong learning and employability. *Official Journal of the European Union, C 243*, 10–25.

The CPD Standards Office. (n.d.). *Digital CPD Certificates.* Retrieved Jun. 29, 2022, from The CPD Standards Office: https://www.cpdstandards.com/digital-cpd-certificates/

Thompson, N. E., & Wheeler, J. P. (2008). Learning environment: Creating and implementing a safe, supportive learning environment. *Journal of Family Consumer Sciences Education, 26*(2), 33–43.

Tlili, A., Zhang, J., Papamitsiou, Z., Manske, S., Huang, R., & Hoppe, H. U. (2021). Towards utilising emerging technologies to address the challenges of using open educational resources: A vision of the future. *Educational Technology Research and Development, 69*(2), 515–532.

Triebstok, K. (2018). *How IPFS is Challenging the Web as We Know It.* Retrieved Dec. 12, 2022, from: https://medium.com/innovation/how-ipfs-is-disrupting-the-web-e10857397822

UNESCO. (2015). *Education 2030: Incheon Declaration and Framework for Action.* Retrieved Sep. 15, 2022, from: http://unesdoc.unesco.org/images/0024/002456/245656e.pdf

Victor, S., & Hart, S. (2016). Distributed Learning: A Flexible Learning and Development Model. In *E-Learn 2016* (pp. 1503–1512). Washington, DC.

Vilchis, N. (2022). *How Do NFTs Support Education?* Retrieved Jul. 11, 2022 from: https://observatory.tec.mx/edu-news/how-do-nfts-support-education

Vollbrecht, P. J., Porter-Stransky, K. A., & Lackey-Cornelison, W. L. (2020). Lessons learned while creating an effective emergency remote learning environment for students during the COVID-19 pandemic. *Advances in Physiology Education, 44*, 722–725.

Wheeler, S. (2012). Distance Learning. In N. M. Seel (Ed.), *Encyclopedia of the Sciences of Learning* (pp. 1018–1020). Boston, MA: Springer.

Willis, B. (1992). *Strategies for Teaching at a Distance.* Syracuse, NY: ERIC Clearinghouse on Information Resources.

Wright, G. B. (2011). Student-centered learning in higher education. *International Journal of Teaching and Learning in Higher Education, 23*(3), 92–97.

Xu, H., Cheng, Y., Li, Z., & You, C. (2021). Content Sharing Network based on IPFS and Blockchain. In *IOP Conference Series: Materials Science and Engineering*, 1043.

5

ADDRESSING LABOUR MARKET CHALLENGES WITH BLOCKCHAIN

Dariusz Put and Jan Trąbka

5.1 Introduction

The biggest challenges faced by the labour market are associated with the concept of Industry 4.0. The term Industry 4.0 was first introduced in November 2011 by the German government and was related to the initiative regarding the high-tech strategy for 2020 (Mohamed, 2018). So far, a number of definitions of this term have emerged (e.g., Deloitte, 2015; Pfohl, Burak, & Kurnaz, 2015). In essence, the term Industry 4.0 includes the interaction between digital and physical processes, a new level of organisation and control over the entire value chain of the life cycle of products, and a technological evolution from embedded to cyber-physical systems. It also emphasises innovations derived and implemented in a value chain to address the trends of digitalisation, automation, transparency, mobility, modularisation, and network collaboration.

Industry 4.0 investments will reduce the employment of the low-skilled labour force while increasing the employment of the qualified labour force in such areas as design and information technology (Bal & Erkan, 2019). Hence, people should adapt their competences to these changes throughout their working life with an emphasis on knowledge and technical skills. Higher education institutions (HEIs) should consider the above-mentioned challenges and adjust their curricula to the labour market expectations.

It would be convenient for businesses if there is a unified, commonly used system for registering the competences and skills of potential employees. Such a system would be an employee database fed by certification organisations (including HEIs) and used by employers to search for suitable

DOI: 10.4324/9781003318736-6

individuals. The design of a uniform system for the identification of qualifications (IQS) within a country and, more broadly, for international organisations, is of significant importance for supporting the labour market and
promoting lifelong learning (Behringer & Coles, 2003). The register of individual competences needs to manage many types of documents, their structures and content, as well as information about the entities issuing them.
Hence, the IT system that would support the functioning of such a register
would have to meet a number of requirements in terms of efficiency, reliability, security, and ease of use. As an underlying technology for such a
system, blockchain can be used. The use of this technology is justified when
a shared, distributed, publicly available database used by a variety of non-
cooperating parties is required, where it is important to maintain the reliability of the information collected and the rules governing the system differ
between participants (Pedersen, Risius, & Beck, 2019).

In the next section, we discuss the expectations and needs of the labour
market from the point of view of employees, employers, and teaching institutions, and the challenges they face in the context of Industry 4.0. Then, we
identify the competences and skills in the light of an evolving labour market.
Finally, we propose a model for competence management, based on blockchain technology.

5.2 Expectations, needs, and challenges of the labour market

5.2.1 Industry 4.0 and its impact on the labour market

With the emergence of Industry 4.0, the labour market faces hitherto
unknown challenges and requires adjustment to the changing environment.
This applies to employers and employees as well as educational institutions,
including HEIs. Robotisation and automation of manufacturing will
demand more advanced skills concerning mechanical engineering. The new
wave of advanced technologies may result in innovative services combined
with significant changes in the workforce. At a high level of industrialisa-
tion, it can be assumed that the process of IT-enabled robotisation will
become increasingly important (Chovancova, Dorocakova, & Malacka,
2018). Industry 4.0 entails the necessity for lifelong learning and the improvement of professional qualifications. The lack of professional career development may result in exclusion from the labour market (Pietrulewicz & Łosyk,
2018).

It is worth noting that Industry 4.0 contributes to the creation of a new
type of interaction between humans and machines. Managers who want to
meet the challenges in the era of the fourth industrial revolution should be
open and flexible, share responsibility and decision-making with their

employees, and these qualities should be systematically developed in a conscious and structured way. They should be able to work in the role of a coach, mentor, and guardian who is able to see the strengths of employees, help them to set a path for building their own competences, and actively support them in their development (Gorecky et al., 2014; Gracel & Makowiec, 2017; Olsen & Tomlin, 2020). The competences that allow a manager to perform these roles towards subordinates include the following abilities (Gracel & Makowiec, 2017):

- to recognise innate talents and strengths,
- to chart career path development that matches both the job requirements and personal aptitudes,
- to look at the sustainability of the team and the company,
- to transfer knowledge,
- to build an appropriate organisational culture.

Thus, the labour market needs potential managers who have these abilities. They have to be prepared to adjust to a constantly changing environment. Also, employees and HEIs need to be aware of the challenges posed by the changes taking place and be able to adapt their activities and expectations to these changes.

5.2.2 Automation and its consequences

Industry 4.0 has been introduced as a popular term to describe the trend towards digitisation and automation (Oesterreich & Teuteberg, 2016). This not only poses a number of challenges to the labour market but also carries several risks. In the United States, the dangers of automation to employment were recognised in the early 21st century (Frey & Osborne, 2017). It was estimated that fewer than 5% of occupations could be entirely automated using new technologies; however, about 60% of occupations could have 30% or more of their constituent activities automated (Chui, Manyika, & Miremadi, 2015). The World Economic Forum (2016) assessed that more than a third of the knowledge and skills, required at that time by the labour market, needed changes within five years. However, it was also recognised that the diffusion of new technologies creates new workplaces (Csugány, 2020). A significant employment growth is expected, e.g. among manufacturers, service providers and installers of industrial robots, and infrastructure providers of cyber-physical systems, including suppliers of security solutions for these systems. The number of people dealing with business intelligence activities and cyber-physical production systems will increase, since the society needs to be prepared to receive, process, and evaluate the rapidly expanding amount of information and knowledge (Simai, 2018).

It should be noted that the demand for highly qualified employees and technician-specialists with competences significantly exceeding their current professional qualifications is expected to rise. Hence, highly qualified employees performing complex tasks will be forced to improve their professional qualifications (Piątkowski, 2020). Along with the technological advancement, low-skilled employees will be re-skilled to perform tasks which are not susceptible to automation, i.e. tasks requiring creative and social competences (Frey & Osborne, 2017).

5.2.3 Generations and their attitudes

When analysing the labour market, the changing attitudes and expectations of the employees should be taken into account. The replacement of each generation brings a major change in society because employers must be able to adapt to what can be offered on the labour market. Generations Y and Z (see Table 5.1 for definitions) are those that constitute a significant group in the labour market now and will have the greatest impact on it in the future. Generation Y is obsessed with technologies. They change their jobs often, looking for better opportunities. In this respect, for Generation Y, the availability of the latest technologies is important in their choice of a potential job. Non-financial motivation factors such as flexible working hours, an opportunity to work from home, an acceptable workload, travel support, and participation in conferences are also important factors for them (Perkune & Līcīte, 2019).

The visions and attitudes of Generation Z are completely different from that of the previous generations, not to mention their values of life and the

TABLE 5.1 Attitude of different generations to work–life balance.

Baby boomers (1946–1964)	Generation X (1965–1979)	Generation Y (1980–1994)	Generation Z (1995–now)
• work ethos • job loss as a motivation for action • live to work	• work is important • work–life balance • prefer better earnings than more free time	• work to live • work–life balance • prefer maximum 8-hour working day • flexible working • approximately two years in one company	• remote working • variety of tasks • challenges • dynamic working environment • freedom

Source: Based on: http://stapler.pl/hydepark/litery-dzielace-generacje-o-roznicach-miedzy-pokoleniem-x-y [access: 27.10.2022]

priorities they set for themselves. The problem-solving methods they use and multitasking operation are just two of the features the would-be engineers have and use during their studies and fulfilment of tasks. They want to be independent faster than their Generation X parents were, since they saw them struggling for and saving money. Their attitude towards financial motivation is different from the previous generations. Generation Z members want to earn money to be independent as much as they can, and they want to do what is most fulfilling for them as individuals. Regarding their future priorities, the most important factors are the following (Szabó & Bartal, 2020): (1) to do in their jobs what they really like doing, (2) to be able to use their skills and talents, (3) to work in a good atmosphere, and (4) to have a good balance between work and private life. Educational institutions and employers need to take these motivations under consideration and try to adjust to them.

5.2.4 Expectations towards HEIs

The labour market is currently undergoing changes that require all its stakeholders to undertake adaptive initiatives. Organisations, such as the United Nations Educational, Scientific and Cultural Organization (UNESCO), the Council of Europe, the European Commission, and the Organization for Economic Co-operation and Development (OECD) have defined policies under the banner of lifelong learning. One of the participants of the labour market are HEIs, which must constantly adapt their educational offer to the concept of lifelong learning, enabling employees to acquire the required competencies and skills in a rapidly changing environment. European policy of lifelong learning illustrates the need for the continuous improvement of skills and participation in the process of learning through the entire period of professional engagement. This is important for all employees, regardless of age, at every stage of professional career development and in each professional group. It means that, apart from HEIs, a significant role in the process of vocational education and professional career development is played by employers who provide their employees with career development and training opportunities (Piątkowski, 2020).

Among the competences for the future, the following are highlighted: capacity for active learning, creativity (also in terms of the artistic domain but primarily technological), digital literacy skills, capacity for knowledge sharing and cooperation, and problem-solving skills (Vuorikari et al., 2016). The combination of skills required on the labour market becomes complex and will continue to change along with the evolution of a workplace increasingly saturated with innovative technologies. It requires the development of digital literacy skills and the capacity for lifelong learning during early education in order to upskill the future generations of staff. It is worth noting that processes requiring problem-solving, intuition, creativity, and persuasive skills are the most difficult to automate (Frey & Osborne, 2017).

Employers not only expect graduates to have the technical competences acquired during professional education but also require graduates to demonstrate a range of broader skills and attributes that include teamwork, communication, leadership, critical thinking, problem-solving, and often managerial abilities. Usually, these broader skills are referred to as soft skills (Lowden et al., 2011). Furthermore, employers indicate trustworthiness, reliability, motivation, communication, and willingness to learn as the most important skills (McMurray et al., 2016). Dubreta and Bulian (2018) have investigated engineering competences and indicated that employers attach great importance to professionalism, which includes the ability to respect deadlines, the ability to follow directions when working on tasks, motivated approach to work tasks, and the ability to work under pressure, i.e. coping with deadlines, downsizings, and demanding clients.

It is expected that HEIs will prepare graduates for the labour market needs, including the development of a range of their soft skills, which were rather underestimated by educators in the past (Stal & Paliwoda-Pękosz, 2019). In addition, HEIs need to be aware of the fact that a pedagogical paradigm-shift is required. Firstly, the students entering HEIs are significantly different from the students of earlier times. Secondly, the era of the digital world is affecting the educators with a much-highlighted impact. Thirdly, the needs and expectations of the labour market are also undergoing a cultural change with respect to the workforce and their habits. The mission of the universities of present days is the following: education, research, and effective usage of knowledge (Szabó & Bartal, 2020).

The competitiveness in economy and industry, the overall standard of living, and even the growth of a nation greatly depend on the workforce consisting of engineers, or in a broader meaning of STEM (science, technology, engineering, math) graduates (Langdon et al., 2011). Hence, STEM jobs are perceived as the jobs of the future. They are essential for developing our technological innovation and global competitiveness (Langdon et al., 2011). Usually, STEM jobs are highly evaluated and well paid in all developed societies (Szabó & Bartal, 2020). It should be noted that skills required in the STEM fields will, in the future, have to be combined with the so-called soft skills in the fields of, for instance, psychology or sociology.

Ongoing technological changes contribute to the fact that the labour market is increasingly looking for employees with competences perceived as practical. Employers are most interested in hiring university graduates who have completed studies with a practical profile. Among the most important factors, when deciding to employ a graduate, the employers indicated the following (Bartosik & Wiścicka, 2021):

- obtained certificates, qualifications, courses, training,
- acquired profession, consistent with the wanted position,
- professional experience.

In the contemporary society, there is a frequently expressed opinion that many have access to university education, but too few of the graduates demonstrate the values, professionalism, and morality, as graduates a few decades ago. Many graduates are dissatisfied because, after completing university studies, they fail to find a job related to their competences and abilities. Universities are not sufficiently involved in the dialogue with the society and are often losing in the competition with other providers of training programmes (Lungu, Braniste, & Calugher, 2019). The adaptation to the labour market requirements cannot be done without applying a new approach to quality by refining the tools used in the monitoring of teaching effectiveness. In this context, the university's primary objective is to assure the quality of the teaching and learning process. The good practices in higher education systems show that effective management of education can be devised and implemented when (Lungu, Braniste, & Calugher, 2019):

- universities actively adapt the educational offer to the expectations of the labour market. Only a regular dialogue with students, graduates, professional associations, and employers can provide the input to achieve a quick adjustment of the educational offer,
- university curricula are designed to lead to the acquisition of specific qualifications and are much more focused on the actual subject matter studied than on content loosely related to the study domain.

Universities develop partnerships with other institutions, corporations and business associations, scientific research groups, professional associations, and non-profit organisations. In order to be effective, the dialogue with the interested entities concerning the performance of universities should be effective in (Lungu, Braniste, & Calugher, 2019; Zgaga, 2007):

- defining the list of skills and abilities they expect from a graduate,
- setting/establishing the purpose of the curriculum with direct involvement of partners,
- inviting specialists working at the partners to present the organisational aspects,
- involving the participation of the most relevant specialists in some teaching activities.

The ongoing changes, described as Industry 4.0, pose a number of challenges to the labour market. Managers must understand the changes taking place and become more flexible, share responsibilities with co-workers, recognise the weaknesses and strengths of employees, and take into account not only their skills but also expectations. Employees must be ready to be "lifelong learners", acquire new skills, and adapt their competencies to the rapidly changing demands of the labour market. In the same vein, HEIs must recognise the changes taking place, constantly analyse the needs of the labour market, and not only adapt their study programmes to the current market needs but also prepare potential employees with the competencies expected in the future.

5.2.5 How blockchain can support education and the labour market

An application of blockchain in HEIs may make a fundamental change in the way teachers deliver educational content, manage courses, and even assess students' work. HEIs can find blockchain useful as it has the potential to change the way of providing certifications and the way knowledge is managed, produced, and shared (Sahonero, 2018). It allows to validate learning records, manage identity, and register publicly available certificates. Institutions may decide with which HEIs they want to share data, avoiding the risk that qualifications (diplomas or certificates) may be counterfeited or falsified (Serranito et al., 2020). Distributed Ledger Technology (see Chapter 2) and a lack of the need for a trusted third party can improve smart contract-based protocols that automatically process contracts with students throughout multiple levels of administration, which constitutes a major advantage of blockchain for higher education (Arndt, 2018).

From the employers' perspective, the lack of trust in candidates that can be observed resulted from the discrepancy between candidates' described and actual skills (Awaji, Solaiman, & Marshall, 2020). Hence, a system storing a reliable set of competences for every candidate could facilitate and speed up the hiring process, reducing the risk of employing incompetent people. Having access to such a system, employers would be able to search for candidates with the confidence that their skills are genuine, as they are validated by credible certification bodies. Employers could also be the providers of information to such a system, thus enriching their employees' portfolios. The use of a system based on blockchain technology will provide such credibility. One of the crucial properties of such a system is also preventing the use of counterfeit or falsified documents. The proposition of such a system is presented in Section 5.4.

5.3 Competencies and skills for the evolving labour market

5.3.1 The problem of term ambiguity

The definition of the term "competence" experiences the problem of ambiguity. Originally, the term "competence" comes from psychology. Initially, competences were seen as certain cognitive predispositions that allow one to learn new things and are the basis for acquiring knowledge and skills (Kocór, 2019). Definitions of competence refer, in a broader context, to a person's knowledge, skills, and experience (Serafin, 2016). In this view, competences encompass the knowledge, skills, predispositions, and attitudes of employees that, when used in the work process, are directed towards fulfilling the organisation's strategy (Juchnowicz, 2014).

There are many approaches to the classification of competences. For example, competences can be divided into behavioural and technical (Guerrero & De los Ríos, 2012). The former refer to behavioural characteristics that affect the achievement of results in the activity undertaken. They can be associated with soft skills, as they are related to such areas as teamwork skills, communication competences, leadership competences, and those involving decision-making. The latter, technical competences, refer to what an employee needs to know and should be able to do (knowledge and skills) in order to undertake and perform specific tasks in his/her position in the organisation. In this perspective, technical competences can be linked to hard skills.

Another classification divides competences into (Armstrong & Taylor, 2014): (1) general and specific (the former relate to the ability, intelligence, personality, and attitudes, and the latter to people working in a given job, without taking into account the organisation they work for or the roles they play), (2) threshold and action (the former are elementary requirements for a given job that do not refer to the division into better or worse performing employees, while action competences refer to such a division), and (3) differentiating (they refer to behavioural traits that are characteristic of good performers, while making it possible to differentiate underperformers).

Competences from different areas interact with each other. With this in mind, core competences can be distinguished, which can be seen as a basis for other competences. This main group of core competences consists of basic human dispositions, among which cognitive, social, and personal competences can be distinguished. The second group includes executive competences, which refer to direct actions and activities in the workplace. Within them, we may discriminate business, company, and managerial competences (Filipowicz, 2004).

5.3.2 Competency formalisation models

Competency-based education and training has gained a growing interest, especially in conjunction with the proliferation of the terms "knowledge society", "citizen mobility", and "globalisation" (Rezgui, Mhiri, & Ghédira, 2012). In order for this approach to be put into practice, it is necessary to identify, classify, and formalise competences.

To this end, a considerable number of models for competence formalisation have been proposed. For instance, the Industry 4.0 competency model based on a behaviour-oriented approach concerns three variants (Prifti et al., 2017): Information Systems, Information Technology, and Engineering. In the model, critical job positions concerning these three areas are identified to effectively and efficiently perform in Industry 4.0. It provides a starting-point for further research regarding employee competences for Industry 4.0. A second example is a unified competency management platform, which serves as a communication layer between the stakeholders interested in the retraining and upskilling of the workforce (Kusmin, Ley, & Normak, 2017). Another model is the competence performance approach, a formal framework developed in cognitive psychology. It is a basis for the Workplace Learning Context Model, providing an integrative view on knowledge of workers by connecting learning, work, and knowledge spaces (Ley et al., 2008).

A context awareness system registering competences and skills may be used by workers to assist them in the development of their professional career (Rosa et al., 2015). An example of such a system, designed to support competence management, is DeCom. The system considers the profiles of employees in organisations and the contexts in which they are involved, looking for opportunities to help them develop their competences (Barbosa et al., 2015). As a part of DeCom, a Context Model is proposed, organised into five elements (Relationship Agent, Competences Agent, Personal Assistant, Administrative Site, and the one containing Profile, Competence and Context Modules), which enable the categorisation of employees' mobility and development using context-based information.

The results of the above-mentioned studies point to the need for education oriented towards competency-based learning. Hence, not only competence description and classification are important, but also the elaboration of solutions to facilitate competence management and comparison between countries.

5.3.3 Typologies of soft skills

The shift from the dominance of the industrial perspective towards the information society results in soft skills being given an increasing importance. Soft skills attribute the greatest importance to integrity, communication, courtesy, and responsibility (Robles, 2012). The key soft competences or skills that have an impact on increasing employability are the following (Andrews & Higson, 2008): professionalism, reliability, the ability to cope with uncertainty, the ability to work under pressure, the ability to plan and think strategically, the capability to communicate and interact with others, either in teams or through networking, good written and verbal communication skills, creativity and self-confidence, good self-management and time-management skills, and a willingness to learn and accept responsibility. Furthermore, work ethic, courtesy, teamwork, self-discipline and self-confidence, and the ability to communicate with clarity are also listed among the most important soft skills (Olsen, 2017). The U.S. Department of Labour identifies six core areas for developing soft skills (Olsen, 2017): communication, enthusiasm and attitude, teamwork, networking, problem-solving and critical thinking, and professionalism.

The phenomenon of the increasing importance of soft competences concerns various types of industries, including those requiring strict, technical skills. In the IT industry, although it is perceived as an area related to analytical skills, soft competences are becoming more and more important, without which it is often impossible to get and keep a job. The important soft competences indicated by IT companies include (Witak, 2013): readiness to learn, ability to organise own work, creativity, communicativeness, teamwork, perseverance, independence, and knowledge sharing.

5.3.4 Evolution of the competence classification system on the example of Poland

It should be emphasised that the problem of competence management is not only an internal matter of one country. Non-uniformity of classification and certification of qualifications in individual countries hinders workers' mobility within all of Europe. Employees and employers looking for offers on the intra-EU market do not have comparisons between the qualification systems. To address this problem, initiatives to create a single system of qualification classification at the EU level have been undertaken. In particular, the European Credit System for Vocational Education and Training (ECVET) (European Centre for Development of Vocational Training, 2023) is an initiative that aims to make it easier for citizens of European countries to acquire certificates and diplomas of vocational qualifications, thus supporting professional mobility and lifelong learning. The use of ECVET is recommended to member states in the Recommendation of the European Parliament and of the Council of 18 June 2009.

Introducing the above-mentioned ECVET recommendations and the implementation of the common qualifications system for lifelong learning in the EU Member States, the so called European Qualifications Framework (EQF), were the first steps to create the system for uniform certification registration. On the basis of it, several EU countries created databases of qualification registers (Austria, Croatia, France, Latvia, Poland, and Slovakia) (Instytut Badań Edukacyjnych, 2020).

Poland has begun to bring the Polish Qualifications Framework (PQF) into line with the EQF. The most significant element of putting the qualification system in Poland in order was the preparation and enactment of the Act on the Integrated Qualification System (IQS) (Ministerstwo Edukacji i Nauki, 2023) in December 2015. The Act defines the conceptual system of the qualifications area, qualification description standards, assignments of qualifications to PQF levels, institutions creating and maintaining IQS, operational processes for the validation and certification of individuals, and a quality assurance system for institutions involved in the learning and certification process.

An important element of IQS is the Integrated Qualification Register (IQR, https://kwalifikacje.edu.pl/integrated-qualification-register-iqr), which is an electronic register that provides an integrated database of all qualifications included in IQS. For example, from the register it is possible to find out what specific requirements need to be met in order to obtain a particular qualification, and which institutions have the authority to grant them. There are many stakeholders of IQR (Instytut Badań Edukacyjnych, 2018). The controlling institutions are the ministries responsible for Polish education at all levels. The certifying institutions are primary schools, secondary schools, and HEIs. Training companies have also been incorporated in the system for awarding market qualifications. IQR recipients are employers, students and parents, teachers, people wishing to improve their professional qualifications, and government officials. The IQR context model presents Figure 5.1.

A set of attributes was defined for each qualification in IQR. Table 5.2 depicts an example of the attributes, illustrated by the qualifications obtained at the Krakow University of Economics, Poland.

IQR is a centralised system. Through the web portal, institutional stakeholders who have been granted access can enter data on individual qualifications. Other stakeholders have access to search the registers. Figure 5.2 shows an example of the IQR portal interface.

IQR is a central database of information on professional qualifications; however, it does not store information about the confirmed qualifications of potential employees. In the next section, we present a proposition of a system for storing data about potential employees. Distributed Ledger Technology (DLT) and blockchain (see Chapter 2) are the basis for designing a register of personal qualifications, accessible in a credible, secure and reliable way.

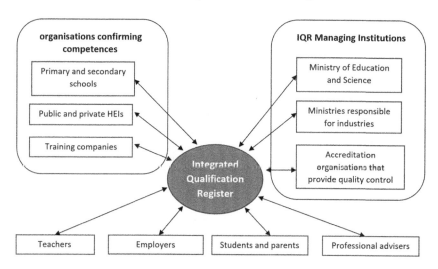

FIGURE 5.1   The Integrated Qualification Register context model.

Note: HEIs – Higher Educational Institutions; IQR – Integrated Qualification Register.

TABLE 5.2 An example of qualification attributes in the Integrated Qualification Register.

Attribute	Example of qualification at the Krakow University of Economics
Qualification code	7P01606309
Full name of the qualification and the document confirming its award	Graduation diploma in the field of accounting and controlling – unique course – Krakow University of Economics; Faculty of Management
PQF level assigned to a given qualification	7
Short characteristic of qualification	Graduates have in-depth knowledge of economics, finance and management sciences and can apply it to solve various economic and financial problems in a company
Educational profile	General academic
Professional/scientific title	Master's degree or other equivalent
Specialisations	Accounting, Controlling
Additional accreditations held	ACCA (The Association of Chartered Certified Accountants) accreditation
ECTS credit points	120
Duration of study	4 semesters
Form of conducting studies	Full-time studies
Language	Polish
ISCED code	0411 – Accounting and Taxes
Certification Authorities (CAs)	Krakow University of Economics
External quality assurance entity	Polish Accreditation Committee

FIGURE 5.2 Integrated Qualifications Register – detailed view of qualifications.

Source: https://kwalifikacje.gov.pl/en/ [access: 8.02.2023]

5.3.5 Proposition of a conceptual model for registering qualifications

To avoid the problem of classification inconsistency, a comprehensive model of vocational qualifications was developed on the basis of IQR. It includes elements of soft competences not considered in IQR. Figure 5.3 presents the model.

Vocational qualifications are a combination of knowledge, skills, experience, and attitudes. They can be divided into hard and soft skills. Hard skills are classified as professional qualifications, as they are always associated with the appropriate certificate. They are defined as a set of learning outcomes with respect to knowledge, skills, and social competences, whose achievement was verified and confirmed by an authorised certifying entity. The basic division of qualifications proposed in the IQR framework is built on the basis of the type of learning cycle, and involves the institutions that validate learning achievements and issue certificates and distinctions. They can be divided into (Dymek et al., 2020):

- **Full qualifications** – obtained through formal education provided by schools and other entities of the educational system. They are awarded after completing specified stages of education.
- **Partial qualifications** – may be awarded not only as a result of formal education, but also by institutions, organisations and associations of different types. These are professional qualifications, confirmed by diplomas and certificates issued after industry exams, awarded after completing postgraduate studies, further education courses and training.
- **Market qualifications** – qualifications that are not regulated by law and are awarded on the basis of professional activity. For example, a qualification in carpentry assembly, a qualification in HDD data recovery.

Soft skills are achieved by non-formal learning; these include psychophysical characteristics and professional experience. Non-formal learning consists of a variety of courses run by private and public educational institutions. Psychophysical features and experience are an important element of the description of a potential employee. Certifications of these competencies are received from former employers or co-workers in the form of reference and recommendation letters.

5.3.6 The competence data structure

Based on the proposed conceptual model, the documents confirming qualifications and skills currently functioning in Poland were identified. During the analysis, they were classified into five basic categories, presented in Table 5.3.

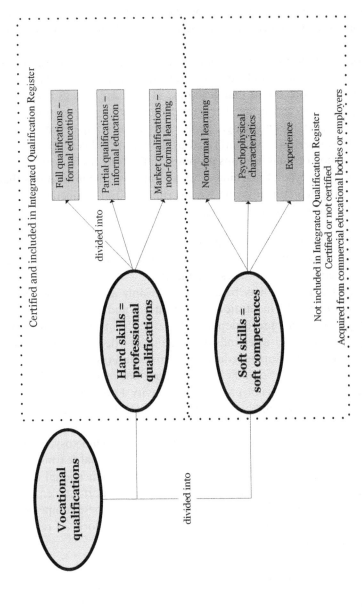

FIGURE 5.3   Conceptual model for registering qualifications.

Source: Based on (Dymek et al., 2020).

TABLE 5.3 Categories of documents confirming qualifications.

	Category	Certification institutions	Types of certificates
1	Formal education	Documents issued by educational institutions on the basis of legal regulations	School certificates, diplomas of studies, degrees
2	Professional entitlements	Documents issued by institutions that are not part of the educational system but have the status of documents formally required by law	Professional qualifications including those requiring state examination (e.g. doctors, architects, electricians, drivers)
3	Formal vocational training	Documents issued by institutions whose educational status is not regulated by law, providing training as part of their own or licensed courses	Industry certifications in various areas and scope, e.g. from companies and professional organisations (if not in the professional entitlements category)
4	Informal vocational training	Documents issued by organisations whose educational status is not regulated by law, which do not verify educational results (certificate of attendance without verification of results) or do not verify personal details (e.g. online courses or examinations without verification of personal details)	Certificates of attendance or course completion issued by various organisations
5	Certification of experience and/or skills	Documents of a formal (e.g. certificate of employment) or informal (e.g. letters of recommendation) nature issued by employers or other organisations, including those of a personal type (e.g. issued by employers employing a person receiving the certificate)	Certificate of employment combined with employer's opinion (positions, skills, internal training), certificates of work in various organisations

Source: Based on (Dymek et al., 2020).

The role of each category of documents is based on separate rules. For documents required by law (categories 1 and 2), the organisations issuing them must be formally accredited by supervisory bodies. In the case of documents certifying vocational training (categories 3 and 4), organisations issuing them are either direct holders of the rights to the given certificate or they operate on the basis of the power granted to them by the holder of such rights (e.g., IT industry certificates of companies such as Microsoft, Oracle, and IBM). In the case of documents certifying experience and/or skills (category 5), the issuer of the document for a given person is the institution where this person used to work (cooperated with), which means that there is no other (external) entity determining the requirements for the structure of these documents.

Based on the identified document categories, we propose the document representation model. The model should be flexible and should enable mapping a document from any of the identified categories. To this end, document characteristics were divided into three separate groups:

* **Formal Document Characteristic** (FDC) – determines which category the document belongs to and indicates, depending on the category, the supervisory authority or the right-holder, the issuing institution, the name of the document (e.g., master's degree in economics), the person to whom it was issued, and the date of issuance (and of expiration if any).
* **General Competence Characteristic** (GCC) – defines basic competences (certified by the document) based on the predefined categories (determined on the basis of models of hard and soft competences and terms used in curricula). The GCC is a partially closed set, i.e. changes to it can only be made in the mode of updating the model by the institutions supervising its use.
* **Detailed Competence Characteristic** (DCC) – is a refinement of the GCC based on concepts and terms that more accurately describe a given competence. DCC is created on the basis of an extended analysis of the curriculum in combination with an analysis of the market employment offers, in a mode similar to the functioning of the so-called keywords, and has a dynamic character, i.e. each issuer of documents can introduce new terms. Additionally, in this group, each issuer can include additional information about the scope of competences by placing a reference to external descriptions (e.g., study programme, scope of training).

Figure 5.4 presents the document representation model.

Having defined the basic data structure for storing all the discussed types of competences, we proceed to the technical phase of designing the register

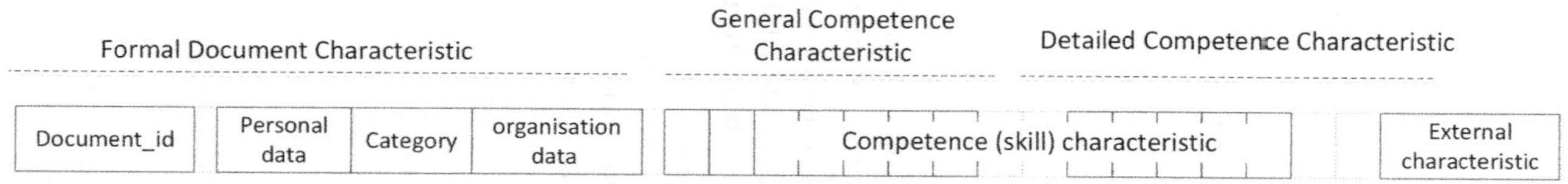

FIGURE 5.4 Document representation model.

Source: Based on (Dymek et al., 2020).

of personal competences based on blockchain, which is discussed in the following section.

5.4 Blockchain in the system of competences management

5.4.1 Related solutions

Competence and qualification management refers, among other things, to diplomas and certificates issued by schools, universities, and other certification bodies. There are examples of using blockchain technology in this area, facilitating the validation of such documents.

The University of Nicosia (UNIC) collects the certificates of its students using blockchain since 2014 (Panagiotidis, 2022). From 2017 UNIC uses the Blockcerts standard in the certificate generation process (Grech, Camilleri, & Inamorato dos Santos, 2017). More insights into UNIC's experience with academic certificates issued on blockchain are described in Chapter 7. In 2017, the Massachusetts Institute of Technology (MIT) offered graduates the opportunity to receive a digital diploma in addition to the traditional paper version. With this digital version, graduates, using applications based on the open Blockcerts standard on their mobile devices, are able to share a digital, MIT-verified diploma with potential employers without having to certify its credibility each time by the issuing university (Prebil, 2018). The OpenCerts project, developed and launched by the Singapore Government Technology Agency in April 2019 in collaboration with the Ngee Ann Polytechnic, aims to provide credible verification of educational credentials in Singapore universities (McDermott, 2019). With the solution provided, employers or educational institutions can verify candidates' certificates and diplomas without a lengthy query-response process. In conjunction with the OpenCerts project focused on the ASEAN region (Association of Southeast Asian Nations), there is the start-up Accredify (https://accredify.io) which offers a comprehensive solution to facilitate the issuance of certificates that can be verified by the OpenCerts platform for educational institutions.

5.4.2 General system overview

On the basis of the developed model of document representation, we propose to create an Integrated Personal Competence Ledger (IPeCoL) system whose task would be to collect and make available information confirming the possession of competences by a given person. The IPeCoL system would act as an integrator of existing registers of issued certificates, and in some cases could replace them over time. In terms of collecting information, each certificate issuer, to the extent of its authority resulting from the category of documents, would place information about the certificate in the system.

As regards access to collected information, the issuers would have access to all documents issued by them. This information would also be accessible to entities supervising particular types of documents, to the extent specified by law or agreement. The person to whom the collected information pertains also has access to it and may grant access (in a specified mode, e.g., temporary, full, partial) to other entities (e.g., a future employer). Placing all the information in a single system allows all its potential users to save a significant effort to maintain, confirm, and verify qualifications.

5.4.3 Justification for the use of blockchain technology

Currently, many organisations are considering setting up a system to support their operations using blockchain technology. When analysing the feasibility of using this technology, it is important to contrast its properties with the kind of information used. In the decision-making process, it may be helpful to consider the following aspects of an organisation's operations (Pedersen, Beck, & Risius, 2019):

- whether the organisation needs a shared common database: blockchain is a shared database, so may be considered as an alternative to traditional databases,
- whether multiple parties are involved: blockchain only makes sense if there are multiple parties,
- do the involved parties have conflicting interests and/or are they trusted: blockchain is appropriate if cooperating institutions experience trust issues or the parties have conflicts of interest,
- do the participants want to avoid a trusted third party: one of the advantages of blockchain is that it enables peer-to-peer transactions without relying on a trusted third-party service,
- do the rules governing system access differ between participants: blockchain architectural design allows for differing rights for users,
- do the rules of transactions remain largely unchanged: for systems where transaction rules change frequently, it would not be advisable to use blockchain,
- is there a need for an objective, immutable log: blockchain stores information and also maintains a log of its history, so it guarantees the validity of transactions,
- is public access required: blockchain solutions can be permissionless, public permissioned, and private permissioned (see Chapter 2),
- where is consensus determined: private-permissioned blockchains determine the validity of transactions within the organisation, in public-permissioned blockchains consensus is established between participating organisations.

In a certificate registration system, it is necessary to use a database shared by different stakeholders (individuals, certifying institutions, HEIs, employees, and employers) who do not directly cooperate, so it is difficult to guarantee credibility. Such a system does not require a third-party as long as it provides reliable information. Moreover, the way in which the system is accessed varies from one stakeholder to another. An important property of this system is the immutability of the documents/certificates placed in it. Furthermore, access to the system should be provided to the public, and different stakeholders would have different rights. Juxtaposing the conditions for the use of blockchain with the characteristics of the certificate registration system, it can be seen that blockchain technology can be successfully used for its implementation.

The minimum requirements for an IT system to support the operation of the IPeCoL shall involve: (1) ensuring data security (taking into account the requirements set out by law, especially those related to personal data), including, but not limited to: full traceability and non-repudiation of the documents issued, lack of the possibility for unauthorised entities to upload documents or modify already stored documents, tracking of access history to documents, (2) access for all issuers to the documents of the relevant categories, (3) access for all persons concerned, with the possibility to grant access in specific modes, and (4) possibility to verify individual documents.

In the IPeCoL, Distributed Ledger Technology, represented by blockchain technology, is used. In this technology, three basic types of systems can be distinguished (Casino, Dasaklis, and Patsakis, 2019): public, private, and hybrid (federated). In public systems, the role of full nodes can be played by any of its users, as all users have the same privileges. The only limitation may be the fulfilment of appropriate technological requirements, e.g., in terms of performance. In private systems, full nodes belong to a single organisation, which may ensure greater control, but may also be a source of limited trust in such a system. An intermediate solution comprises federated (hybrid) systems, in which the list of full nodes is limited and remains under the control of unrelated independent organisations. It is this independence that is one of the guarantees of data security. Each type of system retains the basic features of blockchain technology, in particular confidentiality, non-repudiation, auditability and security. The presented concept of IPeCoL implementation uses a hybrid variant.

In the document representation model (Figure 5.4), each document is described by attributes from three groups. An important part of the document characteristics is the Detailed Competence Characteristic, and in particular the references to external documents describing the competency scope (e.g., training programme). Although it is possible to store such documents in the database itself, it is preferable, from the point of view of efficiency, to store only a link to external registers such as IQS or the websites of the relevant organisations. Only in the case of category 5 of documents (Table 5.3) is it appropriate to store electronic versions of entire documents.

5.4.4 Users and their roles in the system

In the proposed system there are eight basic types of users (Table 5.4).

The certifying institutions are responsible for the management of the attributes, including granting rights of use to subordinates. Certifying authorities CA1 and CA2 are free to use DCC attributes; they also complete the information (links) about the descriptions stored outside the system. CA3 and CA4 complete the list of roles of active users, i.e. those who can place documents in the system or influence their characteristics. AA and CA users have access (viewing) to all certificates issued by themselves or by accredited entities, subject to any legal restrictions. The role of full nodes in the system is performed by organisations belonging to the AA1, AA2, CA1 and CA2 categories. They store the database, are responsible for its management including authorisation of changes, and grant access to the system for other users. Their legal standing and market authority provide assurance of the correct operation of the system.

5.4.5 IPeCoL-based solution architecture

After identifying the stakeholders as well as data and document flows, taking into account blockchain as the leading technology, a solution was proposed with the IPeCoL as its fundamental element. This central element will ensure that the most detailed and multifaceted information about the qualifications of each potential employee is stored and made available. Figure 5.5 presents a diagram illustrating the components and data flows. IPeCoL is a repository of individual competences acquired during the entire professional life. The solution stores in blockchain not only hard (formalised), but also soft competences. Data is supplied by various types of Certifying Institutions (CA). The role of the person (potential employee) is to grant access to their data to interested employers. IPeCoL does not store all information and documents (e.g., scans of paper documents) directly in blockchain: blockchain records include links to external systems such as IQR or other external services or document repositories.

Figure 5.6 shows how the proposed IPeCoL-based solution works. Category AA1-AA2 and CA1-CA2 users act as full nodes responsible for the operation of the system, including storing and sharing data, managing

TABLE 5.4 Users (stakeholders) and their roles in the IPeCOL system.

User	Symbol	Detailed characteristics
Accreditation Authority type 1	AA1	Regulated accrediting bodies. This group includes institutions supervising and authorising other organisations to issue certificates, the nature of which is regulated by law (category 1 and 2). These institutions only occasionally issue certificates themselves, most often delegating these competences to subordinate organisations.
Accreditation Authority type 2	AA2	Accreditation bodies, operating without formal legal regulation. This group includes companies, associations and other organisations that provide training and/or certification of qualifications based on their own requirements ("certificate right holders") (category 3). They may license (accredit) their rights to others, but often issue certificates themselves.
Certifying Authority type 1	CA1	Certification bodies operating in the education system under AA1 accreditation. They can issue certificates (category 1 and 2) in accordance with their credentials, supplementing them with GCC and DCC characteristics.
Certifying Authority type 2	CA2	Certification bodies operating in the education system under AA2 accreditation. They can issue certificates (category 3) according to their credentials, supplementing them with GCC and DCC characteristics.
Certifying Authority type 3	CA3	Training institutions issuing category 4 certificates. They are not subject to accreditation. Their ability to create certificate attributes is, with respect to FDC, significantly limited (e.g., with regard to the type of document to "certify course completion"). In contrast, they have free choice of characteristics with respect to DCC.
Certifying Authority type 4	CA4	Category 5 document issuers. These are not subject to accreditation and in practice any organisation with a formal basis for its operation (which may employ staff) falls into this group. They are free to issue GCC and DCC, with mandatory inclusion of electronic copies of source documents.
Verifying Organisation	VO	Entities that check the credibility of documents presented to them, e.g., as part of recruitment of new employees. Users in this group can verify individual certificates after providing the required information (based, e.g., on the paper version of certificates).

(*Continued*)

TABLE 5.4 (Continued)

User	Symbol	Detailed characteristics
Document Holder	DH	Persons who are affected by the issued certificates. Each person has access to the certificates concerning them and can grant such access under the rules defined by the system (e.g., scope, time).

Document categories according to document characteristics: DCC – Detailed Competence Characteristic; FDC – Formal Document Characteristic; GCC – General Competence Characteristic. Document categories according to the form of education: category 1 – formal education; category 2 – professional entitlements; category 3 – formal vocational training, category 4 – informal vocational training; category 5 – certifications of experience and/or skills (see Table 5.3).

Source: Based on (Dymek et al., 2020).

active users (e.g., accreditation, granting permission to use FDC attributes), validating and accepting new entries.

Depending on the category of documents and accreditations held, active CA1-CA4 users may attach information about issued certificates, and they also have access to the data they post (in read-only mode, blockchain properties do not allow to change them). When attaching documents, they may supplement the information with links to external sources with more detailed information (except for CA4 who posts the full documents). When attaching further documents, a unique code is generated for each document, which allows its direct verification in the system.

Passive users are persons affected by the documents (DH) and entities wishing to verify documents (VO) presented to them. They have access to all documents that concern them (in read-only mode) based on a combination of a digital signatures and selected personal data. DH users can grant access to their own documents (e.g., to a future employer) in modes defined by the system. VO users may verify documents on the basis of their unique code, or after providing the required scope of data corresponding to the content of documents in a traditional paper form. This mode of access allows e.g., a future employer to verify the documents submitted by candidates in support of their qualifications directly in IPeCoL in a reliable manner, while at the same time not increasing the risk of violation of legal rules, e.g., in the area of personal data protection. User roles are not exclusive, e.g., an AA2 organisation can issue certificates, i.e. act as CA2, and at the same time verify candidates (VO role).

The cryptography mechanisms used in blockchain technology ensure the security and integrity of the data, while preserving its privacy. The architecture of the IPeCoL-based solution will allow solving the problem of access to information on individual qualifications at the level of all participants of

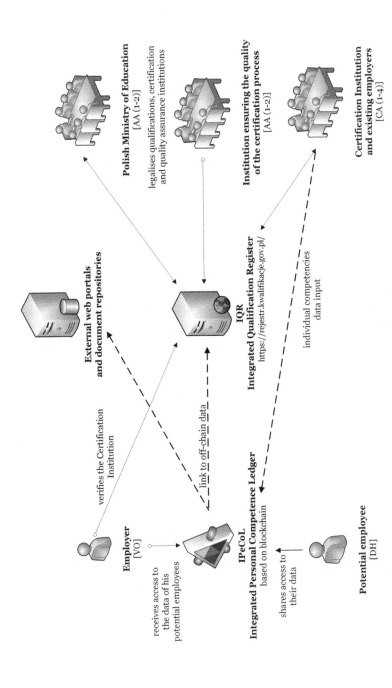

FIGURE 5.5 Components and data flows of the IPeCoL-based solution.

Note: VO – verifying organisation; DH – document holder; AA – accreditation authority; CA – certifying authority.

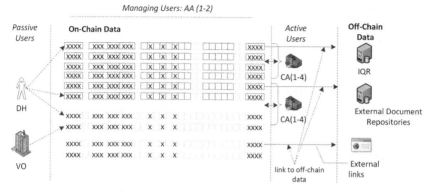

FIGURE 5.6 IPeCoL-based solution design.

Note: VO – verifying organisation; DH – document holder; AA – accreditation authority; CA – certifying authority; IQR – Integrated Qualification Register.

Source: Based on (Dymek et al., 2020).

the labour market. It is worth emphasising that the solution can support not only educational (including HEIs) and business units from one country, but used by organisations from the entire EU can significantly support the policy of lifelong learning.

The IPeCoL system could be extended with additional features without loss of reliability and confidentiality, thanks to the properties of blockchain technology. For example, such additional functionality could make it possible to search the register for people with a specific set of competences, and then, if they have agreed to this in their individual system settings, to send them a job offer without accessing their contact details. Individual users could, in turn, generate access codes to their own data (with time and scope limitation) when looking for a job, thus not having to send extensive documentation proving their own competences.

5.5 Conclusions

Industry 4.0 entails the need for lifelong learning and the continuous improvement of personal qualifications. Progressive automation leads to the disappearance of existing jobs, but also to the emergence of new professions. There is a clear emphasis on expanding professional skills in the field of science, technology, engineering, and math. At the same time, soft competences in the fields of, for instance, psychology or sociology should be developed.

One of the problems of the labour market addressed in this chapter is the lack of commonly accepted tools to track the development of competences of individual people throughout their working life. This problem concerns not only employees but also employers and public and private educational institutions, including HEIs, government institutions, as well as many business organisations. The management of individual competencies can be supported by an IT system that is efficient, reliable, secure, and easy to use. Such a system can be based on blockchain technology. In the contemporary labour market, the possibility of reliable verification of competences and skills is an important issue for both employees and employers. The proposed solution based on the IPeCoL system, incorporating not only a database for storing information on competences but also involving various stakeholders, allows for the unified representation of documents confirming qualifications, and thus can be the basis for building an environment for verifying their credibility. At the same time, the model takes into account the storage of information about soft skills, which have a less formal way of representation. The described concept of the IPeCoL-based solution is the starting point for building a widely available IT system that allows to confirm the credibility of documents while maintaining their privacy and confidentiality. HEIs, as elements of the qualification supply chain, should be involved in building and implementing such systems as IPeCoL. Such activities will allow graduates to function actively and effectively on a difficult, demanding, and quickly changing labour market.

References

Andrews, J., & Higson, H. (2008). Graduate employability, 'soft skills' versus 'hard' business knowledge: A European study. *Higher education in Europe*, *33*(4), 411–422.

Arndt, T. (2018). Empowering university students with blockchain-based transcripts. In *Proceedings of the 15th International Conference on Cognition and Exploratory Learning in the Digital Age*. CELDA, Budapest, Hungary, 21–23 October 2018, pp. 399–400.

Armstrong, M., & Taylor, S. (2014). *Armstrong's Handbook of Human Resource Management Practice*, 13th edition. London: Kogan Page Limited.

Awaji, B., Solaiman, E., & Marshall, L. (2020). Blockchain-based trusted achievement record system design. In *Proceedings of the ICIEI 2020: 5th International Conference on Information and Education Innovations*, London, UK, 26–28 July 2020, pp. 46–51.

Bal, H. Ç., & Erkan, Ç. (2019). Industry 4.0 and competitiveness. *Procedia Computer Science*, *158*, 625–631.

Barbosa, J. L., Kich, M., Barbosa, D. N., Klein, A., & Rigo, S. J. (2015). DeCom: A model for context-aware competence management. *Computers in Industry*, 72, 27–35.

Bartosik, A., & Wiścicka, D. (2021). The importance of training and certificates in the access of university graduates to the labour market. *International Journal of Strategic Management and Decision Support Systems in Strategic Management*, *26*(1), 26–33.

Behringer, F., & Coles, M. (2003). The role of national qualifications systems in promoting lifelong learning. In *OECD Education Working Papers*, 3.

Casino, F., Dasaklis, T. K., & Patsakis, C. (2019). A systematic literature review of blockchain-based applications: current status, classification and open issues. *Telematics Informatics*, *36*, 55–81.

Chovancova, B., Dorocakova, M., & Malacka, V. (2018). Changes in industrial structure of GDP and stock indices also with regard to the Industry 4.0. *Business and Economic Horizons*, *14*(2), 402–414.

Chui, M., Manyika, J., & Miremadi, M. (2015). *Four Fundamentals of Workplace Automation*. Retrieved Sep. 17, 2022, from: http://www.mckinsey.com/business-functions/business-technology/our-insights/four-fundamentals-of-workplace-automation

Csugány, J. (2020). Labour market tendencies in the era of the fourth industrial revolution. In *The 4th Conference on Economics and Management*, EMAN, Belgrade.

Deloitte. (2015). *Industry 4.0. Challenges and Solutions for the Digital Transformation and Use of Exponential Technologies*. 45774A Deloitte Zurich Switzerland 2015.

Dubreta, N., & Bulian, L. (2018). Engineering job skills in Croatian economy. Employers' perspective. *Interdisciplinary Description of Complex Systems: INDECS*, *16*(1), 1–20.

Dymek, D. Konkol, P., Put, D., Stal, J., & Trąbka, J. (2020). Conceptual model of personal competence integrator based on blockchain technology. *AMCIS 2020 Proceedings*, The Association for Information Systems, Atlanta, pp. 1–10.

European Centre for Development of Vocational Training. (2023). *European Credit System for Vocational Education and Training (ECVET)*. Retrieved Jan. 31, 2023, from: https://www.cedefop.europa.eu/en/projects/european-credit-system-vocational-education-and-training-ecvet

Filipowicz, G. (2004). *Zarządzanie kompetencjami zawodowymi*, PWN, Warsaw.

Frey, C. B., & Osborne, M. A. (2017). The future of employment: How susceptible are jobs to computerisation? *Technological Forecasting and Social Change*, *114*(C), 254–280.

Gorecky, D., Schmitt, M., Loskyll, M., & Zühlke, D. (2014). Human-machine-interaction in the industry 4.0 era. In *12th IEEE International Conference on Industrial Informatics (INDIN)*, Porto Alegre, Brazil, pp. 289–294.

Gracel, J., & Makowiec, M. (2017). Core competences of managers in the fourth industrial revolution (Industry 4.0). *Acta Universitatis Nicolai Copernici*, *44*(4), 105–129.

Grech, A., & Camilleri, A. F., Inamorato dos Santos, A. (2017). *Blockchain in Education*. Luxembourg: Publications Office of the European Union, Luxembourg.

Guerrero, D., & De los Ríos, I. (2012). Professional competences: A classification of international models. *Procedia – Social and Behavioral Sciences*, *46*, 1290–1296.

Instytut Badań Edukacyjnych (2020), *Qualifications Registers in Selected European Union Countries*. Retrieved Jan. 31, 2023, from: https://kwalifikacje.edu.pl/wp-content/uploads/publikacje/PDF/Zintegrowany-Rejestr-Kwalifikacji-w-zarysie-1.pdf

Instytut Badań Edukacyjnych (2018), *Zintegrowany Rejestr Kwalifikacji w zarysie*. Instytut Badań Edukacyjnych, Warszawa.

Juchnowicz, M. (ed.). (2014). *Zarządzanie kapitałem ludzkim. Procesy – narzędzia – aplikacje*. Polskie Wydawnictwo Ekonomiczne, Warszawa.

Kocór, M. (2019). *Nadwyżka czy deficyt kompetencji? Konsekwencje niedopasowania na rynku pracy*. Wydawnictwo Uniwersytetu Jagiellońskiego, Kraków.

Kusmin, K.-L., Ley, T., & Normak, P. (2017). *Towards a Data Driven Competency Management Platform for Industry 4.0*. Redwood City: Course Hero.

Langdon, D., McKittrick, G., Beede, D., Khan, B., & Doms, M. (2011). *STEM: Good Jobs Now and for the Future. ESA Issue Brief #03-11. July, 2011*. Retrieved Nov. 15, 2022, from: https://files.eric.ed.gov/fulltext/ED522129.pdf?fbclid=IwAR 24WKq0PYerEK_QNGR1kgGoi050sFXiZEjEibL8SGpTjRXaP69QgN OE3X8

Ley, T., Ulbrich, A., Scheir, P., Lindstaedt, S., Kump, B., & Albert, D. (2008). Modeling competences for supporting work-integrated learning in knowledge work. *Journal of Knowledge Management 12*(6), 31–47.

Lowden, K., Hall, S., Elliot, D., & Lewin, J. (2011). *Employers' Perceptions of the Employability Skills of New Graduates*. Glasgow: The SCRE Centre Research in Education, Edge Foundation, University of Glasgow.

Lungu, E., Braniste, G., & Calugher, V. (2019). The adaptation of physical culture higher education offer to the labour market. In *Education and Sports Science in the 21st Century. Proceedings of the International Congress of Physical Education, Sports and Kinetotherapy. Education and Sports Science in the 21st Century, Edition dedicated to the 95th anniversary of UNEFS, (ICPESK 2018)*, 14–16 June, 2019, Bucharest, Romania.

Ministerstwo Edukacji i Nauki. (2023). *Coordination Point for Polish Qualifications Framework*. Retrieved Jan. 31, 2023, from: https://prk.men.gov.pl/en/2en/

McDermott, D. (2019). *Blockchain Set to be Vital Tool for ASEAN HE Mobility*. University World News. Retrieved Nov. 10, 2022, from: https://www.university worldnews.com

McMurray, S., Dutton, M., McQuaid, R., & Richard, A. (2016). Employer demands from business graduates. *Education + Training, 58*(1), 112–132.

Mohamed, M. (2018). Challenges and benefits of industry 4.0: An overview. *International Journal of Supply and Operations Management, 5*(3), 256–265.

Olsen, L. (2017). A hard look at soft skills. *Administrative Professional Today. 43*(11), 7. Capitol Information Group.

Olsen, T. L., & Tomlin, B. (2020). Industry 4.0: Opportunities and challenges for operations management. *Manufacturing & Service Operations Management, 22*(1), 113–122.

Oesterreich, T. D., & Teuteberg, F. (2016). Understanding the implications of digitisation and automation in the context of Industry 4.0: A triangulation approach and elements of a research agenda for the construction industry. *Computers in Industry, 83*, 121–139.

Panagiotidis, P. (2022). Blockchain in education – The case of language learning. *European Journal of Education, 5*(1), 66–83.

Pedersen, A. B., Risius, M., & Beck, R. (2019). A ten-step decision path to determine when to use blockchain technologies. *MIS Quarterly Executive, 18*(2), 99–115.

Perkune, L., Līcīte, L. (2019). Labour market expectations of generation. In *Proceedings of the 2019 International Conference "Economic Science for Rural Development,"* vol. 52, LLU ESAF, Jelgava, 9–10 May 2019, pp. 119–126.

Pfohl, H.-Ch., Burak, Y., & Kurnaz, T. (2015). The impact of Industry 4.0 on the supply chain. In *Innovations and Strategies for Logistics and Supply Chains:*

Technologies, Business Models and Risk Management. Proceedings of the Hamburg International Conference of Logistics (HICL), vol. 20, pp. 31–58.

Piątkowski, M. (2020). Expectations and challenges in the labour market in the context of industrial revolution 4.0. The agglomeration method-based analysis for Poland and other EU member states. *Sustainability, 12*, 5437.

Pietrulewicz, B., Łosyk, H. (2018). Social and education problems at the working space in the fourth-generation industry context. *Problemy Profesjologii, 2*, 69–77.

Prebil, M. (2018). *Blockchain for Education and Skills? A Big Maybe*. New America. Retrieved Jan. 21, 2022, from: https://www.newamerica.org [access: 21.1.2022].

Prifti, L., Knigge, M., Kienegger, H., & Krcmar, H. (2017). A competency model for Industry 4.0 employees. In *13th International Conference on Wirtschaftsinformatik*, February 12–15, St. Gallen, Switzerland.

Rezgui, K., Mhiri, H., & Ghédira, K. (2012). Competency models: A review of initiatives. In *2012 IEEE 12th International Conference on Advanced Learning Technologies*, pp. 141–142.

Robles, M. (2012). Executive perceptions of the top 10 soft skills needed in today's workplace. *Business Communication Quarterly 75*(4), 453–465.

Rosa, J. H., Barbosa, J. L. V., Kich, M., & Brito, L. (2015). A multi-temporal context-aware system for competences management. *International Journal of Artificial Intelligence in Education, 25*, 455–492.

Sahonero, G. (2018). Blockchain and peace engineering and its relationship to engineering education. In *Proceedings of the 2018 World Engineering Education Forum – Global Engineering Deans Council*, Albuquerque, NM, USA, 12–16 November 2018.

Serafin, K. (2016). Kompetencje pracownicze determinantą kreacji wartości kapitału intelektualnego organizacji. Studia Ekonomiczne. *Zeszyty Naukowe Uniwersytetu Ekonomicznego w Katowicach, 283*, 16–28.

Serranito, D., Vasconcelos, A., Guerreiro, S., & Correia, M. (2020). Blockchain ecosystem for verifiable qualifications. In *Proceedings of the 2020 2nd Conference on Blockchain Research and Applications for Innovative Networks and Services*, BRAINS, Paris, France, 28–30 September 2020, pp. 192–199.

Simai, M. (2018). A felsőoktatás jövője, az élethosszi tanulás és a globális kihívások. [Future of higher education. life-long learning & global challenges.] *Magyar Tudomány, 179*(1), 90–98.

Stal, J., & Paliwoda-Pękosz, G. (2019). Fostering development of soft skills in ICT curricula: A case of a transition economy. *Information Technology for Development, 25*(2), 250–274.

Szabó, C. M., Bartal, O. (2020). The relation of contemporary labour market skills and the future engineers' visions. In *III Annual International Conference "System Engineering"*, KnE Engineering, pp. 59–66.

Vuorikari, R., Punie, Y., Gomez, S. C., & Van Den Brande, G. (2016). *DigComp 2.0: The Digital Competence Framework for Citizens. Update Phase 1: The Conceptual Reference Model*. Joint Research Centre, Luxembourg.

Zgaga, P. (2007). *Higher Education in Transition: Reconsiderations on Higher Education in Europe at the Turn of Millennium*, Umeå: Umeå University.

Witak, K. (2013). *Kompetencje miękkie w IT kluczem do sukcesu. Computerworld*. Retrieved Nov. 7, 2022, from: https://www.computerworld.pl/news/Kompetencje-miekkie-w-IT-kluczem-do-sukcesu,392040.html

6

TEACHING BLOCKCHAIN

The case of the MSc in Blockchain and Digital Currency of the University of Nicosia

Marinos Themistocleous

6.1 Introduction

On October 31, 2008, an individual or group known as Satoshi Nakamoto published a groundbreaking paper about the development of a Peer-to-Peer (P2P) electronic cash system called Bitcoin (Nakamoto, 2008). That paper outlined a decentralised P2P protocol that addresses the double-spending problem – a key solution that enables digital money to be used securely among complete strangers without the need for a traditional trusted third-party like a bank. The proposed open-source solution rests on the use of an append-only ledger, replicated across a network of peers that use a Proof of Work (PoW) consensus to validate and register new transactions. The Bitcoin protocol is transparent, immutable, censorship resistant, and secure, thus building trust among participants.

On January 3, 2009, Bitcoin blockchain and cryptocurrency were launched, and since then have been disrupting various sectors of public and private domains. The adoption of blockchain technology has been growing, with Cunha et al. (2021) reporting that education, sourcing, and regulation can significantly speed up its widespread use.

Recognizing the potential of digital currencies and blockchain technology, the University of Nicosia (UNIC) in Cyprus began investigating these areas in 2012. UNIC identified a need for academic programmes offering education and certification in this emerging field. As a result, UNIC initiated the development of the world's first MSc programme in Blockchain and Digital Currency in 2013. The programme was officially launched in 2014 and, until 2018, remained the only academic programme of its kind

DOI: 10.4324/9781003318736-7

globally (Themistocleous et al., 2020). During its early years, the programme gained a reputation as the most successful and disruptive in the field. Over 110,000 participants attended its first course, a free Massive Open Online Course (MOOC) and more than 1,150 students from 120 countries graduated from the programme. Notably, 54% of these graduates found blockchain-related employment during or immediately after their studies. The programme's success attracted international attention, and influential players within the blockchain ecosystem, such as Coinbase and Ripple, offered sponsorships to support its endeavors.

This chapter aims to shed light on this success story by presenting and analysing its evolution. The remainder of this chapter is structured as follows: Section 6.2 reports on the early years of the programme from conception to development and launch of the programme. Thereafter, Section 6.3 navigates through the first cycle of success followed by the revision of the programme and its big bang (Section 6.4). Section 6.5 analyses the future developments of the programme, while Section 6.6 presents lessons learnt and Section 6.7 gives the conclusions.

6.2 Episode I: Programme conception and launch

In 2012, UNIC members attempted to transfer Bitcoins from one country to another. Few minutes later they surprisingly observed that the Bitcoins arrived in Cyprus without the intervention of banks or other intermediaries.

At that time, sending and receiving Bitcoins was more difficult than today as there was a lack of advanced tools and knowledge. Additionally, there were only a few exchanges that facilitated the trade of cryptocurrencies or other crypto-financial transactions (e.g., Kraken, the first crypto exchange was established in mid-2011 (Holmes, 2018)). Furthermore, only a small number of people around the globe knew how to use it. Training and education were also scarce. People were able to find out how to use Bitcoin and blockchain through their participation in self-organised local community events (e.g., meetups) or by experimenting. The normative literature on this topic was limited, and there were only a small number of online resources available. Industry-led educational programmes on this area were also limited at that time. There were no academic courses on blockchain and cryptos. Clearly, there was a huge gap in this area and UNIC spotted the opportunity and recognised the importance of developing an academic programme to (a) assist people to learn how to use the technology and digital currency in practice and (b) support sourcing and widespread adoption of blockchain and cryptocurrency.

The UNIC Council discussed the proposal for the new MSc and, recognising that this disruptive technology can potentially have a considerable impact on society, public and businesses, it decided to invest time and resources in its development. The Business School (BuS) was considered as the most appropriate to host the programme. Since the plan was for the programme to be used as a vehicle for speeding up the adoption of blockchain and cryptocurrencies, it was decided that it should cover key business, financial, legal, regulatory, and technical aspects of blockchain. Initially, there was no interest from the BuS faculty but after a couple of meetings the school decided to undertake this task.

In November 2013, UNIC made two important announcements: (a) to develop and offer an MSc programme on digital currencies in English and (b) to accept Bitcoins as payment for tuition fees. As a result, it became the first University in the world to support payments in Bitcoins. A few weeks later, UNIC received its first Bitcoin from a student. To further promote the use of cryptos, UNIC offered a discount to all students paying with this type of currency.

On April 2, 2014, UNIC announced the launch of the first free MOOC on the introduction of digital currencies (Southhurst, 2014). The course started on May 15, 2014, and it was the first course of the MSc in Digital Currency. Due to public resistance to Bitcoin, cryptos, and blockchain at the time, the University decided not to name the programme "MSc in Blockchain and Cryptocurrency". Instead, a more generic name was adopted and finally the programme was launched as "MSc in Digital Currency".

6.3 Episode II: From small wins to success

The MSc programme in Digital Currency is structured in three semesters with a duration of 1.5 years and a total workload of 90 European Credit Transfer and Accumulation System (ECTS) points. During the first-year, students attend compulsory courses. In the last semester they select three electives or one elective and a master thesis/project. All courses have a workload of 10 ECTS except the master thesis/project, which totals 20 ECTS. Table 6.1 describes the structure of the MSc in Digital Currency.

> **Courses' evaluation**: Courses are evaluated through: (a) interactive activities, (b) individual and/or group assignments/projects, and (c) final written exams. Interactive activities cover (a) student-to-content, (b) student-to-student, and (c) student-to-instructor interactivity and assessment of learning objectives. These activities are assigned every session starting from session 1 to session 12 and use multiple types of

TABLE 6.1 The structure of the MSc in Digital Currency.

Type	Course	Semester	ECTS
Core	Introduction to Digital Currencies	1	10
Core	Money and Banking	1	10
Core	Regulation and Digital Currencies	1	10
Core	Principals of Disruptive Innovation	2	10
Core	Blockchain Technology and Applications	2	10
Core	Open Financial Systems	2	10
Elective	Emerging Topics and Practical Considerations in Blockchain	3	10
Elective	Cryptographic Systems Security	3	10
Elective	Digital Currency Programming	3	10
Elective	International Currency Markets	3	10
Elective	Digital Currencies in the Developing World	3	10
Elective	Financial Markets and Alternative Investments	3	10
Elective	Master Thesis	3	20
Elective	Master Project	3	20

interactivity such as quizzes, collaborative wikis, simulation, interactive learning games, hands-on activities, scenarios for problem-solving, and bringing students to real-life situations so that they can take decisions and study the consequences of their decisions.

Exams invigilation: Exams take place online and are invigilated using a specialised service called Proctorio (https://proctorio.com/), a tool that is used by more than 850 universities. Final exams are open book essay based and are available for a duration of 40 hours as students live in different time zones. Technology offered by Proctorio and practices adopted by the programme prevent cheating and preserve the integrity of both the exam content and UNIC. For each course a pool of exam questions has been created. Each pool consists of questions which are sorted by book chapter or lecture. During the exams a rule-based system creates an exam paper for each student by randomly selecting questions from the pool.

Learning Management System (LMS): Moodle LMS (moodle.org) is used to support courses delivery and it facilitates the sharing of course material and communication among instructors, teaching assistants and students. Each course has its own space on Moodle through which the teaching material, the schedule of the classes, and the interaction between students and teaching staff is facilitated. Teaching material including PowerPoint presentations with extended descriptions and explanations, asynchronous video presentations, additional readings (journal articles and/or e-books), access to additional videos and commercials related to the course, synchronous meetings (through Webex), forums, chats, case studies, interactive activities, and other formative and summative assessments are provided. For each week of delivery, the teaching material is released in advance and students are required to study it before the live session.

Live sessions take place every week through which instructors deliver their lecture and answer to students' questions. In many live sessions, invited speakers (experts in the field) present their own point of view and share their knowledge with the class. In some cases, there is a panel discussion during the live session in which two or more experts participate. Although live sessions are synchronous, they are video recorded and offered to students in an asynchronous mode too. This is very useful for the class as not all the students can attend the live sessions due to time zone differences.

Diplomas on blockchain: Students who graduate from the programme receive their diplomas in two formats. The first one is the traditional hard copy diploma that is given to students during the graduation ceremony. The second one refers to a digital certificate (diploma) that is anchored on the blockchain. The technology for the issuance of the blockchain-based diplomas was developed inhouse by the UNIC faculty using Bitcoin blockchain. See Chapter 7 for more details about academic certificates issued on blockchain by UNIC.

The strategic objectives, set in 2014, for the MSc in Digital Currency were to:

• educate as many people as possible around the world, to speed up blockchain and digital currency adoption and help graduates acquire and advance their competences. To promote this goal, it was decided to deliver the programme online (E-learning) instead of on-campus, as this would allow participants to enrol without relocating to Cyprus,

• overcome resistance to change and open a new avenue in business and computer science studies. Back in 2014, it was extremely difficult to persuade students to start an MSc in digital currency or blockchain, as most of them had their reservations. At the time, many people believed that blockchain and cryptocurrencies are only for computer nerds. Others had the perception that it was only for drug dealers, gamblers, or money launderers (Singh, 2015). To overcome this barrier UNIC decided to offer the first course of the MSc programme for free, not only for its MSc students but also to anybody who was interested in this area. The first course (MOOC) is literally open access and free. In addition, Andreas Antonopoulos, a Bitcoin enthusiast and best-selling author of the books "Mastering

Bitcoin" and "Mastering Ethereum" (Antonopoulos, 2014; Antonopoulos & Wood, 2018), agreed to co-teach this course as he shared UNIC's vision:

- be financially self-sustained in the sense that it does not generate a financial loss,
- use the revenue generated from the MSc programme to establish and run an institute dedicated to blockchain and cryptocurrency research.

The programme was launched in May 2014 and offers two student intake periods per annum, in Fall and Spring. During the first year of its operation participation was low but soon after UNIC saw a steady increase in the number of students and participants for both the MSc programme and the MOOC.

On June 30, 2016, the graduation of the first students was widely reported in the mass media and on specialist blockchain/crypto outlets (Bitcoin.com, 2016). As a result, the programme has attracted global attention and many people expressed their interest in enrolling. Soon the number of registered students significantly increased. Additionally, since 2016, blockchain and cryptocurrencies attracted a lot of interest. On the one hand, there was a high demand from enterprises; on the other hand, there was a shortage of people with blockchain-related skills (e.g., programmers, advisors, consultants). The launch of Ethereum, on July 30, 2015, with its enhanced functionality along with smart contracts and the evolution of decentralised applications (dApps), has significantly increased the need for employees and freelancers with relevant skills. Besides, in 2017, the euphoria due to the rising price of Bitcoin, along with the fact that UNIC accepts tuition fees in this currency, led some additional people to sign up for the programme.

The data clearly demonstrates that the programme achieved its initial goal, which was to generate interest on this field and educate as many people as possible. It is worth noting that, up to now, over 110,000 have attended the MOOC and more than 1,150 students have graduated from the MSc. The income generated from the MSc programme was re-invested in building a strong research team in blockchain. For that reason, UNIC established the Institute for the Future (IFF) as its main vehicle for scientific and applied research in blockchain and cryptocurrency (IFF, 2022). Faculty members who teach on the programme work together with dedicated teams of doctoral students, postdocs, and other researchers on various projects. Apart from EU-funded projects, IFF participates in applied research sponsored by organisations like Ripple, Stellar, Energy Web, etc., and has delivered high-quality research (e.g., Karamitsos et al., 2022; Christodoulou et al., 2022; Kapassa et al., 2021; Pressmair et al., 2021; Christodoulou et al., 2020). IFF is also the only academic member of the EU Blockchain Observatory and Forum (EUBOF), which is a European Commission initiative to accelerate block-chain innovation and the development of the blockchain ecosystem within the EU (EUBOF, 2022). UNIC has the role of the academic partner, recog-nised as a pioneer in studying blockchain in the context of higher education. The University of Nicosia assists the EUBOF in filling the gap that exists today between the supply of and demand for academic knowledge in block-chain. It has a crucial contribution to the project, providing know-how and experience in the field and working in close collaboration with other partners. In addition, IFF has recently signed a contract with the European Central Bank (ECB) for strategic consultation, training, and software development services on key emerging technologies, such as blockchain.

A survey about the employability and job descriptions of the students and alumni of the programme was conducted between 2018 and 2019. The data collected from 179 respondents revealed that programme graduates have the opportunities for employment in a variety of institutions, such as public and private organisations, including consulting, software companies, banking institutions, and start-ups. Figures 6.1 and 6.2 demonstrate the graduates' professions and the changes in their careers since the beginning of their studies at UNIC.

Clearly, the empirical data shows that the MSc programme has helped the graduates in advancing their careers, by being employed in fields where their studies are relevant. It appears that 54% of the programme graduates move to a blockchain-related field during their studies of immediately after. Those

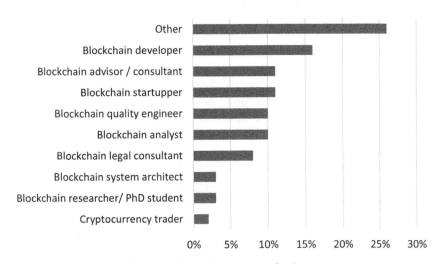

FIGURE 6.1   Students' and graduates' current profession.

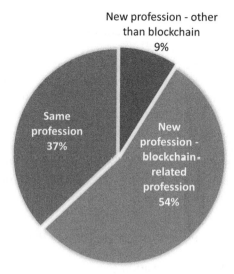

New profession - other
than blockchain
9%

Same
profession
37%

New
profession -
blockchain-
related
profession
54%

FIGURE 6.2   Changes in the profession since the beginning of the MSc in Blockchain and Digital Currency.

who have a blockchain-related profession work as cryptocurrency traders (2%), blockchain researchers/PhD student (3%), blockchain system architects (3%,) blockchain legal consultants (8%), blockchain analyst (10%), blockchain quality engineers (10%), blockchain startuppers (11%), blockchain advisors/consultants (11%), and blockchain developers (16%). The remaining 26% of respondents reported other profession within the blockchain and cryptocurrency space without specifying it.

6.4 Episode III: Continued improvements maintain success and protect competitive advantage

Blockchain technology is a rapidly changing field that has gone through different stages of evolution such as: (a) cryptocurrencies, (b) smart contracts, (c) decentralised applications, (d) interoperability and scalability, and (e) Central Bank Digital Currencies (CBDCs) and Non-Fungible Tokens (NFTs) (Cunha et al., 2021). The MSc in Digital Currency was introduced before the second stage of blockchain evolution (smart contracts). In 2018–2019 it was obvious that the programme should go through a redesign to update and upgrade its content and include new courses. As a result, UNIC decided to revise the content, introduce new topics, remove or merge courses, and, in general, create a new curriculum that will offer students enhanced and up-to-date knowledge. During this process, the latest developments in blockchain technology, as well as students' and faculty's feedback, were taken into consideration.

In November 2019, the revised programme was submitted to the Cyprus Agency of Quality Assurance and Accreditation in Higher Education (CYQAA) for accreditation along with an application for the establishment and accreditation of a new department that will run the new programme. The creation of the department of Digital Innovation was the result of an internal reform of the BuS. CYQAA appointed a panel of external experts from the United Kingdom, Austria, and Spain who evaluated the revised programme and department. In Fall 2020, and following the positive evaluation of the external experts, CYQAA accredited the:

- Conventional MSc programme of studies in Blockchain and Digital Currency,
- Department of Digital Innovation.

Furthermore, in May 2021 the new e-learning MSc in Blockchain and Digital Currency was also accredited, leading to its launch in Fall 2021–2022.

The new programme has a similar structure to the previous one and it consists of six compulsory courses offered during the first two semesters, followed by several electives. Each course has a workload of 10 ECTS, except for the MSc thesis that counts for 30 ECTS. Students who select the thesis option are allowed to complete their studies in one calendar year instead of one and a half. Table 6.2 shows the new structure of the MSc in Blockchain and Digital Currency. As shown in Table 6.2 and compared to Table 6.1, courses like (a) International Currency Markets, (b) Digital Currencies in the Developing World, and (c) Financial Markets and Alternative Investments were removed from the programme. They were replaced by a set of five more advanced electives, namely: (a) Token Economics, (b) Emerging Topics in Fintech, (c) Emerging Topics in Law and Regulation, (d) Smart Contract Programming, and (e) Permissioned Blockchain Programming. There was also a redesign of other existing courses to enrich their syllabus with cutting-edge topics. The revised programme is now offered in both conventional and e-learning modes of delivery.

The amendments to the course structure, syllabus, and programme name have been beneficial. They have led to an all-time high in terms of student enrolments for the online programme for the academic year 2021–2022. Additionally, a class of students signed up for the on-campus programme. Moreover, MOOC participants have significantly increased in numbers, to almost double, compared to the previous version. These numbers are

TABLE 6.2 The structure of the MSc in Blockchain and Digital Currency.

Type	Course	Semester	ECTS
Core	Blockchain and Digital Currency	1	10
Core	Blockchain Systems and Architectures	1	10
Core	Law and Regulation in Blockchain	1	10
Core	Emerging Topics in Blockchain and Digital Currency	2	10
Core	Blockchain and Entrepreneurship Management	2	10
Core	Principles of Money, Banking and Finance	2	10
Elective	Digital Currency Programming	3	10
Elective	Smart Contract Programming	3	10
Elective	Permissioned Blockchain Programming	3	10
Elective	Cryptographic Systems Security	3	10
Elective	Emerging Topics in Fintech	3	10
Elective	Emerging Topics in Law and Regulation	3	10
Elective	Token Economics	3	10
Elective	Open and Decentralised Financial Systems	3	10
Elective	Master Thesis	3	30

consistent in the Fall 2022–2023 intake period as well, with increased numbers of new MSc students for e-learning and on-campus programmes as well as MOOC participants.

In Fall 2021, the MSc in Digital Currency stopped its operation, and its students were transferred to the new MSc programme. The transition from the 2014 programme to the 2021 one was smooth, as there were clear rules in place for the transfer of credits (ECTS) and the mapping of courses among the two programmes.

Beside the improvements in terms of the programme, the Department of Digital Innovation decided to replace its tools for its online delivery. As a result, Webex was replaced by Engageli software (https://www.engageli.com/). From the students' evaluations it appears that students:

- like the content of the new courses and programme, which they find excellent,
- are impressed by the Engageli software, as it significantly increases inter-activity and improves the quality of delivery and interaction among students and teaching staff,
- many of the students who enrolled before the launch of the new programme expressed their interest in attending additional courses, as the new programme offers more advanced topics compared to its previous version.

6.5 Episode IV: Shaping the future

UNIC continuously stays tuned with the latest technological innovations, monitors state of the art technologies, and puts enormous effort in creating high-quality programmes for the benefit of the society and the economy. In this context, the Department of Digital Innovation developed a new MOOC course that focuses on Decentralized Finance (DeFi) and offered it for free in Fall 2021 (UNIC, 2021). Since then, the course has been repeated twice a year (Fall and Spring semesters) and has attracted a lot of interest. The data about student enrolment shows that 17,000 participants have attended the course so far.

In addition, in November 2021, UNIC announced its Open Metaverse Initiative (OMI) (OMI, 2021). One of the main goals of OMI is to introduce a new MSc programme in Metaverse. The Department of Digital Innovation prepared the application for this MSc programme and submitted it for accreditation to the CYQAA in October 2022. It is estimated that the new MSc in Metaverse will be accredited by Spring 2023 and launched in Fall 2023–2024. It is expected that this will be the first MSc programme about the metaverse in the world.

Similar to the MSc in Blockchain and Digital Currency, the first course of the MSc in Metaverse is offered as a free MOOC (UNIC, 2022). On September 26, 2022, the MOOC was launched in an innovative manner: it is offered on-chain and in the metaverse. The MOOC, entitled NFTs and the Metaverse, has been attended by 24,500 participants (Themistocleous et al., 2023).

6.6 Lessons learnt

In the previous sections, the case of the UNIC MSc in Blockchain and Digital Currency was reported and discussed. Based on the first-hand experience of designing and delivering the curriculum, combined with the analysis of the empirical data, a number of lessons learnt are derived and are reported below. These lessons learnt may be useful to other universities, blockchain organisations, researchers, and academics when designing or redesigning their programmes.

- **Lesson 1. Think Big**: "Think Big" is the motto of the University of Nicosia. The motto suggests that when someone thinks creatively and expansively, significant achievements or breakthroughs can occur. This approach encourages individuals to disregard existing boundaries and limitations and embrace a disruptive innovation approach. An interesting lesson that can be learned from this practice is the importance of thinking outside the box. By challenging conventional wisdom and exploring new possibilities, individuals and institutions can uncover innovative solutions and create something remarkable. The University of Nicosia exemplifies this mindset by not limiting its programs to local students. Instead, it designed and delivered an MSc (Master of Science) program that has the potential to attract students from all over the world. This strategy demonstrates a willingness to embrace diversity and openness, enabling the university to tap into a global pool of talent and perspectives. This practice was repeated in the case of the new MSc in Metaverse and its successful MOOC in NFTs and the Metaverse. It is worth noting that University of Nicosia is located in Cyprus, a small European country with a population of less than a million citizens.

- **Lesson 2. Be there, be on time, and be good**: The history of blockchain and cryptocurrencies does indeed suggest that being a first mover can often lead to greater success compared to latecomers. A notable example of this is Bitcoin, which is not only the first cryptocurrency but also the most prominent and widely recognized one. Its early entry into the market and the network effect it has established over time have contributed to its dominant position. Another example is Ethereum, which pioneered the concept of smart contracts and blockchain as a platform for decentralized applications. By being an early mover in this space, Ethereum has gained significant traction and has become a preferred platform for developers and projects looking to leverage blockchain technology. Similarly, the UNIC MSc in Blockchain and Digital Currency, as mentioned, positioned itself as a first mover in the field of academic education in this domain. By recognizing the emerging importance of blockchain and digital currencies and offering a high quality program dedicated to it, the UNIC MSc was able to fill a significant gap in the market. This early entry likely contributed to its success, as it attracted students who were eager to gain expertise and knowledge in this rapidly evolving field. Buntinx (2017) and NOWPayments (2020) support the claim that the UNIC MSc program has been recognized as the most successful program in this area. The early establishment of the program allowed it to establish a strong reputation, build a network of industry connections, and attract top students and professionals interested in blockchain and digital currencies.
- **Lesson 3. Seek growth**: The purpose of UNIC was not to offer another MSc programme to increase its income. The goal was to create an innovative programme to allow UNIC to grow and become one of the leading institutions in academia in this field. For that reason, UNIC reinvested the income generated by this programme to build a strong research institute on blockchain and other technologies of the Fourth Industrial

Revolution. In doing so, UNIC managed to create one of the biggest research teams in Blockchain and Digital Currency.

- **Lesson 4. Openness, scalability, and interoperability**: It appears that factors like accessibility, scalability, and interoperability were significant for the success of the programme. The e-learning mode of delivery enabled the programme to scale. The use of English language offered interoperability, while the use of MOOC supported the programme to educate tens of thousands of people. All these contributed to the success of the programme.

- **Lesson 5. Quality and continuous improvement**: The insights reported in this chapter demonstrate that programmes that deal with advanced technological fields like blockchain should be revised and upgraded every few years. As reported in the previous section, UNIC is looking forward to introducing new electives to the MSc just a year after the accreditation of the second edition of the programme. This indicates that programmes that focus on fast evolving technologies should have a mechanism for continuous improvement. This resembles a business process improvement scenario, where every 1–2 years there are small improvements to the process followed by a bigger business process reengineering every 3–5 years.

- **Lesson 6. Be generous**: The generous sponsorships provided by UNIC to students pursuing the MSc in Blockchain and Digital Currency are a crucial success factor. The annual sponsorship amount of 300,000€ demonstrates the university's commitment to supporting students in this field. By offering sponsorships, UNIC enabled many talented students to access higher education and continue their studies in blockchain and digital currency. This is particularly significant for students from less-developed countries who may face financial difficulties in pursuing advanced degrees. The sponsorships provided them with the opportunity to gain specialized knowledge and skills in this emerging field. The impact of these sponsorships extends beyond education. Graduates who received the sponsorship were not only able to study from their home countries but also went on to establish their own businesses after graduation. This demonstrates the practical application of their education and the empowerment they received through the MSc program. Furthermore, these successful graduates acted as role models and ambassadors for blockchain adoption. Through their achievements and entrepreneurial endeavors, they inspired others to follow in their footsteps. By promoting and advocating for blockchain technology, they contributed to its wider adoption and dissemination.

- **Lesson 7. Involve practitioners**: Having a close collaboration with the industry is indeed crucial in a rapidly evolving field like blockchain. UNIC's experience highlights the significance of involving practitioners in the educational process to enhance the learning experience for students. By inviting industry practitioners as guest speakers and co-tutors, UNIC provides its students with valuable insights from professionals who have hands-on experience in the field. These practitioners can share their expertise, practical knowledge, and real-world examples, which enriches the academic curriculum and provides students with a more comprehensive understanding of blockchain. The involvement of well-established industry experts as guest lecturers or panel participants during live sessions of the MSc courses is highly appreciated by the students. It allows them to learn from industry leaders who are at the forefront of blockchain developments. This collaboration helps bridge the gap between theory and practice, enabling students to see the practical applications of the concepts they learn in class. Additionally, industry experts' participation in panel discussions and live sessions offers students an opportunity to ask questions, engage in discussions, and gain insights into the current trends, challenges, and opportunities in the blockchain industry. It also allows students to network and build connections with professionals in the field, which can be valuable for their future career prospects.

6.7 Conclusions

The University of Nicosia's launch of the first MSc program in Blockchain and Digital Currency in 2014 marked a groundbreaking moment in the field. This program quickly gained worldwide recognition as the most successful MSc in this domain, and its success can be attributed to several key factors. Firstly, the university's systematic and continuous improvement strategy played a crucial role. By consistently reviewing and refining the program, UNIC ensured that it stayed at the forefront of blockchain education. This proactive approach allowed UNIC to adapt to the rapidly evolving nature of the technology and provide students with the most up-to-date knowledge and skills.

Moreover, UNIC made breakthrough decisions that contributed to the program's success. By focusing on growth rather than profit, the university demonstrated an innovative and forward-thinking mindset. Their goal was not just to educate a limited number of students but to contribute to the widespread adoption of blockchain technology and educate a global audience. The program's scalability and interoperability were also key factors in its success. UNIC designed a program that could accommodate a large number of participants from diverse backgrounds and geographical locations. This approach enabled them to educate over 110,000 participants from 120 countries, transcending traditional boundaries and making a global impact.

The continuous improvement of the program, both in terms of the syllabus and the tools used for delivery, ensured that students received a high-quality and relevant education. UNIC's commitment to staying abreast of industry advancements and incorporating them into the curriculum helped produce well-rounded graduates with a comprehensive understanding of blockchain technology. Lastly, UNIC's social responsibility and generosity in offering sponsorships to students showcased their commitment to making education accessible. By providing financial support to deserving students, including those from less-developed countries, the university demonstrated its dedication to empowering individuals and promoting equal opportunities in blockchain education.

Overall, the success of the University of Nicosia's MSc programme in Blockchain and Digital Currency can be attributed to its breakthrough innovation in education, out-of-the-box thinking focused on growth and impact, continuous improvement, and social responsibility. It showcases that, regardless of size or location, an institution can become a global leader by addressing emerging needs, embracing innovation, and prioritizing the betterment of society.

References

Antonopoulos, A. (2014). *Mastering Bitcoin: Unlocking Digital Cryptocurrencies.* Newton, MA: O'Reilly Media.

Antonopoulos, A., & Wood, G. (2018). *Mastering Ethereum: Building Smart Contracts and dApps.* Newton, MA: O'Reilly Media, Inc.

Bitcoin.com. (2016). *Students Graduate from First Ever Blockchain Master's Program.* Retrieved Jan. 27, 2023 from: https://news.bitcoin.com/students-graduate-blockchain-masters/

Buntinx, J. P. (2017). *Top 5 University Bitcoin Courses.* Retrieved Jan. 12, 2023, from: https://themerkle.com/top-5-university-Bitcoin-courses/

Christodoulou, C., Katelaris, L., Themistocleous, M., Christoudoulou, P., & Iosif, E. (2022). NFTs and the Metaverse Revolution: Research Perspectives and Open Challenges. In M. Lacity, H. Treiblmaier (Eds.), *Blockchains and the Token Economy: Theory and Practice* (pp. 139–178) Cham: Palgrave Macmillan.

Christodoulou, K., Iosif, E., Inglezakis, A., & Themistocleous, M. (2020). Consensus crash testing: Exploring ripple's decentralization degree in adversarial environments. *Future Internet, 12*(3), 53.

Cunha, P. R., Soja, P., & Themistocleous, M. (2021). Blockchain for development: A guiding framework. *Information Technology for Development, 27*(3), 417–438.

EUBOF. (2022). *EU Blockchain Observatory & Forum.* Retrieved Oct. 22, 2022, from: https://www.euBlockchainforum.eu/

Holmes, J. (2018). Kraken: An overview of one of Europe's top Bitcoin exchanges. *Bitcoin Magazine.* Retrieved Oct. 16, 2018, from: https://Bitcoinmagazine.com/reviews/kraken-overview-one-europes-top-Bitcoin-exchanges

IFF. (2022). *UNIC Institute for the Future*. Retrieved Jul. 19, 2022, from: https://www.unic.ac.cy/iff/

Kapassa, E., Themistocleous, M., Christodoulou, K., & Iosif, E. (2021). Blockchain application in internet of vehicles: Challenges, contributions and current limitations. *Future Internet, 13*(12), 313.

Karamitsos, I., Papadaki, M., & Themistocleous, M. (2022). Blockchain as a service (BCaaS): A value modeling approach in the education business model. *Journal of Software Engineering and Applications, 15*(5), 165–182.

Nakamoto, S. (2008). *Bitcoin: A Peer-to-Peer Electronic Cash System*. Retrieved Jul. 11, 2013, from: https://bitcoin.org/bitcoin.pdf.

NOWPayments. (2020). *Top 5 Universities Offering Courses in Blockchain in 2020*. Retrieved Jan. 18, 2023, from: https://www.unic.ac.cy/top-5-universities-offering-courses-in-blockchain-in-2020-4/

OMI. (2021). *The UNIC Open Metaverse Initiative*. Retrieved Aug. 22, 2022, from: https://www.unic.ac.cy/openmetaverse/

Pressmair, G., Kapassa, E., Casado-Mansilla, D., Borges, C., Themistocleous, M. (2021). Overcoming barriers for the adoption of local energy and flexibility markets: A user-centric and hybrid model. *Journal of Cleaner Production, 317*(2021), 128323.

Singh, K. (2015). The new wild west: Preventing money laundering in the bitcoin network. *Northwestern Journal of Technology and Intellectual Property, 13*(1), 37–64.

Southhurst, J. (2014). *University of Nicosia Launches Free 'Introduction to Digital Currencies' Online Course*. Retrieved Mar. 12, 2015, from: https://www.coindesk.com/markets/2014/04/02/university-of-nicosia-launches-free-introduction-to-digital-currencies-online-course/

Themistocleous, M., Christodoulou, K., Iosif, E., Louca, S., & Tseas, D. (2020). Blockchain in Academia: Where do we Stand and Where Do We Go? In *Proceedings of the Fifty-third Annual Hawaii International Conference on System Sciences (HICSS 53)*, January 7–10, 2020. Maui, Hawaii, USA (pp. 5338–5347). Los Alamitos, CA: IEEE Computer Society.

Themistocleous, M., Christodoulou, K., & Katelaris, L. (2023). An Educational Metaverse Experiment: The First On-Chain and In-Metaverse Academic Course. In Papadaki, M., Rupino da Cunha, P., Themistocleous, M., & Christodoulou, K. (Eds.), *Information Systems. EMCIS 2022. Lecture Notes in Business Information Processing*, vol. 464 (pp. 678–690). Cham: Springer.

UNIC. (2021). *Free DeFi MOOC*. Retrieved Sept. 26, 2022, from: https://www.unic.ac.cy/Blockchain/free-defi-mooc/

UNIC. (2022). *NFTs and the Metaverse*. Retrieved Sept. 26, 2022, from: https://www.unic.ac.cy/openmetaverse/mooc-nfts-metaverse/

7

ACADEMIC CERTIFICATES ISSUED ON BLOCKCHAIN

The case of the University of Nicosia and Block.co

Marinos Themistocleous, Klitos Christodoulou and Elias Iosif

7.1 Introduction

Certificates are highly beneficial and used by a wide array of individuals and entities in the public and private sectors alike. Millions of certificates are issued daily for various purposes like birth certificates, divorce decrees, vaccination status (e.g., COVID-19), and professional licences (Papadaki et al., 2021; Karamitsos et al., 2022).

Their importance is profound for individuals and organisations relying on them (Earle, 2010). Certificates are issued by trusted third parties known as Certificate Authorities (CAs) like government agencies, educational institutions, and private companies (Boiral, 2012). They are utilised for a variety of reasons such as to: (a) prove ownership of property and vehicles, (b) verify one's identity in situations where there is doubt (e.g., passport) or (c) prove eligibility for government benefits such as unemployment insurance (Capece et al., 2020). They also help protect against identity theft and fraud by providing a way to verify that documents have not been tampered with in any way. Certificates are the foundation for many aspects of our daily lives, from opening a bank account to buying a house or car and without them the world would be a chaotic mess.

A common type of certificate is an academic degree which proves that an individual has met all the requirements for graduating from a particular school or programme (Castro & Au-Yong-Oliveira, 2021). The holders of academic diplomas can demonstrate to their potential employers that they have been properly vetted and they have the qualifications for the job they

DOI: 10.4324/9781003318736-8

are applying for. It is important for organisations to be able to trust these documents (Capece et al., 2020). If certificates are not trusted, then there are serious consequences for those who rely on their validity and accuracy to function properly.

Due to their importance, certificates are often stolen or counterfeited. If a certificate is compromised, it can result in economic harm to the owner of the certificate and may have serious consequences for society as well (Castro & Au-Yong-Oliveira, 2021). There are different ways that certificates can be compromised including forgery of the digital signature on them. In other cases, dishonest individuals can create fake diplomas or certificates to use them for illegal purposes (Sayed, 2019). There are several ways to create a fake academic degree or any other kind of certificate. In particular, someone can use an image editing software to manipulate an existing certificate into something new. It is also possible to find old diplomas online and modify them using the same methods. In addition, there are websites that offer the option to create fake academic diplomas. Although most of them were developed for fun, there are people who use them to create fake certificates to obtain jobs that require a certain level of education but they do not have it. The advanced technology that is used to produce these fake diplomas makes it very difficult for people who are not experts in this field to determine whether a diploma is real or fake. For that reason, there is a need for more advanced certificate issuance techniques that will assure that their results (diplomas) are authentic. These methods should also provide an easy to verify mechanism that ensures the recipient of a digital diploma about its authenticity (Capece et al., 2020).

In this chapter, we explore the case of Block.co, the University of Nicosia, Cyprus (UNIC) spinoff that focuses on providing solutions to the above-mentioned problem by issuing digital certificates that are anchored on the blockchain and are verifiable in an easy and user-friendly way. The remainder of this chapter is structured as follows: in Section 7.2 the limitations of the existing centralised certificate issuance systems are presented and analysed followed by the solutions that blockchain technology can offer in this area. The next section presents the case of Block.co and the chapter closes with lessons learnt and conclusions.

7.2 Limitations of the existing centralised systems for the issuance of diplomas

The traditional centralised practices for the issuance of certificates have many limitations, and the current certificate authority model is often not transparent. There are many cases where the people who operate these CA services make arbitrary decisions about what certificates they issue or the sources they trust. This leads to a lack of accountability and can be problematic if anyone of these entities decides to abuse their power or collude with an attacker. In addition, CAs are prone to fraud and manipulation as a result of their centralised nature. The process of issuing certificates is slow, cost inefficient and not very transparent (Sayed, 2019). The process of managing certificates is also inefficient, complex and lengthy, and often requires manual intervention by third parties. It also involves substantial paperwork, which makes it difficult to ensure that processes are being followed correctly.

The issuance of certificates by a centralised authority points to a single point of failure. This makes the system vulnerable and can lead to security breaches. The lack of transparency and trust for these systems also means that users have no way of verifying how their data is being used or what it is being used for. According to breach-level-index (www.breachlevelindex. org), a database that can be used for identifying cases of data breaches, data records are lost or stolen at a very high frequency. It is estimated that 2,262,217,440 records are lost/stolen per annum as illustrated below:

- Every day: 6,197,856
- Every hour: 258,244
- Every minute: 4,304

The increasing number of fake certificates is another significant issue that causes enormous problems to organisations and society (Sayed, 2019). From time to time there are breaking news reporting people who work in critical positions or services without the right qualifications and put the lives of innocent people in danger. An example is the case of a conwoman who worked for 22 years in the British National Health System (NHS) with fake degrees (Greenfield, 2018). Clearly, that lady put in danger the lives of thousands of patients and led NHS to review the records of 3,000 staff members.

The increasing volume of fake certificates along with the enormous number of stolen or lost records signify the need for change to embrace advanced technologies like blockchain that can help us to overcome these problems.

7.3 Blockchain meets the potential

In October 2008, Satoshi Nakamoto, the inventor of Bitcoin, introduced an innovative way to publish data on an open source, distributed ledger that supports the sharing of trusted, immutable data across a decentralised network (Nakamoto, 2008). Blockchain stores data in a series of tamper-proof blocks where blocks are added to a chain in a linear, chronological order with each of them containing a timestamp, a link to the previous block, and a series of transactions (Antonopoulos, 2014).

Blockchain creates trust in two ways. First, it establishes trust between parties that may not otherwise trust each other (Touloupou et al., 2022a). Second, it creates a system of record that is immutable and unchangeable by design (Touloupou et al., 2022b). As a result, blockchain allows users to create unchangeable transactions without relying on any single authority or third party such as universities, banks, or governments. In doing so, blockchain has revolutionised the way we think about trust.

In terms of the issuance of certificates, distributed ledger technologies can be considered as suitable solutions for education as they provide a secure and reliable way to store and share records of academic achievement (MIT Media Lab, 2016; Capece et al., 2020; Castro & Au-Yong-Oliveira, 2021). Blockchain also eliminates the need for third-party verifiers, such as government agencies or professional associations, which often charge high fees for their services.

The University of Nicosia became the first university to recognise the importance of blockchain technology in issuing and verifying digital certificates (Wong, 2014). In 2015, UNIC issued the first academic digital diplomas on Bitcoin blockchain to help prevent fraud in the issuance of certificates. In doing so, UNIC demonstrated that blockchain technology can enable students, faculty, and staff to share their diplomas with anyone in the world in a friendly and usable manner without the intervention of an intermediate or a government agency.

Since then, many other universities have followed suit such as MIT in 2016 with Blockcerts, its own solution (https://www.blockcerts.org/) and the British University in Dubai, in 2018 that adopted UNIC solution (Jones, 2017; MIT Lab, 2016). In January 2022, European Union (EU) adopted an initiative that aims to support more than 60 European universities to issue their certificates using the European Blockchain Services Infrastructure (EBSI) (Erudera News, 2022). EBSI is meant as a horizontal infrastructure enabling the utilisation of blockchain power at the EU level across different domains spanning from public entities to businesses ant their respective networks/ecosystems including citizens.

7.4 The case of Block.co: Issuing, validating and revoking certificates on blockchain

7.4.1 Block.co – The current solution

For the purpose of this chapter, we conducted interviews with key players at UNIC and Block.co, UNIC's spin off that runs the issuance of blockchain certificates. Due to confidentiality reasons, we refer to those players using the coded names interviewee A, B, or C. The participants hold different positions and have had an active role in the analysis, design, development, maintenance, and management of the solution.

The University of Nicosia is a pioneer in blockchain education and research with a mission to empower the global blockchain community through innovative educational programmes, support sourcing, and spread its adoption. In 2013, UNIC begun its journey in this area and a year later it launched the first MSc programme in blockchain and digital currency in the world (Themistocleous et al., 2020; Cunha et al., 2021). UNIC continued to innovate and in 2015 it developed an in-house solution to anchor the university's diplomas on the blockchain. That was the first-of-its-kind achievement and a major step towards the future of education. In 2017, UNIC achieved another important goal by publishing all university diplomas on the blockchain. Since 2017, all UNIC diplomas are issued in both traditional hard copy and blockchain-enabled digital formats.

To better understand the background behind the development of such a solution, we asked interviewee A to explain the reasoning and the series of events that took place. Interviewee A reported the following:

For us it was like being in the early 90s where we started researching and teaching Internet but we had not built a solution to demonstrate its usage. At that time, we had a theoretical understanding but not a good practical experience. It was like talking about e-business and the things we can do with Internet but without having deployed a web server or developed a web application. We wanted to enhance our practical knowledge as it is one thing to teach a topic that you read in a book and another thing to combine your practical, theoretical and research experience and share it with your students. So, our goal was to get a better understanding of the blockchain technology and how it works. For us it was important to understand how to build a blockchain solution on Bitcoin protocol and explore how to integrate it into a web application that will allow others to use it. We also wanted to implement a solution that is relevant to our core business; a solution that can be used by our students. And of course, the result was to build a blockchain application for the issuance of UNIC certificates on Bitcoin blockchain.

In further exploring this case, we requested from Interviewee B to explain the whole process and describe its main stages. According to Interviewee B, the solution has three distinct phases: certificates issuance, validation, and revocation as these are depicted in Figure 7.1 and described in the following paragraphs.

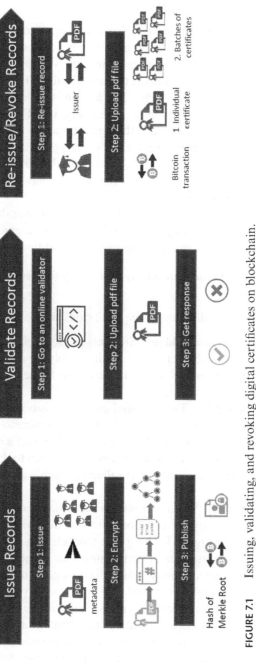

FIGURE 7.1   Issuing, validating, and revoking digital certificates on blockchain.

Issue records. The process begins with the issuance of the certificates which is done in the following ways:

- **Step 1: Issue**. A digital replica of a hard copy certificate issued by UNIC is created in the pdf format. Like the hard copy diploma, the pdf version includes data such as student name, surname, year of graduation, issue date, degree name, etc. In addition to these, the digital certificate contains metadata (related to the respective blockchain issuance itself such as the issuing address). Using the UNIC private key, UNIC signs the contents of the digital certificate and adds the signature to the diploma.
- **Step 2: Encrypt**. Then using the SHA-256 encryption algorithm (Christodoulou et al., 2020; Antonopoulos, 2014), a hash is created for the document. The hash is used to confirm that no one has tampered with the content of the digital diploma.
- **Step 3: Publish**. The UNIC private key is used to anchor the certificate on the blockchain. In this way, the digital diploma of a graduate is issued/published on the blockchain at a specific date and time.

The above-described procedure allows us to verify the issuer and validate the certificate content.

Validate records. The validation of the certificates takes place in an easy way:

- **Step 1: Go to an online validator**. Students receive their digital certificates electronically (as a pdf file) and when they apply for a job position or in any other case, they submit the digital certificate to the potential employer or corresponding organisation.
- **Step 2: Upload pdf file**. The potential employer visits the site of block.co and drags and drops the digital certificate to the online validator.
- **Step 3: Get response**. Then block.co reports whether this is a true copy or a fake degree. In the first version of the system, validation took place manually but later Block.co created the online validator which is an easy-to-use tool.

Re-issue/revoke records. When it comes to the issuance of certificates using blockchain technology, the question is how we deal with their revocation. Many people have argued for long that blockchain is not an appropriate technology for the issuance of certificates. This is because blockchain is designed around immutability, which means once data has been written onto a chain it cannot be changed. This can lead to problems, especially if the issuing authority decides to revoke a certificate later. For instance, a female student may decide to change her surname after the graduation because of a marriage, divorce, or for any other reason. To overcome this limitation UNIC designed and implemented the following simple solution:

- **Step 1: Re-issue record**. A new transaction is recorded on the blockchain reporting that a specific certificate will be amended.
- **Step 2: Upload pdf file**. The revised certificate is issued and anchored on the blockchain.

7.4.2 Block.co – Moving forward

In 2019, UNIC established a spin-off company under the name Block.co (www.block.co) to extend and commercialise the idea of blockchain-based self-verifiable certificates. As a result, Block.co was launched to further advance this concept. Due to its revocation feature, Block.co promotes its solution as "the only one decentralised revocation in the world".

One of the first actions of Block.co was to offer its solution in the form of Software as a Service (SaaS) product and platform. Then Block.co decided to move to Litecoin to monitor the transaction cost. The solution was further extended in a way that it can be used by organisations that issue any kind of certificates like degrees or legal documents (e.g., contracts, marriage certificate, driving licences, shipping documents). For shipping only, the company provides 19 different types of certificates (for each role/responsibility, e.g., first aid, firefighting).

With the rapid rise of the Non-Fungible Tokens (NFTs) (Christodoulou et al., 2022), Block.co has moved to the issuance of NFTs certificates on Ethereum and Polygon networks. During the last few months, Block.co further extended its solution and moved into the area of Soul-Bound-Tokens (SBT), a new classification of NFTs introduced by the Ethereum co-founder Vitalik Buterin, Puja Ohlhaver, and Eric Glen Weyl in May 2022 (Sergeenkov, 2022; Weyl et al., 2022). An SBT is a classification of tokens that aims to overcome existing problems in the tokens market related to digital identification. For instance, existing NFTs can be traded, but they are not tied with a particular organisation or individual.

Soul-bound NFTs refer to tokens that are non-transferable. They do not have monetary value and cannot be bought or sold. This kind of NFTs can be issued by organisations or individuals upon the completion of an achievement (e.g., studies). For that reason, Block.co adopts this new practice and has become the first organisation to issue SBT NFTs in academia.

We asked the interviewee C to explain the process and he reported the following:

- The issuing organisation gains access to Block.co platform and drags and drops any number of documents in jpg, png, jif, and 3D formats. In doing so, the issuing organisation publishes the SBT NFT certificate and sends it to the user (student/graduate) by a message.

- An email or text message is sent to the user to claim the certificate. The message includes a link that diverts to a page where the NFT is minted. Alternatively, the user can claim it through a QR scan.
- The user creates a wallet and adds the soul-bound NFT certificate to his/her wallet. In case the user has a crypto wallet, Block.co sends the SBT NFT certificate to the wallet directly.
- There is a smart contract for each collection of certificates in which the issuer specifies the number of NFTs that are part of that collection (e.g., the collection Graduation MSc diplomas for the class Blockchain and Digital Currency, 2022, includes 146 NFTs diplomas).
- The verification is done through Etherscan (an online service which can be used for accessing analytics about a number of Ethereum networks)
- Users can exhibit their NFTs certificates and potential employer can have a look to the NFT and then visit Etherscan (Antonopoulos & Wood, 2018) to verify that this is a valid one.
- In case a user loses access to his/her wallet there is a process for burning the NFT and reminting from the image in Inter-Planetary File System – IPFS (a distributed system for storing and accessing files).

It appears that Block.co responds to the latest technological evolutions in blockchain and tokens areas. As reported by interviewee C the updated process allows Block.co to adopt NFTs and SBTs and we expect that such move will offer it a competitive advantage as its product clearly differentiates from the other vendors.

7.5 Lessons learnt

Based on the case presented in this chapter a number of lessons learnt are presented below.

- **Lesson 1. The future of the certificates' issuance is decentralised**: As it is reported in Section 7.2, existing centralised certificate issuance systems are vulnerable and lead to security breaches. As a result, the number of records that are stolen/lost annually is extremely high. In addition, fake diplomas are easy to be produced and difficult to be traced which lead to significant trust issues. The use of blockchain technology supports organisations to overcome these problems as it provides a trusted and transparent solution where certificates are recorded on a distributed ledger. The issuance of blockchain-based academic certificates was first introduced in 2015 and since then a number of universities have adopted it so far. Currently, European Union is pushing towards that direction too and it is expected that in the next coming years we will have many organisations that will move towards the issuance of blockchain-based certifications.

- **Lesson 2. Revocation of blockchain-based certificates is feasible**: In very specific cases certificates that are anchored on a blockchain can be revoked. Although, for quite some time, there was a long debate about this topic, it was proved that certificates can be revoked without deleting data from the blockchain. The process is easy to be followed, secure and transparent. Recent data demonstrate that the Block.co solution is not the only one that achieves this result. Other solutions like the MIT application Blockcerts.com permits the revocation of the certificates. Revocation allows certificate issuers to "amend" specific data on a blockchain by issuing two new transactions: (a) the first informs the blockchain that there will be a change of a specific transaction and (b) the second writes the "revised" data in the blockchain ledger. Of course, revocation takes place only under very specific circumstances based on well-defined rules (e.g., surname change in case of a marriage, divorce).

- **Lesson 3. Soul-Bound-Tokens will drive future developments in decentralised certificates**: As mentioned in the previous session, Soul-Bound-Tokens represent a new generation of tokens that have no monetary value and they cannot be transferred, bought or sold. SBTs are tied with an identity and are given under the accomplishment of an achievement (e.g., graduation). The Block.co case demonstrates that these new type of tokens can be used for the certificates' issuance. We expect that in the future a series of non-transferable certificates like birth certificates, educational degrees, driving or professional licences, marriage or divorce decrees, and identification documents (passports, ids) will be issued as SBTs and stored in a digital wallet. This will result in a more secure, trusted, reliable and transparent future that will bring significant benefits to public and private domains.

7.6 Conclusions

High volumes of certificates are issued daily for various reasons with many private and public organisations relying on their use. Due to their importance, many people attempt to use them in an illegal way. As a result, more than 2.2 billion records are stolen or lost annually. There are also many others who generate and use fake diplomas. In addition to these, the verification of traditional certificates is a costly and time consuming task that requires a certain level of expertise. Given the fast pace of technological advancements it is difficult to validate traditional certificates. The normative literature and the press reported many cases of employees who got a job using fake diplomas and many of them served in critical areas like healthcare, shipping, transportation, and aviation putting human lives in danger.

A response to this problem comes from the area of blockchain technology. Blockchain was initially evolved to offer a new decentralised, transparent, immutable, and trusted way to overcome existing problems (e.g., double spending) and to introduce new ways of doing business. This technology can be used in many different ways for both the public and private domains. In this chapter we explored the case of the issuance, validation and revocation of blockchain-based digital certificates and we shed light to the case of the University of Nicosia and its spin-off Block.co. UNIC recognised the importance of blockchain and in 2015 broke ground by issuing the first blockchain-enabled academic certificates in the world. Since 2017 it has published all its academic certificates on the blockchain using its own application that offers a secure, trusted and transparent way to issue and validate certifications on blockchain. Its solution supports the certificates revocation of certificates, a very important function which permits under very specific circumstances the amendment of a certificate. In 2019, UNIC established Block.co, its spin-off company, to further disseminate, commercialise and enhance its solution. Since then, Block.co has followed the blockchain evolution and has upgraded its solution accordingly. The application initially operated in Bitcoin protocol and later moved to Litecoin to monitor cost. Block.co now offers certificates in the form of NFTs and extended its application to offer solutions on Ethereum and Polygon blockchains. The new developments in the area of NFTs and SBTs have led the company to upgrade its solution to issue, validate and revoke certificates in the form of SBT NFTs, a first-of-its-kind achievement. Clearly, the case of Block.co demonstrates a successful case where academic research and innovation has resulted in outputs that improve the quality of services, at a lower cost and in less time. Block.co is fast responding to the latest technological innovation and it now offers its products not only to academia but also to many other sectors.

Furthermore, the overall NFTs (and any derived tokens) model can be generalised by considering NFTs multimedia objects. This view 'enables the tokenisation' of (literally) any digital object going beyond the traditional modalities of text and images. Consider such a generalised NFT supporting other modalities like audio and speech as well as haptic signals. Specifically, for the case of verifiable certificates this consideration enables the incorporation of additional features and advanced functionality. This can advance the current state-of-the-art across different dimensions: from the enhancement of the uniqueness of NFTs to the further customisation. For certificates, this can be translated, among others, to increased security as well as user experience.

References

Antonopoulos, A. (2014). *Mastering Bitcoin: Unlocking Digital Cryptocurrencies*. Newton, MA: O'Reilly Media.

Antonopoulos, A., & Wood, G. (2018). *Mastering Ethereum: Building Smart Contracts and dApps*. Newton, MA: O'Reilly Media, Inc.

Boiral, O. (2012). ISO certificates as organizational degrees? Beyond the rational myths of the certification process. *Organisational Studies, 33*(5–6), 633–654.

Capece, G., Levialdi Ghiron, N., & Pasquale, F. (2020). Blockchain technology: Redefining trust for digital certificates. *Sustainability, 12*, 8952.

Castro, R. Q., & Au-Yong-Oliveira, M. (2021). Blockchain and higher education diplomas. *European Journal of Investigation in Health, Psychology and Education, 11*(1), 154–167.

Christodoulou, C., Katelaris, L., Themistocleous, M., Christoudoulou P., & Iosif E. (2022). NFTs and the Metaverse Revolution: Research Perspectives and Open Challenges. In M. Lacity, H. Treiblmaier (Eds.), *Blockchains and the Token Economy: Theory and Practice* (pp. 139–178) Cham: Palgrave Macmillan.

Christodoulou, K., Iosif, E., Inglezakis, A., & Themistocleous, M. (2020). Consensus crash testing: Exploring ripple's decentralization degree in adversarial environments. *Future Internet, 12*(3), 53.

Cunha, P. R., Soja, P., & Themistocleous, M. (2021). Blockchain for development: A guiding framework. *Information Technology for Development, 27*(3), 417–438.

Earle, D. (2010). *Benefits of Tertiary Certificates and Diplomas: Exploring Economic and Social Outcomes*. Wellington, New Zealand: Ministry of Education.

Erudera News, (2022). *EU to Expand 60 Universities with over 500 HE Institutions by Mid-2024*. Retrieved Jan. 16, 2023, from: https://erudera.com/news/eu-to-expand-60-universities-with-over-500-he-institutions-by-mid-2024/

Greenfield, P. (2018). *Fake Psychiatrist Case Puts Thousands of Doctors under Scrutiny*. Retrieved Jan. 16, 2023, from: https://www.theguardian.com/uk-news/2018/nov/19/thousands-of-doctors-under-scrutiny-after-fake-qualifications-case

Jones, B. (2017). *MIT Has Started Issuing Diplomas Using Blockchain Technology, Futurism*. Retrieved Jan. 16, 2023, from: https://futurism.com/mit-has-started-issuing-diplomas-using-blockchain-technology

Karamitsos, I., Papadaki, M., & Themistocleous, M. (2022). Blockchain as a service (BCaaS): A value modeling approach in the education business model. *Journal of Software Engineering and Applications, 15*(5), 165–182.

MIT Media Lab (2016). What we learned from designing an academic certificates system on the blockchain. *Medium*. Retrieved Jan. 16, 2023, from: https://medium.com/mit-media-lab/what-we-learned-from-designing-an-academic-certificates-system-on-the-blockchain-34ba5874f196#.4m4bmwcm0

Nakamoto, S. (2008). *Bitcoin: A Peer-to-Peer Electronic Cash System*. Retrieved Jul. 11, 2013, from: https://bitcoin.org/bitcoin.pdf

Papadaki, M., Karamitsos, I., & Themistocleous, M., (2021). Covid-19 digital test certificates and blockchain. *Journal of Enterprise Information Management, 34*(4), 993–1003.

Sayed, R. H. (2019). *Potential of Blockchain Technology to Solve Fake Diploma Problem*. University of Jyväskylä. Retrieved Jan. 16, 2023, from: https://jyx.jyu.fi/handle/123456789/64817

Sergeenkov, A. (2022). *What Are Soulbound Tokens? The Non-Transferrable NFT Explained.* Retrieved Jan. 16, 2023, from: https://www.coindesk.com/learn/what-are-soulbound-tokens-the-non-transferrable-nft-explained/

Themistocleous, M., Christodoulou, K., Iosif, E., Louca, S., & Tseas, D. (2020). Blockchain in Academia: Where Do We Stand and Where Do We Go? In *Proceedings of the Fifty-third Annual Hawaii International Conference on System Sciences (HICSS 53)*, Jan. 7–10, 2020. Maui, Hawaii, USA (pp. 5338–5347) Los Alamitos, CA: IEEE Computer Society.

Touloupou, M., Themistocleous, M, Iosif E., & Christodoulou, K. (2022a). A systematic literature review towards a blockchain benchmarking framework. *IEEE Access*, 10, 7630–7644.

Touloupou, M., Christodoulou, K., Inglezakis, A., Iosif, E., & Themistocleous, M. (2022b). Benchmarking Blockchains: The Case of XRP Ledger and Beyond. In *Proceedings of the 55th Hawaii International Conference on System Sciences. (HICSS 55)*, January 4-7, 2022. Maui, Hawaii, USA, Los Alamitos, CA: IEEE Computer Society. Retrieved Jan. 16, 2023, from: https://scholarspace.manoa.hawaii.edu/bitstream/10125/80070/0586.pdf

Weyl, E. G., Ohlhaver, P., & Buterin, V. (2022). Decentralized society: Finding Web3's soul. Available at SSRN 4105763.

Wong, J. (2014). *University of Nicosia Issues Block-Chain Verified Certificates.* Retrieved Jan. 16, 2023, from: https://www.coindesk.com/markets/2014/09/16/university-of-nicosia-issues-block-chain-verified-certificates/

8

BLOCKCHAIN'S IMPACT ON EDUCATION

Current landscape and prospects for the future

Dariusz Dymek and Janusz Stal

8.1 Introduction

New digital technologies, including blockchain, are seen as the main drivers of the Forth Industrial Revolution (4IR) which is the common term for social and market changes related to globalisation and digitalisation (Schwab, 2016; Xu, David, & Kim, 2018). Together with market changes, a generational change takes place. New generations, marked as Y and Z are entering adulthood and are starting to affect many aspects of social life (Bencsik, Horváth-Csikós, & Juhász, 2016). Both mentioned phenomena have a significant impact on education as a whole, but in particular on higher education, which is linked with a strong pressure from the labour market. Higher education institutions (HEIs) must face the demands of the labour market and (future and current) students, resulting in the need to change the approach to the teaching process and the way they operate (Chaka, 2022). The general concept of these changes is referred to as Education 4.0.

Blockchain has significant potential to support the shift of HEIs towards Education 4.0. Education is indicated as one of few areas of blockchain technology (BC) application (Sunny et al., 2022) with many examples of concepts, designs of systems, and ongoing or finished projects (Fedorova & Skobleva, 2020; Loukil, Abed, & Boukadi, 2021). As in the case of every new technology, there are two approaches to its adoption or, in other words, ways of innovation introduction. The first, more common approach, consists of replacing the existing solutions with a new technology that, thanks to its new features, improves their performance. The second approach is

DOI: 10.4324/9781003318736-9

trying to take advantage of new opportunities and to create an entirely new system with unique functionalities, not seen before (Capetillo, Camacho, & Alanis, 2022).

The aim of this chapter is to analyse the existing and potential impact of blockchain technology on higher education. It starts with the indication of possible areas of blockchain adoption and description of concepts concerned with how this technology can influence education. Next, a few examples of successfully completed blockchain-based projects are presented. Since an adoption of every technology is related to both benefits and risks, the challenges to blockchain implementation with indication of potential future risks are discussed in Section 8.2. The chapter ends with considerations of the possible impact of BC application on education, in particular on the functioning of HEIs in the context of Education 4.0.

8.2 Promising areas of blockchain application in education

8.2.1 Education as a potential area of blockchain application

In the last few years, education has become one of the major areas of blockchain applications (Sunny et al., 2022). One of the reasons for this is that the changes in education forced by such phenomena as digitalisation and associated transformation of the labour market, new generation of young people entering the education process and later the labour market, referred to as Education 4.0, require the strong support from information technology (Fernández-Caramés & Fraga-Lamas, 2019). In searching for technological support in solving the problems of higher education institutions related to Education 4.0, many new digital technologies like blockchain, artificial intelligence, mixed and virtual reality, Internet of Things, big data, and cloud computing have been analysed and checked for possibility of their adoption (Chaka, 2022; Hernandez-de-Menendez, Escobar Díaz, & Morales-Menendez, 2020) (see Chapter 1).

Education was found to be one of the seven most frequently mentioned disciplines of BC applications in research publications since 2015 (Sunny et al., 2022). However, only two areas of BC applications in education have been indicated: certificate management and student loan management. The third area mentioned, i.e. "data science", is an example of BC usage for implementing the open-badges concept that can be treated as an element of certificate management. A similar analysis conducted by Akram et al. (2020) identified education as one of the 14 blockchain-based social applications, indicating the possible areas of usage such as certification management, identity management, and copyright management.

A more detailed approach, concentrated only on BC usage in education, presented by Fedorova & Skobleva (2020) distinguished eight potential areas of using blockchain technology in education:

- issuance and storage of certificates and diplomas,
- identification solutions,
- protection of intellectual property,
- new network of cooperation between students and their professors,
- formation of an academic passport (portfolio),
- payment for studies with cryptocurrency,
- accreditation of educational institutions,
- administration of educational processes.

Another review classified the variety of blockchain applications for educational purposes into 12 categories (Alammary, Alhazmi, Almasri, & Gillani, 2019):

- certificates management,
- competencies and learning outcomes management,
- evaluating students' professional ability,
- protecting learning objects,
- securing collaborative learning environment,
- fees and credits transfer,
- obtaining digital guardianship consent,
- competitions management,
- copyrights management,
- enhancing students' interactions in e-learning,
- examination review,
- supporting lifelong learning.

The first six above-listed categories are mentioned by many authors, while the last six ones appear rarely, sometimes only in one publication. This suggests that the list of potential areas of BC usage in education is not closed and is still under development.

A similar analysis identified five major areas of BC application (Loukil, Abed, & Boukadi, 2021):

- certificate/degree verification and revocation,
- user-centric educational record management,
- students' professional ability evaluation,
- BC-based educational institute systems,
- online learning environment.

The difference between the above classifications is mainly associated with the level of detail. According to the individual approaches, authors define their own classification, often differently naming the same category, or use more detailed criteria. However, some of the indicated areas are common in all categories and are discussed in the following section.

8.2.2 Approaches to blockchain adoption in education

First and foremost, BC has great potential to solve the problems related to certifications management, including: issuing, validation, and authentication of certificates. These topics concern not only educational institutions and students but also widely affect the labour market. The high level of fraud concerning the different types of certificates is a serious issue and generates a significant cost (Awaji & Solaiman, 2022). BC, with its features such as immutability, reliability, transparency, availability, and trust, is now probably the best technological choice for solving that problem in an efficient way on the larger scale, extending beyond the individual organisation. The idea of issuance and storage of certificates and diplomas with the support of BC has many implementations within the educational institutions, e.g., at the University of Nicosia (Cyprus) (see Chapter 7), Massachusetts Institute of Technology (MIT, USA), and the Open University (United Kingdom) (Fedorova & Skobleva, 2020).

Similarly, students' exchanges among the different HEIs and verification of their educational achievements can also be supported by BC. Many students change the HEI during study and need to provide proof of the results from the previous place of study. Though Allamary et al. (2019) treat this category separately as "competencies and learning outcomes management" and Loukil (2021) classifies it as a part of "user-centric educational record management", from a technical point of view it is very similar to certificate management and requires similar technological solutions. An example of such a solution is EduCTX platform (Turkanović, Hölbl, Košić, Heričko, & Kamišalić, 2018) (see Chapter 3). It uses the concept of the European Credit Transfer and Accumulation System (ECTS) which was developed in 1989 to support the student exchange programme (Erasmus). ECTS credits, based on the learning results and associated workload, express the learning effort. Many HEIs from different countries participate in the Erasmus programme, and this leads to the problem with certification and verification of ECTS credits gained by an exchange student. EduCTX is a blockchain-based platform, in which every student holds a dedicated EduCTX blockchain wallet and may collect ECTX tokens, i.e. the value of ECTS credits assigned by the HEI to completed courses. A student is able to globally prove completion of courses without any administrative effort by simply presenting tokens from the EduCTX wallet.

Second, the financial aspects of study can also be supported by BC. The simplest idea is to use cryptocurrencies to pay for study (Devine, 2015), while the more advanced ideas concern the usage of smart contract for sponsoring studies (Rashid et al., 2019), based on "pay-for-success" schema (Capetillo, Camacho, & Alanis, 2022). In this schema, a student gets a certain amount of digital currency for, e.g., passing the exam or completing a year of study, which is guaranteed and fully automatic by the usage of smart contracts. Payment for study using cryptocurrency is available at, e.g., the University of Nicosia (Cyprus) (see Chapter 6), King's College (USA), and Woolf University (the United Kingdom).

Third, protection of intellectual property comprises a promising area of BC applications. The general idea of BC applications in this category is to record the authorship for resources (intellectual works) such as teaching materials, scholarly articles, artworks, and new ideas. Such an immutable record can become a part of the student e-portfolio, proving individual intellectual effort during the student's study. A good example of implementation of that concept is a system operating in the Open University. In this system, using the OpenLearn platform, students can earn the OpenLearn badges which are available in a student Learning Passport (Capetillo, Camacho, & Alanis, 2022). The usage of BC for a protection of intellectual properties (including copyright management) can also support the librarians in gathering, preserving, and sharing authorship information, supporting the verifiable records of academic achievements (Hoy, 2017). This area also includes the Allamary's et al. (2019) category "protecting learning objects" which concerns the problem of protecting learning items from destruction and unauthorised change.

There are a few concepts belonging to the intersection of several categories, especially when the technological aspects of BC implementation are taken into consideration. For example, a Kudos concept (Sharples & Domingue, 2016) was developed building upon the idea of a so-called new digital economy, an idea which is the basis of such well-known companies as AirBnB, Uber, or Kickstarter. The main component of this concept is the development of a permanent distributed record (based on BC) of intellectual efforts and associated reputational rewards. Each involved educational or academic institution, innovative organisation, and any intellectual worker (e.g., writer, artist) is given an initial quantity of "educational reputation currency", called Kudos. This initial quantity reflects some existing metric like rankings of the universities or H-index for academics. In that way the reputation market is created. A student can gain some Kudos for passing a test, completing the course, and paying for the mentoring, e.g., in cryptocurrency. This concept is a combination of institutional records, tuition fee system payments, and academic passports. It also has the potential in the area of accreditation of educational institutions.

A related concept, which can be limited to an individual educational organisation or a consortium, uses the idea of cryptocurrency for enhancing students' interactions in e-learning. Students can gain the virtual currency for participating in community activities and later can use this currency to get access to additional learning resources. At the same time, it allows to track students' learning progress and can serve as a learning certificate (educational record management) (Zhong, Xie, Zou, & Chui, 2018).

An increasing number of e-learning platforms and courses offered create the need of a reliable system of their rating. In this respect, Garg et al. (2022) proposed the blockchain-based Online Education Content Rating system which was modelled on the Zapid system, a solution developed to provide trust among Amazon sellers, consumers, and reviewers.

Another possibility of the use of BC is derived from the properties of Non-Fungible Tokens (NFT) (Wang, Li, Wang, & Chen, 2021). NFTs are a type of cryptocurrency derived from smart contracts. NFTs are unique and cannot be exchanged, and this makes them the perfect candidate for identity management. Students' IDs can be converted into tokens and can be used for any purpose which requires the proper identification, e.g., access to resources, tracking learning progress, and educational record management (Capetillo, Camacho, & Alanis, 2022).

8.2.3 Benefits of blockchain adoption in education

Adoption of BC in education can have a positive impact on educational institutions. Table 8.1 contains the list of benefits highlighted by authors of the above-cited reviews.

All pointed out benefits can be divided into three major categories. The first category deals with improving the management of HEIs at the institutional level. This category contains benefits concerning such areas as data management (including certificates, students' records, intellectual property), security (including access to restricted resources, identity authentication, preserving privacy), and cost reduction. With respect to the last area, cost reduction can be obtained by cutting the administrative expenses related to the first two areas (Alammary, Alhazmi, Almasri, & Gillani, 2019). These management-related benefits are not limited to education and are largely common for other domains of BC application. It means that HEIs can adopt the BC-based solution worked out by organisations from other industries. A similar characteristic has the second category which is related to the partnership of students and HEIs represented by teachers and administration. Creating the atmosphere of mutual trust, being one of the benefits of BC

TABLE 8.1 Benefits of blockchain adoption in education.

	Alammary et al. (2019)	Loukil et al. (2021)	Sunny et al. (2022)
Benefits related to management at the institutional level			
Better control of data access	✓	✓	✓
Improving the management of students' records	✓	✓	✓
High security	✓	✓	✓
Preserving students' privacy		✓	
Identity authentication	✓		✓
Costs reduction	✓		✓
Benefits related to partnership of students and institution			
Enhancing trust	✓		✓
Enhancing students' assessments	✓		✓
Enhancing accountability and transparency	✓	✓	
Supporting learners' career decisions	✓		
Benefits related to educational process			
Enhancing learners' interactivity	✓	✓	

application, results in establishing the friendly environment supporting learning, teaching, and administrative processes. The third category of benefits is related to educational process. This category includes enhancing learners' interactivity.

To properly evaluate the benefits of BC adoption in education, all major stakeholders' point of view should be considered. The main stakeholders of the higher education are students (future graduates who will enter the labour market), HEIs (teaching staff, administration and management personnel), employers (representing the labour market), and policymakers (e.g., accreditation boards) (De la Torre, Rossi, & Sagarra, 2019). All of them can be beneficiaries of the blockchain-based system implementations.

The multiple-stakeholder impact can be demonstrated on an example of benefits related to data management. Improvement of the students' records management has a positive effect on HEI's administration processes in terms of possible acceleration and automation of processes resulting in cost reduction. An enhancement of accountability and transparency allows to evaluate a student's performance efficiently and quickly. This is a very important topic for teaching staff. At the same time, it allows to comply with clear and transparent assessment rules, which is important not only for students but also for HEI accreditation bodies (reliable learning results). Certificate management

systems that belong to this category allow employers to easily verify achievements and authorise certificates, which results in measurable financial
benefits.

A more detailed analysis of BC applications and benefits, based on practical examples, is presented in the subsequent sections of this chapter.

8.3 Current landscape: Lessons learned from practice

8.3.1 Overview of current blockchain implementations

There are a number of areas of blockchain technology adoption in the
higher education domain. The main discussion was carried out in the second
chapter. Overall, research shows that it is possible to distinguish the following areas:

- issuing certificates and diplomas,
- protecting intellectual property, especially study materials,
- disseminating, exchanging, and evaluating ideas,
- enabling payment for studies, including the use of cryptocurrencies,
- establishing a learning environment that connects students and educators
  using an online platform.

However, it is worth noting that although the number of blockchain-based
applications in higher education is increasing, few of them have been made
available to the public. The main area of BC adoption in higher education is
mainly related to the management of certificates and their verification.

8.3.2 Certificates and diplomas verification

Several initiatives have started using and testing BC to store academic certificates and allow graduates to have a greater control over document distribution
(e.g., Blockcerts developed at the MIT and Learning Machine, OpenCerts
developed by the government of Singapore, or BTCert developed by the
University of Birmingham). The University of Nicosia (UNIC), a pioneer in
blockchain education and research, developed a solution to store university
diplomas using blockchain in 2015. This has led to all university diplomas
being issued in both traditional paper forms and blockchain-enabled digital
formats.

Originally, the solution was offered in the form of Software as a Service
(SaaS) product and platform. Then it was extended to be used by organisations that need all kinds of certificates like degrees and legal documents, e.g.,
contracts, marriage certificate, or driver's license. Based on the experience of

using blockchain to permanently store university diplomas, some lessons learned have been formulated (see Chapter 7):

- The future of certificate issuance is decentralised as existing centralised certificate issuance systems are vulnerable and lead to security breaches, which results in an increasing number of counterfeit diplomas, leading to a decrease in confidence in their authenticity. Using BC helps overcome these issues as it provides a trusted and transparent solution where certificates are registered in a distributed ledger. Such a solution is supported by numerous countries and organisations, including the European Union, which indicates the possibility of issuing certificates based on blockchain.
- Revocation of blockchain-based certificates is feasible and can be used in very specific cases (e.g., changing a graduate's name). In general, the modifiability of data was one of the central issues in connection with the collection and storage of university degree certificates based on blockchain. The available solutions indicate that such an operation is possible and allows certificate issuers to "correct" specific data in the blockchain.
- Future development of decentralised certificates may be based on Soul-Bound-Tokens (SBT), which are characterised by being tied to an identity, awarded upon completion of some achievements (e.g., graduation), cannot be transferred, bought, or sold. SBT can therefore be used to issue certificates, and it seems that in the future a number of non-transferable certificates, such as diplomas of graduation or identity documents, will be issued as SBT and stored in a digital wallet.

Another promising example that relates to storing academic certificates concerns Blockcerts (BCC), a set of standards for digital academic certificates on the blockchain, consisting of open-source libraries, tools, and mobile apps that enable a decentralised, standards-based, recipient-centric ecosystem and support trusted verification through blockchain technologies (Schmidt, 2016). BCC offers a decentralised authorisation system. The blockchain acts as a provider of trust, resulting in credentials being tamper-proof and verifiable. BCC can be used in the context of academic, professional, and work-related qualifications. Developed by MIT Media Lab and Learning Machine, the solution was deployed in 2017. After that, at least a hundred of MIT students received their diplomas in a digital form using blockchain technology.

An essential component to manage the certifications and the verification process is the BCC Wallet, a mobile app available on students' mobile phones to handle the required technical complexity of public key cryptography concepts. The wallet manages the creation of students' public and private keys and signs their diploma, allowing the student to later prove ownership and verify integrity.

One of the universities that tried to implement BCC was the University of Fernand Pessoa (Vidal et al., 2019). The main focus was on the cost of issuing the diploma. The results show that the cost of issuing one or three diplomas was similar. For the three diploma transactions, BCC combines all three and generates a single hash. The results of the conducted research indicate that issuing individual diplomas is too expensive. However, according to the BCC specification, up to 2000 awards can be combined into a single block. Therefore, bulk issuance of diplomas would be cost-effective, at least on Bitcoin-like networks, since the cost of a 2000 diploma transaction would be $0.0025 per a single certificate.

It should be emphasised that the modification of data of an issued certificate, e.g., when an issued certificate expires, e.g. a language certificate, is still a challenge. Nevertheless, some solutions are proposed as the one developed by the UNIC and mentioned in the previous example and described in Chapter 7. In the case of the Ethereum network, it is possible to use smart contracts to address this issue (Santos & Duffy, 2017).

8.3.3 Intellectual property rights

In recent years, online education has started to play a key role. In distance learning, teaching materials are stored in a digital form and made available on the Internet. Therefore, intellectual property, especially in a digital form, can easily be copied, stolen, or used in violation of property rights. This entails protection of intellectual property, managing copyright in digital educational resources, and ensuring the security of access to digital data or its distribution. At the same time, generation, recognition, protection, and trading of intellectual property rights face unprecedented challenges. Unfortunately, the traditional system of intellectual property rights, originally designed to protect the works of innovators and encourage progress, cannot keep up with the speed of development of methods and forms of education. Furthermore, contemporary digital teaching aids and tools make such a system even more complicated. At the same time, there are suggestions that the knowledge should be accessible to the public and that the ownership should be based on the expectations of both creators and users.

BC seems to have the potential to manage, protect, and monetise intellectual property rights. It is an open ledger that records verified transactions from different nodes, hence it is considered transparent and immutable. On the other hand, intellectual property (IP) refers to all created elements used in the educational process (e.g., texts, images, multimedia) that are legally recognised and protected. A BC-based intellectual property management and protection framework should include intellectual property registration, authorship verification, and use of smart contracts to transfer intellectual property assets (Bonnet & Teuteberg, 2022).

Unfortunately, little work has been done on the practical use of blockchain to protect property rights. Existing studies mainly focus on theoretical considerations, highlighting numerous limitations of using BC in the field of intellectual property and determining what are the predominant benefits of and challenges to the application of distributed ledgers in intellectual property management. Currently, implementations of such systems are practically absent (Wang et al., 2019). A critical look at the application of blockchain with regard to its ability to manage intellectual property mainly points to two types of challenges (Ito & O'Dair, 2019; Bonnet & Teuteberg, 2022):

- operational – inability to guarantee authenticity and provenance with certainty; at the same time, cryptocurrencies are too unpredictable to be adopted for royalties,
- implementational – blockchains are optimised for cryptocurrencies; therefore, there are problems in managing intellectual property from storing original files and metadata to transferring licenses.

In summary, the studies carried out indicate that, despite the enormous potential, Distributed Ledger Technology is still immature and is in the initial phase, especially from technological and legal points of view (Bonnet & Teuteberg, 2022). However, blockchain and Distributed Ledger Technology can significantly impact the development of intellectual property solutions. In particular, the potential of blockchain technology for managing, protecting, and monetising intellectual property rights seems very promising.

8.4 Prospects of reshaping the Education 4.0 ecosystem

8.4.1 General challenges to blockchain adoption

Previous sections, presenting the areas of BC application in education, concentrate on predicted benefits with justification grounded in real examples of systems based on BC. To create a bigger picture, it is still necessary to take into account the challenges, problems, and risks that have to be faced. BC is a relatively new technology and despite the fact that it has been known for more than a decade (Nakamoto, 2008), it is still not widely spread and might be considered immature.

Regardless of the domain, BC applications are affected by many factors that can be divided into three main categories: institutional, market, and

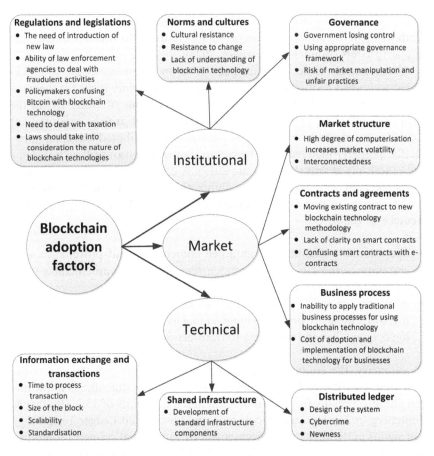

FIGURE 8.1 Blockchain technology adoption factors.

Source: Based on (Jansen, Weerakkody, Ismagilova, Sivarajah, & Irani, 2020).

technical (Jansen, Weerakkody, Ismagilova, Sivarajah, & Irani, 2020). Figure 8.1 presents these factors with division into categories and subcategories.

The institutional category covers the factors that set requirements on BC design or are affected by the blockchain application. The most numerous in this category is the subcategory "*Regulations and legislations*" related to the influence of law regulation and government agencies. The importance of these factors cannot be overestimated because they can slow down or even prevent the application of blockchain in certain areas. "*Policymakers confusing Bitcoin with blockchain technology*" is a good example of such factors. It deals with the problem of perceiving the blockchain through the lens of cryptocurrencies, in particular Bitcoin, which many people (including decision-makers) associate with tax evasion or even with the illegal market. The next subcategory

"*Governance*" reflects the need to work out the appropriate governance frameworks or tailor the existing frameworks to the functionality and features of BC. This should mitigate the risk of market manipulation and unfair practices, which can have the direct impact on the third subcategory "*Norms and culture*" that covers the factors related to individual or group attitudes to BC application.

Factors from the market category refer to the operation of an organisation in its environment and are divided into the following subcategories: *Market structures, Contracts and agreements,* and *Business processes.* The names of subcategories identify the main components of business environment and the factors themselves indicate the anxieties of market participants and challenges faced by blockchain technology.

The last category deals directly with technical features of BC and with the various shapes and the design choices of its applications (e.g., private/public, permissioned/permissionless, type of consensus algorithms). The *Information exchange and transactions* subcategory describes the challenges concerning the size of data volume and the efficiency of data processing. Next, the *Distributed ledger* subcategory gathers the challenges with data distribution and related risk of an unauthorised access to them (cybercrime). These issues are very important considering the fact that blockchain is a rather new technology and some information systems do not have well-developed security mechanisms. By the same token, the third subcategory: *Shared Infrastructure* highlights the problem of a complex, multilayer, and distributed infrastructure. It should be noted that the lack of standardisation at different levels ranging from technical protocols to smart contracts can be treated by decision-makers as an argument against BC application.

8.4.2 Challenges to blockchain applications in education

The presented classification does not consider the areas of application; nevertheless, many of the discussed considerations are relevant to education. In an analysis limited only to challenges to blockchain application in education, similar factors were listed (Alammary, Alhazmi, Almasri, & Gillani, 2019): scalability, security and privacy, cost of adopting, trust (in technology), setting the boundaries, immutability, immaturity, data unavailability, and weakening the value of the traditional school. Some of them like *scalability, immaturity,* and *data unavailability* are similar to global challenges presented above. Other elements, e.g., *weakening the value of the traditional school*, are the exemplification of the factors from the "*Norms and culture*" subcategory. Interestingly, *immutability*, which is one of the original properties of blockchain, is mentioned as a challenge. This stems from the concern that immutability could make it difficult for educational institutions to apply new information storage laws or correct inaccurate data. In turn, *setting the boundaries* deals with the decision problem which data and services should be offered through the blockchain network. This challenge can be classified as a lack of understanding of blockchain technology (*Norms and culture* subcategory).

A more detailed analysis of challenges to BC application regarding education is presented by Mohammad and Vargas (2022). On the basis of semi-structured interviews with experts working on blockchain projects in HEIs including the academic (professor/associate professor, researcher, and Ph.D. student) and administrative (IT division manager, developer, and decision-maker) staff from six countries, they have identified 15 barriers for blockchain adoption in HEI's, in which they distinguished three categories: technological, organisational, and environmental. The barriers from technological and environmental categories are similar to factors pointed out by (Jansen, Weerakkody, Ismagilova, Sivarajah, & Irani, 2020) (see Figure 8.1). Organisational barriers are more interesting. Except for the financial barrier (cost of adopting), which appears in many analyses, Mohammad and Vargas identify two less often pointed out challenges: a lack of adequate skills and a lack of management commitment and support. While the latter is a typical risk factor for implementation of any software system, the former highlights the problem of availability of properly educated and experienced professionals. Although the term "blockchain" is widely known among IT professionals, there are very few specialists with a deeper knowledge and experience in the development of blockchain based applications. A relatively small number of projects based on BC implies that, compared to other technologies, specialists in this area are not widely sought after on the labour market. This, in turn, means that there is no strong pressure (both from students and the labour market) on HEI's to educate in this area. Hence, despite the apparent popularity of BC, still few universities offer studies in this field when compared to other technologies.

Analysing the research works concerning the challenges to BC adoption in education, it can be seen that they focus mainly on development-related aspects like technological and legal barriers. This is rather understandable because developers meet these challenges in their work and, due to this, these categories of challenges are more easily identified by them. Park (2021) takes an attempt to have a deeper approach. Quoting A. Watters' question: *"What problems (…) might the blockchain's adoption in education create?"* (Watters, 2016), he is trying to focus on potential long-range effects which can have negative consequences for some participants. A good example of this can be one of basic blockchain features: "immutability". It is mainly treated as a challenge in the context of possible difficulties for educational institutions while applying new information storage laws or correcting inaccurate data. However, there is a risk that it can be used for social control and perpetuation of power (Park, 2021).

8.4.3 Blockchain as a support for Education 4.0

The concept of Education 4.0 is an answer of the educational institutions to the challenges posed by social and market changes. Social changes are related to new generations entering higher education, and next as graduates entering the labour market. In turn, market changes are related to the phenomena of globalisation and digitisation of production processes and services, collectively referred to as the Fourth Industrial Revolution. Education 4.0 can be treated as an educational derivative of 4IR and in this sense is shaped by the same flagship technologies which powered the 4IR (Chaka, 2022). Education 4.0 must meet the expectation of young people (entering the education process) and labour market (graduates as a future employees). Although the Education 4.0 concept covers all levels of education, inclusion of labour market expectation allows to narrow down these considerations only to the higher education (sometimes named Higher Education 4.0).

Education 4.0 redefines the roles of students and HEIs staff (teachers, administration, managers) in the educational process (Himmetoğlu, Ayduğ, & Bayrak, 2020). The core components of Education 4.0 are Competencies, Learning Methods, Information and Communication Technologies (ICT), and Infrastructure (Miranda et al., 2021). Their interconnection looks as follow: technologies, by supporting the infrastructure at the classroom and institutional level, create the friendly environment for using new learning methods which allow students to obtain expected competencies. A significant role is played by the current and emerging so-called disruptive technologies. Each of technologies has its own area of usage, supporting the HEI's in facing the challenges posed by Education 4.0. In this context, the following question can arise: *How blockchain technology adoption can help HEIs in their shift towards Education 4.0?*

As mentioned in the previous sections, BC applications cover areas mainly related to supporting infrastructure at the institutional level like data management and security. BC is less supportive at the level of classroom, where only one expected direct benefit "enhancing learners' interactivity" is pointed out (Alammary, Alhazmi, Almasri, & Gillani, 2019; Loukil, Abed, & Boukadi, 2021). However, even in the case of this benefit, it requires the system support at the institutional level.

Education 4.0 puts emphasis on the role of a student as a main stakeholder in the educational process and on the effects of this process expressed in terms of competencies (see Chapters 1 and 4). Treating a competency as the ability to effectively perform specific actions by a person, the competency is assigned to the person and not to the process of its obtaining. In this context the competencies are independent of the method of their authentication (certification management). It allows to concentrate on a student's role in the educational process and narrow down the consideration to BC as an infrastructural backbone at the institutional level.

A modern approach to students' role in educational processes is described as a "student-centred" or "learner-centred" education (see Chapter 4). It is defined by six basic categories (Bremner, 2021): active participation (including interaction), adapting to needs (including human needs), autonomy (including metacognition), relevant skills (including real-life skills and higher level skills), power sharing (involve students in decision-making about what they learn, how they learn and how they are assessed), and formative assessment. These categories describe a student-friendly environment that creates conditions for effective education, but it also sets the high demands for HEI as an institution. Establishing such an environment requires flexible administrative procedures to ensure the security and reliability of all data related to the student, their learning progress and achievements. This is the area in which BC can play a significant role. Examples of possible benefits of BC adoption for different stakeholders are presented in Table 8.2.

The usage of BC needs time to yield the real effects. In this respect, Camilleri, Inamorato dos Santos, & Grech (2017) presented eight scenarios of blockchain adoption in education, dividing them into three categories according to time needed to implementation and visible effects. Three short-term scenarios include permanently secure certificates, verification of a multi-step accreditation, and receiving payments. Four medium-term scenarios cover automatic recognition and transfer of credits, lifelong learning passports, student identification, and tracking the intellectual property and rewarding its use and re-use. The eight long-term scenarios deal with providing students with government funding via vouchers. Nowadays, it can be said that seven short- and medium-term scenarios partially became a reality. By analysing ongoing or completed projects, examples of the implementation of these scenarios can be identified. The problem is that except the permanently secure certificates and lifelong learning passports, there are very few examples of other scenarios. The eighth scenario is still at a conceptual stage.

When considering an impact of BC on education, two more perspectives, i.e. the category and type of innovation, should be taken into consideration. The results of an analysis of 13 ongoing project in this context made by Capetillo, Camacho, and Alanis (2022) show that ten of them are in "Sustaining" category, which means that they mainly focused on a replacement of technology, changing the previously used tools or methods in new

TABLE 8.2 Results of blockchain technology applications.

Areas of application	Expected effects	Results from stakeholders' points of view
Certifications and diplomas management	Issuance, validation, and authentication of students' competencies and achievement	Reliable portfolios (labour market) Facilitating continuous education (lifelong learning) (student)
Improvement of the management of students' records	Reliable data on students' learning progress and results Preserving privacy	Changing the HEI during study (student) Participation in international exchange programmes (like Erasmus) (student) Adaptation to students' needs: individual programme and course of study (student, HEI) Enhancing students' assessments (student, teacher) Supporting autonomous learning experience (student, teacher) Enhancing learners' interactivity (student, teacher)
Identity verification	Preserving privacy	Access to restricted resources (student, HEI) Participation in formal procedures (student, HEI)

Source: Based on (Fedorova & Skobleva, 2020; Capetillo, Camacho, & Alanis, 2022; Loukil, Abed, & Boukadi, 2021; Bartolomé, 2020; Bozkurt & Ucar, 2020).

ways based on BC. Only three are classified as a "Disruptive" innovation, which means that they developed new ways to carry out the activities of a given kind. A similar situation occurs when analysing the type of innovation. Nine projects are classified as "Core", which means that they concentrate on an improvement of activities which are currently carried out. Two projects are classified as "Related" i.e., they added features which were previously unavailable. One project was classified as "Disruptive" and one as "New", where *disruptive* means that the project enabled new dynamics or mechanisms to allow access for new users (e.g., new mechanism of payment for education), and *new* refers to projects enabling the introduction of new user groups and new markets. This analysis shows a conservative approach to adaption of newest technology, including blockchain, by HEIs managers (decision-makers). It is easier to use a new technology at well-known and precisely defined areas than trying to do something completely different, with the possible risk of failure.

8.5 Conclusions

Blockchain technology as every other technology is only the tool which can be used for solving the problems or to seize opportunities resulting from its unique properties. Therefore, it is important to start by asking: *What problems blockchain technology can solve?* or *What opportunities blockchain technology offers to us?*

A good example of an answer to the first question is certificate management, probably the most popular BC application related to education. It brings the benefits to all stakeholders and illustrates the common approach: the feasibilities of new technology allow to solve a well-known problem almost without changing the mode of operation of its participants. More confusing is an answer to the second question. It needs a deep understanding of the BC and, after identification of related opportunities, it requires the civil courage, enthusiasm, and proper circumstances to make an effort to put it into practice. The first step, identification of possible applications and anticipation of potential benefits, is done quite often, resulting in many concepts for the adoption of BC. The next step, implementation of the concept is much less common. The possible reasons can be a lack of understanding of BC by decision-makers, lack of well-experienced professionals, or simply, management's reluctance to change.

It is also worth remembering that each new technology, apart from potential benefits, may carry various risks. It is very important to try to anticipate the potential risks and to take action to minimise them. In particular, some essential features like immutability and distributed data storage pose a number of challenges that might not be responded to in the near future.

Summing up, blockchain technology has a potential to support HEIs in their shift towards Education 4.0. However, it might be a time-consuming process. Ongoing projects that use BC play a significant role in this transformation. Their failure can slow down the process of blockchain technology adoption, but their success will most likely attract more institutions and make the whole community more open to BC applications.

References

Akram, S. V., Malik, P. K., Singh, R., Anita, G., & Tanwar, S. (2020). Adoption of blockchain technology in various realms: Opportunities and challenges. *Security and Privacy*, *3*(5), e109.

Alammary, A., Alhazmi, S., Almasri, M., & Gillani, S. (2019). Blockchain-based applications in education: A systematic review. *Applied Sciences*, *9*(12), 2400.

Awaji, B., & Solaiman, E. (2022). Design, Implementation, and Evaluation of Blockchain-Based Trusted Achievement Record System for Students in Higher Education. In *14th International Conference on Computer Supported Education – ESEDU 2022*. Retrieved from: arXiv:2204.12547

Bartolomé, A. (2020). Blockchain in Educational Methodologies. In D. Burgos (ed.), *Radical Solutions and eLearning* (pp. 63–79). Singapore: Springer.

Bencsik, A., Horváth-Csikós, G., & Juhász, T. (2016). Y and Z generations at workplaces. *Journal of Competitiveness, 8*(3), 90–106.

Bonnet, S., & Teuteberg, F. (2022). Impact of blockchain and distributed ledger technology for the management, protection, enforcement and monetization of intellectual property: A systematic literature review. *Information Systems and e-Business Management*, 1–47.

Bozkurt, A., & Ucar, H. (2020). Blockchain Technology as a Bridging Infrastructure Among Formal, Non-Formal, and Informal Learning Processes. In H. Y. R. Sharma (Ed.), *Blockchain Technology Applications in Education*, (pp. 1–15). Hershey, PA: IGI Global.

Bremner, N. (2021). The multiple meanings of 'student-centred' or 'learner-centred' education, and the case for a more flexible approach to defining it. *Comparative Education, 57*(2), 159–186.

Camilleri, A., Inamorato dos Santos, A., & Grech, A. (2017). *Blockchain in Education*. Luxembourg: European Commission, Joint Research Centre, Publications Office.

Capetillo, A., Camacho, D., & Alanis, M. (2022). Blockchained education: challenging the long-standing model of academic institutions. *International Journal on Interactive Design and Manufacturing (IJIDeM)*. Retrieved January 25, 2023, from: https://doi.org/10.1007/s12008-022-00886-1

Chaka, C. (2022). Is education 4.0 a sufficient innovative, and disruptive educational trend to promote sustainable open education for higher education institutions? A review of literature trends. *Frontiers in Education, 7*(82497), 1–14.

De la Torre, E. M., Rossi, F., & Sagarra, M. (2019). Who benefits from HEIs engagement? An analysis of priority stakeholders and activity profiles of HEIs in the United Kingdom. *Studies in Higher Education, 44*(12), 2163–2182.

Devine, P. (2015). Blockchain Learning: Can Crypto-Currency Methods be Appropriated to Enhance Online Learning? In *ALT Online Winter Conference 2015*.

Fedorova, E. P., & Skobleva, E. I. (2020). Application of blockchain technology in higher education. *European Journal of Contemporary Education, 9*(3), 552–571.

Fernández-Caramés, T. M., & Fraga-Lamas, P. (2019). Towards next generation teaching, learning, and context-aware applications for higher education: a review on blockchain, IoT, fog and edge computing enabled smart campuses and universities. *Applied Sciences, 9*(21), 4479.

Garg, A., Sharmila, A., Kumar, P., Madhukar, M., & Layola-Gonzalez, O. (2022). Blockchain-based online education content ranking. *Education and Information Technologies, 27*, 4793–4815.

Hernandez-de-Menendez, M., Escobar Díaz, C., & Morales-Menendez, R. (2020). Technologies for the future of learning: state of the art. *International Journal on Interactive Design and Manufacturing (IJIDeM), 14*, 683–695.

Himmetoğlu, B., Ayduğ, D., & Bayrak, C. (2020). Education 4.0: Defining the teacher, the student, and the school manager aspects of the revolution. *Turkish Online Journal of Distance Education-TOJDE, 21*, 12–28.

Hoy, M. B. (2017). An introduction to the blockchain and its implications for libraries and medicine. *Medical Reference Services Quarterly 36*(3), 273–279.

Ito, K., & O'Dair, M. (2019). A critical examination of the application of blockchain technology to intellectual property management. *Business Transformation through Blockchain*, 2, 317–335.

Jansen, M., Weerakkody, V., Ismagilova, E., Sivarajah, U., & Irani, Z. (2020). A framework for analysing blockchain technology adoption: Integrating institutional, market and technical factors. *International Journal of Information Management*, 50, 302–309.

Loukil, F., Abed, M., & Boukadi, K. (2021). Blockchain adoption in education: a systematic literature review. *Education and Information Technologies*, 26, 5779–5797.

Miranda, J., Navarrete, C., Noguez, J., Molina-Espinosa, J., Ramírez-Montoya, M., Navarro-Tuch, S. A., …Molina, A. (2021). The core components of education 4.0 in higher education: Three case studies in engineering education. *Computers & Electrical Engineering*, 93:107278.

Mohammad, A., & Vargas, S. (2022). Barriers affecting higher education institutions' adoption of blockchain technology: A qualitative study. *Informatics*, 9(64).

Nakamoto, S. (2008). *Bitcoin: A Peer-to-Peer Electronic Cash System*. Retrieved January 26, 2023, from: https://bitcoin.org/bitcoin.pdf

Park, J. (2021). Promises and challenges of Blockchain in education. *Smart Learning Environment*, 8(33).

Rashid, M., Deo, K., Prasad, D., Singh, K., Chand, S., & Assaf, M. (2019). *TEduChain: A Platform for Crowdsourcing Tertiary Education Fund using Blockchain Technology*. Retrieved January 25, 2023, from: https://arxiv.org/pdf/1901.06327.pdf

Santos, J., & Duffy, K. H. (2017). A Decentralized Approach to Blockcerts Certificate Revocation. In *The 5th Rebooting the Web of Trust Design Workshop*, Boston.

Schmidt, P. (2016). *Blockcerts - An Open Infrastructure for Academic Credentials on the Blockchain*. MLLearning, Retrieved January 26, 2023, from: http://www.mllearning.com

Schwab, K. (2016). *The Fourth Industrial Revolution*. Cologny/Geneva, Switzerland: World Economic Forum.

Sharples, M., & Domingue, J. (2016). The Blockchain and Kudos: A Distributed System for Educational Record, Reputation and Reward, Adaptive and Adaptable Learning. In K. Verbert (Ed.), *European Conference on Technology Enhanced Learning EC-TEL 2016 (LNCS 9891)* (pp. 490–496).

Sunny, F. A., Hajek, P., Munk, M., Abedin, M. Z., Satu, M. S., Efat, M. I., & Islam, M. J. (2022). A systematic review of blockchain applications. *IEEE Access*, 10, 59155–59177.

Turkanović, M., Hölbl, M., Košić, K., Herićko, M., & Kamišalić, A. (2018). EduCTX: A blockchain-based higher education credit platform. *IEEE Access*, 6, 5112–5127.

Vidal, F., Gouveia, F., & Soares, C. (2019, October). Analysis of Blockchain Technology for Higher Education. In *2019 International Conference on Cyber-Enabled Distributed Computing and Knowledge Discovery (CyberC)* (pp. 28–33). IEEE.

Wang, Q., Li, R., Wang, Q., & Chen, S. (2021). *Non-Fungible Token (NFT): Overview, Evaluation, Opportunities and Challenges*. Retrieved January 25, 2023, from: https://arxiv.org/abs/2105.07447

Wang, J., Wang, S., Guo, J., Du, Y., Cheng, S., & Li, X. (2019). A summary of research on blockchain in the field of intellectual property. *Procedia Computer Science*, 147, 191–197.

Watters, A. (2016). *The Blockchain for Education: An Introduction*. Retrieved January 23, 2023, from: http://hackeducation.com/2016/04/07/blockchain-education-guide

Xu, M., David, J. M., & Kim, S. H. (2018). The fourth industrial revolution: Opportunities and challenges. *International Journal of Financial research, 9*(2), 90–95.

Zhong, J., Xie, H., Zou, D., & Chui, D. K. (2018). A Blockchain Model for Word-Learning Systems. In *5th International Conference on Behavioral, Economic, and Socio-Cultural Computing (BESC)* (pp. 130–131).

INDEX

Pages in *italics* refer to figures and pages in **bold** refer to tables.

academic certificates: blockchain
168–169; certificates' issuance is
decentralised 174–175;
confidentiality reasons 169;
distributed ledger technologies 169;
issuance of certificates 167–168;
issue records *171*, 172; Non-Fungible
Tokens (NFTs) 173–174; overview
166–167; re-issue/revoke records *171*,
172–173; revocation of blockchain-
based certificates 175; Soul-Bound-
Tokens (SBT) 173, 175; validate
records *171*, 172

accessing educational content:
blockchain and IPFS 111–112, *112*;
collaboration 107; creation and
distribution 108; intellectual
property rights 110–111; open
educational resources 108–109;
public digital key 109; quick and
convenient access 108; traditional
approach 108

accreditation process: blockchain-based
accreditation system 85–87, *86*;
delivered results 81; domain
accreditation institutions 82; higher
education institutions (HEIs) 83, **84**,
85; motivation and stakeholders

81–83; state accreditation
institutions 82; verifiability 85
adaptive learning 2, 8, 23
Akram, S. V. 180
Alanis, M. 180, 183–184, 194
Allamary, A. 182–183
application programming interface
(API) 48, 75
AS-IS process modelling 68
Attewell, P. 16

Berriman, R. 11–12
bitcoin blockchain 44, 150, 154,
169–170
blended learning/hybrid learning 27, 52,
98–99
Blockcerts (BCC) 138, 169, 175, 187
Blockchain of Learning Logs (BOLL)
106–107
blockchain recommendations, BPM
lifecycle: adaptation phase 71;
analysis phase 69; discovery 69;
execution phase 71; identification 69;
implementation phase 71;
monitoring phase 71; redesign phase
69, 71
blockchain technology (BC):
accreditation system 85–87, *86*;

adoption benefits 184–186, **185**, *190*, **195**; advantages 38; Bitcoin cryptocurrency transactions 47; challenges in education 53–56; competences management 138–146; competitive advantage 62–63; digital badges 101; disruptive technologies 29, 195; distributed and distance learning 102; DLT 38; Education 4.0 1–5; in higher education (HE) 49–53; higher education institutions (HEIs) 63; impact on education *see* education impact, BC; implementation of 48–49; interoperability 48; management of HEIs 87, *87*; micro-credentials 100; norms and culture 191; processes and IS infrastructure *66*; reshaping education 5; scalability 48; SWOT analysis 47

Block.co: confidentiality reasons 169; issue records *171*, 172; Non-Fungible Tokens (NFTs) 173–174; re-issue/revoke records *171*, 172–173; validate records *171*, 172

Bulian, L. 124

Business Process Management Systems (BPMS): analysis phase 68; blockchain recommendations 69–72, *70*; discovery phase 68; identification phase 67; implementation phase 68; lifecycle 67–68; monitoring and controlling phase 68; process approach 64–65; process-oriented management 65–67; redesign phase 68

Business Process Re-engineering (BPR) 64

Buterin, V. 173

Camacho, D. 180, 183–184, 194

Camilleri, A. 62–63, 96, 101, 104, 138, 194

Campus Management Systems (CAMS) 67–68, 71

Capetillo, A. 180, 183–184, 194

Champy, J. 64

Chou, H. 107, 110

Christodoulou, K. 4, 155, 166–176

Ciccio, C. D. 77

competence and qualification management: IPeCoL-based

solution architecture 141–145; justification for BC 139–141; OpenCerts platform 138; overview 138–139; UNIC's experience (University of Nicosia, Cyprus) 138; users and roles in the system 141

competence data structure: conceptual model 133, *134*; detailed competence characteristic (DCC) 136; document representation model 136, *137*; documents confirming qualifications **135**; formal document characteristic (FDC) 136; general competence characteristic (GCC) 136

competency-based learning: focus on skills in education **19**, 18–20; Industry 4.0 18–20; labour market impact on learning approaches 17–18

COVID-19 pandemic 13, 27, 52, 95, 98, 166

Cunha, P. R. 1, 53, 96, 150, 157, 170

Cyprus Agency of Quality Assurance and Accreditation in Higher Education (CYQAA) 158, 160

Davenport, T. H. 64

Delegated PoS (DPoS) 43

digital badge 100–101

Dikusar, A. 28

disruptive technologies *26*; artificial intelligence 28–29; big data systems 27; blockchain 29; cloud computing 27; existing teaching process 26; extended reality 28; flagship 26; hologram 30; Internet of Things (IoT) 29; metaverse 30; robotics 30; smart sensors 31

Distributed Ledger Technology (DLT): blockchain technology (BC) 38; block generation process 43; challenges 41; consensus algorithm 42–44; cryptographic encryption 39; data (transaction) persistence 40; data provenance 40; decentralisation 39; decentralised data processing 39; distributed consensus on the ledger state 40; education 46; energy domain 46; features of 39; finance 45; government 46; healthcare big data 46; hybrid 40; immutability and irreversibility 40; intellectual

property rights 46–47; IPeCoL 140; manufacturing and supply chain 46; peer-to-peer (P2P) network 38; permissioned networks 40; permissionless 40; potential applications 44–47; reliability in trust-less environments 39; retail services 45; smart cities 46–47; smart contracts 44; trade 45; transparency and trust 39; transport and tourism 45; working principle 41–42
Domina, T. 16
Dubreta, N. 124
Dymek, D. 2, 4, 7–31, 98, 133, 179–196

Education 4.0: blockchain technology 1–5; click technology 22; digital tools 22; flipped classroom technology 22; Industry 4.0 revolution 26; instant web response tool 22; intelligent tutoring systems 22; skills expected from student **22**; social media technology 22; video learning resources and social media 22
education impact, BC: applications in education 191–193; approaches 82–184; categories of 181; certificate management 180; certificates and diplomas verification 186–188; challenges to blockchain adoption 189–191, *190*; current blockchain implementations 186; EduCTX platform 182; financial aspects of study 183; intellectual property 183; intellectual property rights 188–189; potential areas of using BC 181; student loan management 180; support for Education 4.0 193–195, **195**
Ethereum blockchain 74, 77, 81, 85
Ethereum Virtual Machine (EVM) 74
EU Blockchain Observatory and Forum (EUBOF) 156
European Blockchain Services Infrastructure (EBSI) 79–80
European Digital Economy and Society Index (DESI) 7
event-based learning 23

Fedorova, E. P. 49, 179, 181–182
flipped classroom technology 22–23

gamification 23
Garg, A. 184
General Data Protection Regulation (GDPR) 56, 79, 100–101, 105–106, 113
Goel, S. 11–12
Grabowski, M. 3, 62–89, 94–113
Grech, A. 62–63, 96, 101, 104, 138, 194
Guardia, L. 23–24

Hammer, M. H. 64
Hart, S. 87, 97
Hawksworth, J. 11–12
higher education (HE): blockchain limitations *54*; certificates 49–50, 52; COVID-19 pandemic 52; credentials 50; dissemination 50; educational administration 52; educational process *51*; intellectual property assets 50; learning environment 50; non-technological challenges 55; payments 50; shared documents 53; social issues 55; teaching process 20, *21*; technology-related factors 54–55; university education process 50
higher education institutions (HEIs): accreditation process 63, 83, **84**, 85; blockchain implementations 63; BPMN notation 72, 74; certification organisations 119; collaboration process 72; delivery process 76; educational cycle process 65; Factory contract 74, 76; interfaces/triggers 75; management and administrative process 65; management of 87, *87*; process of handling tenders *73, 75*; Purchasing Department 72, 74, 76; research process 65; tendering process 76; untrusted business process 72, 76

IDEAS pedagogy framework *24*, 24–25
Inamorato dos Santos, A. 138, 194
Industry 4.0 1–3, 7–8, 18–20, 25, 31, 37, 72, 77, 81, 113, 119–121, 126, 128, 145
Information and Communication Technologies (ICT) 1–2, 7, 13, 15, 18, 22–23, 25, 95–96, 99, 193
Integrated Personal Competence Ledger (IPeCoL) system 138, 140–141, 143, *144–145*, 146; accreditation

authority (AA) 143; certifying
authority (CA) 143; components and
data flows *144*; cryptography
mechanisms 143; Distributed Ledger
Technology 141; document holder
(DH) 143; reliability and
confidentiality 145; solution design
145; users and roles 142–143;
verifying organisation (VO) 143
Integrated Qualification Register (IQR)
130, *132*, 133, 141; context model
131; qualification attributes **131**
Integrated Qualification System (IQS)
120, 130, 141
inter-organisational processes: added
value to HEIs 77–78; EBSI 79–80;
EduCTX 80–81; overview 76–77;
QualiChain 78–79
InterPlanetary File System (IPFS) 101,
110–113, *112*, 174

Kamišalic, A. 49, 80
Kant, N. 62–63, 102
Konkol, P. 2–3, 7–31, 94–113

labour market: ambiguity 127;
automation and its consequences
121–122; blockchain in HEIs 126;
challenges 119; classification of
qualifications 129–130, *131*, *132*;
competences management 138–146;
competency formalisation models
128; expectations towards HEIs
123–126; full qualifications 133;
generations and attitudes 122–123;
Industry 4.0 and its impact 120–121;
market qualifications 133; non-
formal learning 133; ongoing
technological changes 124; partial
qualifications 133; typologies of soft
skills 128–129; vocational
qualifications 133
lifelong learning: benefits and
opportunities 103; blockchain-based
tokens 104–107; challenges 103–104;
continuing professional development
(CPD) 102; GDPR requirement 105
Loukil, F. 179, 181–182, 193

Massive Open Online Course (MOOC)
151–152, 155, 158–162
Mendling, J. 64–65, 67, 69, 72

Meng, N. 111
Metaverse 30
Milstein, M. B. 87
Mohammad, A. 192
MSc in Digital Currency 152, **153**;
changes in the profession *157*;
strategic objectives 154–155;
structure of **159**; students' and
graduates' current profession
156, *156*

Nakamoto, S. 38, 150, 168, 189
new learning methods and forms:
IDEAS pedagogy framework *24*,
24–25; stakeholders of educational
process 20, *21*, **22**; teaching methods
and digitalisation 22–23
Non-Fungible Tokens (NFTs) 101, 104,
157, 160–161, 173–174, 176, 184

Ocheja, P. 106–107
Ohlhaver, P. 173
Organization for Economic
Co-operation and Development
(OECD) 11, 15, 18, 123

Park, J. 54, 192–193
Peppers, D. 96
Polish Accreditation Committee (PAC)
82–83
Polish Qualifications Framework (PQF)
130
Put, D. 3, 18, 37–57, 119–146

QualiChain project 105, *106*

reshaping management *87*, 87–88
rhizomatic learning 23
Riley, R. 9
Rogers, M. 96

Saurbier, A. 78, 81–83, 86
Short, J. E. 64
Skobleva, E. I. 49, 179, 181–182
Soul-Bound-Tokens (SBT) 173–176,
187
spaced learning 97–98
Stal, J. 3–4, 18, 37–57, 179–196
student-centred learning: accessing
educational content 107–112; active
participation 194; blockchain
support 100–102; distance education

98–100; distributed learning 97–98; identification 96; individualisation 96; integration 96; integrity 96; interaction 96; lifelong learning 102–107; overview 94–95
Swan, M. 96

teaching blockchain: courses' evaluation 152–153; decentralised applications (dApps) 155; diplomas on blockchain 154; e-learning mode 162; EUBOF 156; exams invigilation 153; learning management system (LMS) 153–154; lessons learnt 160–163; live sessions 154; maintain success and protect competitive advantage 157–159; MOOC 155; MSc in Digital Currency 152, **153**; overview 150–151; programme conception and launch 151–152; strategic objectives 154–155
Themistocleous, M. 4, 78, 89, 96, 150–164, 166–176

TMchain system 110
Total Quality Management (TQM) 64, 67, 82
Trąbka, J. 3, 18, 62–89, 119–146

University of Nicosia, Cyprus (UNIC) 88, 138, 150–158, 160–163, 167, 169–170, 172–173, 176, 186, 188

Vargas, S. 192
Victor, S. 97
Viriyasitavat, W. 72
vom Brocke, J. 69

Watters, A. 192
Weber, I. 69, 72, 74, 77
Weyl, E. G. 173
workflow management systems (WfMS) 64–65, 68

Zhang, S. 111